AF333739

MORE CHAPEL MESSAGES

Linton C. Johnson, L.H.D.

Randall House Publications
114 Bush Road – P.O. Box 17306
Nashville, Tennessee 37217

More Chapel Messages
©Copyright 1983
Randall House Publications
Nashville, Tennessee
ISBN 0-89265-087-7

All rights in this book are reserved. No part of the text may be reproduced in any manner without permission in writing from the publisher except in the case of brief quotations for purposes of a review.

Printed in the United States of America

INTRODUCTION

The greatest revelation of what a man is undoubtedly comes out in the home environment. It lays bare one's true character.

Insights are gained into the character of Dr. Linton C. Johnson by the statement of many principles of purity he directed to his own daughter, Mary Nell, who was entering her teenage years. The letter was written during the 1950's.

THINGS A FATHER WOULD LIKE HIS DAUGHTER TO KNOW

As you approach womanhood, there are some things that are very important for you to know. As your father I thought I could best discuss these things with you by writing you this letter.

First, I think it will help you to realize the wonderful position God has placed you in. You remember, God did not put His final amen on His creation until He made woman. Woman was created to make man's life complete. Her highest service is performed when she is being a helpmate to her husband and making his life complete. I believe, and I know you do, that our greatest peace and happiness are attained when we serve in the capacity God ordained for us. There is no such thing as an inferior position in God's order of things. Everything is superior when it is as God planned it.

Another thing you want to remember is that every day is a chapter written in the book of your life. The way you write these chapters will determine whether the book is good, mediocre, or bad. In other words, now is the time for you to start planning to be the kind of person you are going to be. Perhaps this will include being a wife and mother.

Let me first discuss the matter of self-respect. Every one of us has to live with himself. Be true to your better self. Do only those things which meet your highest standards. You will be tempted at times by your friends to trade your high, clean standard for a lower and more questionable one. The lower, cheaper standard may seem more practical and expedient for the moment; but if you break your moral code you will lose your self-respect. Of course, you understand that we both believe that our moral code should be based upon the Word of God. I warn you against letting other people set your standards for you. Sometimes friends of yours who have cheapened themselves would persuade you to come to their level in order to give them company and somehwat justify themselves and their standards. You will always have more respect for yourself if you make your decisions on the basis of what you know is right, rather than the persuasion of those about you.

Next, I think the matter of faithfulness is very important. You have many things to be faithful to. Be faithful to God and the teachings of the Bible. Be faithful to the training we have given you at home. Be faithful to the deep inner desire to be honest, truthful, and pure. Be faithful to the future and all that you might be if you live true, pure and godly. Be faithful to the husband you might have one day. Be faithful to the children that might be born to you. It is too late to start being faithful after you have been unfaithful. Some things cannot be salvaged or regained. Damaged goods can be used, but they are never worth as much; they never give pride of ownership like the new or unsoiled goods. So now is the time to begin being faithful; after a while could be too late.

Purity to a girl is of untold value. It seems to mean more to them than to boys. It should not. But the flower of purity seems to bloom fairer and be more fragrant in a girl's life than anywhere else in God's garden. That is the reason, I suppose, that when this rose of purity is plucked from a girl's life it is missed so much and leaves such an ugly scar. Those who steal the rose of purity from a girl usually leave her to her own shame when they are ready to marry, for they too desire to be presented a garland of purity on their wedding night. They want their children to have that kind of mother. There is only one flower of purity in every girl's garden.

So guard it with your life and present it to your husband on your wedding night. He will value it as long as he lives. You too will be glad that you could make him happy with this bouquet of purity. He will be looking for it. Do not disappoint Him.

Then some day you may have the privilege of looking into the face of your own new-born daughter, you may have the right to hope that she too will live a pure life if you have been pure before her.

CONTENTS

December 10, 1974
Scripture: 1 Corinthians 15:58
Subject: Don't Quit!

DON'T QUIT!

Now then this morning I want to call your attention to a very familiar passage of Scripture found in 1 Corinthians 15, the last verse. This is the "resurrection chapter." Paul tells us about the resurrection of these bodies. God is going to raise them up in the last day. Some wonderful truths are in this chapter. Some mysteries that Paul said, "I show you a mystery." "We shall not all sleep," and so on. He closes this chapter with these words that on the surface may not seem to fit in to what he had been saying. I think there is a definite purpose for his saying this as he closes this great chapter on the resurrection. "Therefore, my beloved brethren," that is, in the light of all that he had said. "Be ye stedfast, unmoveable, always abounding," notice these words now. "Stedfast, unmoveable, abounding, always abounding in the work of the Lord, forasmuch as ye know that your labour is not in vain in the Lord." I want to read that again, even though we could quote it:

> Therefore, my beloved brethren, be ye stedfast, unmoveable, always abounding in the work of the Lord, forasmuch as ye know that your labour is not in vain in the Lord.

A lot of people get discouraged because they are not sure of this last statement, that our labor, our work, our faithfulness for God are not in vain. A brother preacher said to me a few days ago, "I have been trying to evaluate my ministry." And he added, "I am not happy with what I see." He continued, "I am (so many years old)." He is approaching middle age, and he said, "I cannot find much that I have done that I can evaluate." Now you say, "Well, he is lazy." No, he is not lazy. This preacher is a hard worker. He has what we would call a good church, a growing church. Wherever this pastor has been, the work blossomed, and yet he was saying, "I am not happy with what I see when I evaluate my ministry." Now he said, "I may have 15 or 20 good years left if the Lord is good to me, and I want to make these years count." And he wanted to discuss it with me. Well, I do not think that he was discouraged to the point that he was going to quit; but here was a man wondering if all the years that he had spent working for the Lord had really been profitable.

Many men are dropping out of the ministry. Many missionaries are leaving the field. Many laymen are slacking in their work because they are not sure that what they are doing is really worthwhile. We have students who drop out of this school. They cannot see for the life of them how being here, doing without, going to school, the monotony of bells ringing, and going to this class and that, how anything is going to contribute to their lives. It seems vain; it seems useless. They think they need to get out there and start doing something that they can see. They get discouraged and quit.

As I think back over my own life, and I do not want to preach to you my life history, it was just ordinary, nothing out of the ordinary at all. I can look back at certain key crossroads when I considered quitting many times, the things that I was doing. Every man I suppose faces that. I thank God that during some of those critical times, some way God nudged me on and I did not quit. I went to college in the depression years. I was the only student graduating in my high school class (that has been more than 40 years ago) that went to college that fall. I lived in perhaps as poor a town as you could have found in the state of Georgia. Every bank had closed. Nobody had any money. I suppose every town like that felt it was the poorest town. But I went to college that year right in the heart of the depression.

I gave out of money. I did not give out; they gave out of keeping me without money. I was without money all the time, but they said, "Your bill is not paid. You will have to go home." I was not alone in this. I borrowed. I am just telling you a little something here. You think you have had hard times. I borrowed 10 cents and hitch-hiked home. I bought the biggest, they called it, what was that kind of a bun? I forgot what it was. Some of you oldtimers might remember. I bought the biggest bun that 10 cents would buy, and I ate it that day and hitchhiked home. I got home way in the night. A fellow put me off the truck, and I walked on home. I surprised the family.

I could have quit. I had sisters that were teaching school, and the school officials could not pay them for their teaching; the county was broke. They could not get their money. My father was a farmer. He owned several farms. He could not sell his produce. Most of the good men in the county were losing their farms. My father happened to hold on to his. But you could not sell anything; nobody could buy it. You had to trade your corn and potatoes for other produce. No money was exchanged, and it would have looked a little odd for me to have driven up to the college with a load of potatoes. So, I had to have some money. I do not know how I got it, but I went back, and I stayed in school, in the depression.

Well, I am not going to tell you all the story, but later on, I went back to college after that year and still no money. Still depression years, and we did without. On the campus of a college about the size of ours, there was not but one automobile owned by a student. It was a *Model A Ford*. Troy Johnson owned it. He was from Fuquay Springs, North Carolina. He drove it up there, but he did not have money to buy gasoline so he parked it. It stayed parked there on the campus. One student; one car in a college about this size; now we cannot find parking space here.

Now there have been a lot of quitting places. Many times I wanted to when I went back to college. I met a girl there from Pennsylvania and those slow Georgia boys are no match for those northern girls. She got me interested in getting married. I did not have any money to go to school, I thought, and here I was wanting to get married. That is a good excuse: to drop out of school and get married. I do not know how she figured I could feed her if I could not feed myself. She was blind to that. But anyway, it was a good stopping place. I could have a good face-saving reason and talked myself into it, so we planned to get married. I would have dropped out of school again.

But there was an old man; he was a miser. Everybody considered him a miser down in my part of the country. And the reason that he had money was that he was a miser. Everybody despised that old man until they needed some money. He was a miser, but he had a little money. Now I never have figured this one out. He heard that I was not going back to school. The only time that I ever remember that old man from an adjoining community going to our church was on this occasion, and I preached that day, just a boy preacher. He asked somebody what I was going to do. They said, "Well, I guess he will not go back to school." "Why?" "Well, he does not have any money." "Well," he said, "I might have a little bit. Tell him to come to see me." Well, I planned to get married, but here was an opportunity to go back to school. So I went to see him. He said, "Yes, I can let you have a little." It was 10 percent interest. I did not know what interest was. I did not know how to figure it. I was glad I did not. If I had sat down and figured it up, I would have said I cannot take it. But I took it, and I called my wife-to-be and said, "We will not be getting married." We postponed our marriage about 3 years, and I went on and finished college.

That was a good quitting place. We did our courting by mail for about 3 years. I had not seen her in 11 months when we met to get married. It was a good quitting place, but thank God, someway, God just kept nudging me on. I do not know how, He just kept me going; I did not quit. I am just telling you this to show you that you do not have to quit. People call in here and say, "We would like to have somebody to work." It was not like that when I went to college.

Now, "be ye stedfast." If God has saved you, if Jesus Christ is your Savior, if He lives down in your heart, and if He means anything to you, you have got to listen to Him. These people who can turn Jesus off and just make Him a convenience, I do not understand their salvation. I do not understand their type of Christianity. They do not have to ask Jesus anything. They just decide what they are going to do, and they run their own lives without taking God into account. They rationalize, just do anything they please. I do not understand it. When God takes control, you have lost control. You do not do what you want to do.

When I go home, people keep asking me when am I going to retire. I do not know. I should not say this here before the board. They may do it before this session is over but sometimes I sort of wish they would fire me. Then I would pass the responsibility on to them. I would not have to make the decisions. That is not a suggestion, gentlemen. But I do not know when I am going to retire. I did not start this just because I chose it, and I cannot stop it just because I choose to. I am going to have to get an inner release, or either God is going to have to take me some other way. I am going to have to find out what God wants. See, you are tied to the horns of the altar. You are bound there. You are a sacrifice; you have been tied to the altar. And only God can cut those cords and loose you. You are bound there forever. You are not your own. You have been bought with a price.

Do not come around talking to me about your Christianity if you are going to take your own life into your own hands and make your own decisions for your own convenience. You had better find out whether you are saved or not. You had better find out if you really meant business when you talked to the Lord because we are not our own; we are His. We are bondslaves, tied, and owned by another. And do not go around making your plans or talking yourself into things until you know that you are in the will of God. You will make serious mistakes, and God will mark you off. You will limp into Heaven by the skin of your teeth, if you get there at all.

"Be ye stedfast, unmoveable, always abounding in the work of the Lord." Now I have not qualified there. I wish I could be "always abounding." But let me tell you; the spring has not always gushed up like I would like it, but when you get down to business with God, you will find there is a spring in your soul. There is a freshness there when you are doing the will of God. You can look up through your tears and while you weep with your eyes, you rejoice with your heart and soul when you are in the will of God. And listen, if you cannot do that, if you cannot weep and rejoice at the same time, then you need something to happen in your heart and in your life. "Always abounding," never giving up, never turning back. Lord, you saved me and when you saved me, I became your servant, your slave.

You know I have wished many times the Lord would change His plans for my life. I am glad He has not. All I say, Lord, is help me to be faithful; help me to be faithful. "Always abounding in the work of the Lord forasmuch as ye know." Do you know it? Are you sold on this? Do you know that labor is not in vain?

I was like this preacher. He said, "I cannot see anything. I went back to a church recently that I had pastored. I had stayed there a certain number of years, and it bloomed and blossomed. I went back and I couldn't find my tracks there. Those years of labor seemed to be lost." And he said, "I do not want that to happen." Well, we cannot always evaluate our lives, our fruit. I do not know whether I have any fruit over there or not. You know, the people that I thought got saved under my ministry, I know some of them did, but I have not kept any scoreboard because when I get up there and I take my list and go around looking for them, they may not be there. I may be counting some fruit that is not there. I am going to have to leave that to God. But I will tell you when you put your life into the hand of God, you can be sure that you are not living in vain. Just doing the will of God from day-to-day. Saying, "Thank You, Lord, for what You give me. Lord, I will do this task as best I can."

Do not measure yourself by others. Oh, this is the greatest

measuring age you have ever been in. We are all just backing up to one another and measuring, taking our height, and we are so frustrated because I cannot measure up to you and you to me. God pity us; we do not know how to measure ourselves. You just put your life into the hands of God and say, "Lord, I will have to trust You for the results." And then when you get up there, the books will be opened, and there will be some fruit.

Your labor is not in vain. Oh, you say, "I cannot sing." Well, maybe you cannot, but what about enjoying that song that is in your heart? For some reason, I do not have people asking me to sing before an audience, but you know, I sing. I sing while you are singing. I may not open my mouth, but every child of God has a song in his heart that God put there. And so God is taking note. God has a tape recorder, and He picks that tune that is in my soul, and He may play it for me in Heaven. And it will be a beautiful tune; in fact, it will be an anthem. All the songs that I have sung in my soul, God knows about. There is a record. It is not in vain.

Every cup of cold water that you might give, God takes note of it, and it will be there when you stand before God. You are not living in vain. You say, well, I cannot talk. Nobody is going to call me to pastor. Well, all right if they do not call you to pastor.

You know, one of the best soul winners, I do not know whether he was *the* best soul winner, but he made the best effort of any student I have known that has gone out from this school. Some of you know whom I am talking about. A boy that could not talk plainly. He had a nervous problem. He wanted to preach and he *does* preach. I see his name in the paper now, asking for opportunities to preach. I do not know how many souls that fellow is going to win, but I will tell you one thing: I do not want to stack my record up against his when I get to Heaven. A boy that could not talk so you could understand him. He is energetic, begging for places to preach; he would go up and down the streets when he was a student here, and he would talk to people, more people about the Lord, than any 10 students we had. As far as I know, he has done it throughout his ministry. Here was a boy with all the handicaps that would justify anybody quitting, but he has not quit.

Now your labor is not in vain in the Lord, so therefore, "Be ye stedfast, unmoveable, always abounding in the work of the Lord." Some of you are going to quit at the end of this semester. Now as I said the other day, it may be in God's will for some of you to make some changes, but the vast majority of you , you have not finished the job. If for no other reason, for character's sake, some of you ought to finish at least one job in your life. Some of you have never driven the last nail that should have been driven.

I have told this many times, but I think it illustrates something. There was a tenant farmer that lived on one of our farms one time, and for some strange reason, he would not ever finish a field. He would plow today in the field, and tomorrow you would find him over there. You would say, "Well, did he finish?" No. He would just move from field to field. He had to have a new field every day. My father did not keep him but one year. No use to waste that time jumping from field to field. Finish a field and then move on to another field. I do not know why that fellow did that.

You know some people are like that; they never finish a field. They plow a little here, and then they plow a little there; and they are always looking for something sensational, glorious, and glamorous and never finishing a job. I think some of you need to stay if for no other reason than just to say, "I finished at least one year, in one place," and have the thrill of knowing that you finished something. And then some of you need to stay because you have not really dedicated your heart to the Lord. You are making plans, your plans. You are going to get out of the will of God. "Be ye stedfast, unmoveable, always abounding." Listen, there will never be any abounding if you are not steadfast. You will always have a guilt complex. You will look in the mirror, and you will say, "I am a quitter."

I would not marry a fellow that could not wait at least one year to get married. I would not marry a girl that put pressure on me to get married. I would take off in the other direction as fast as I could because if she is going to put pressure on me to get married, think of the pressure she is going to put on me after she does get me. I do not want to live under that pressure. I want somebody that has got character to say, "I have got a duty. I am going to do my duty and not my pleasure." And life is made up of duties and not pleasures.

May we stand.

PRAYER

Our Father, be with us this day. Meet all of our needs. Help us to do Your will. In Jesus' Name. Amen.

2

January 21, 1966
Scripture: Proverbs 10:1-10
Subject: Wisdom From Proverbs

WINKING, BLINKING, AND NOD

I was reading the tenth chapter of Proverbs the other day, and there are a few things that are very practical that I want to point out. There is one good thing about preaching from Proverbs. You do not have to have an outline. There is no outline to it. These proverbs are just lined up, one after another, and they are not put in any particular order—that is, some of them.

"The proverbs of Solomon. A wise son maketh a glad father . . . ." Now you are not in a position yet to realize this, but you ought to think about it. You are in the position of being sons and daughters, and you have never thought about how your dad and mother feel about things. We do not begin to realize this until—well, most of the time until we have children of our own. Then we can look back and say, "My, I must have been very thoughtless. I could have pleased my parents much more than I did." By this time, your dads and mothers are getting your report cards. They are looking them over. Mom goes to the mailbox, and she yells out for dad and says, "Look! John made good grades!" And there are beams in their eyes. He must be studying. They are as proud as they can be. They call the neighbors, and of course during the conversation, incidentally, they just tell the neighbors about John. You know. And they are just as pleased as they can be.

Good grades mean you have been wise in the use of your time. You have spent your time wisely up here. You did not give way to the temptation to join in the "bull session." You did not waste your time when you should have been studying. Some of you did that. Others of you, when you should have been studying, were arguing theology. You can always argue theology. There is never an end to it, and there are no conclusions. It is a deep well that has no bottom, and you enjoy it. All of us enjoy it, but there comes a time to study.

All right. A wise son maketh a glad dad, when he gets the report card. He feels that the investment he made in you was worthwhile. That money that he had to go down to the bank and borrow was for your benefit. It may have been on next year's crop, if he farms. He may not know whether he is going to be able to pay it off or not. But he wanted you to have the best. Maybe he did not want you to have to work, and your mother—that new dress that she would like to have—she did not buy because she wanted to keep you in school. A wise daughter makes a glad mother. Now, listen, you ought to think about those things.

We are starting a new semester, a new start. You did not do as well as you should have done or could have done last semester. You know where the mistakes were made. You know right where the trouble was. You can correct it if you want to. Now, an unwise son makes a dad's heart grieve, and mother's too. They get your report card, and they do not call the neighbors. And if the neighbors ask, How is John doing? They change the subject. They do not want to talk about it. You have wasted your time. You did not do what you should have done. So now, let us not waste our time. Let us get started off right.

You owe something to your parents. They are investing in you. And in most instances, this is a sacrifice. So make them glad when they get the report cards. One of the saddest things that we have to do here in dealing with students, occasionally when the penalty is severe, is to call them or write them (dad and mother) and disappoint them. You know, it would be just as easy to call them up and say, "Your son was killed in an accident," as to call them up and say, "Your son, or your daughter, has messed things up and we are sending them home." I do not know that the grief would be any harder to bear. It is a hard thing to do. We think about it. We do not do it lightly. It is a sad thing for a child to break a mother's heart or a father's heart, when you do not have to do it. And you do not have to do it.

"Treasures of wickedness profit nothing . . . ." Just put your bank full, and it does not profit. I saw three gamblers, notorious gamblers, in this city. Their pictures were in the paper the other day. They were dressed like millionaires. Perhaps they were. Well-dressed men, intelligent men. They have made fortunes gambling. They were connected with the under-world activities of this city. Their names are known to all citizens of Nashville who read the newspapers. But they were found guilty. They are going to prison. Now the treasures of wickedness profit nothing. The devil will tell you different. He will tell you that it pays off. He glamorizes. You know, he is the greatest glamorizer in all the world. He can take a pit of sin, the slime of sin, and put neon lights around it and glamorize it and fool people. And they come and they are deceived. But the treasures of wickedness do not profit.

Listen, if you earn a grade in this school that is not an honest grade, you did not get it honestly, it is not going to do you any good. Sooner or later it will hurt you. Sin never pays off. Sin *never* pays. The fingerprints of sin are never rubbed out. Everything sin touches, it mars or defaces; and the thing that it touches loses its value. In your life you can be forgiven of your sins, but still you are the loser. There are people in this audience no doubt today that their sins have been forgiven by the grace of God, but their lives will never be what they could have been because they have been marred by sin. Some things you cannot rub out. They will follow you to your grave. So, sin does not pay.

" . . . But righteousness delivereth from death. The LORD will not suffer the soul of the righteous to famish: but he casteth away the substance of the wicked." You hear a lot of complaining and griping: "The world is in an awful condition." And it is. There is no bright star shining on the world's scene today. It is a foggy gray every way you look—at the world around you. There is no comfort in it.

This situation in Vietnam—now I am not trying to hook up prophecy here. I do not know enough about it—but I know this: that some time or other, whether this is it or not, I do not know, some time or other the world is going to get bogged down in a great war in the East. I do not know whether this is it or not. It could be, but I do not know. But I know one thing: If we are stuck with a war in Asia, we can spend the next millennium shooting at those Asian people, and they will still be coming over the hills. You cannot win a war in Asia. Not when you get involved with the Chinese and all those people of those islands there. Why, they will be born faster than you can kill them. We will wear ourselves out. We will spend our resources, and I do not care how rich we think we are; there is a limit to our resources. Have you been noticing something just recently? You know all these years past we have had a farm surplus. The government did not know what to do with it. They could not find storage houses for all that was being produced. Just recently the tide has shifted. Now they are talking about a possible shortage. All of a sudden it hits you like that. Here we go along, too much, too much, cut back, cut back. And all of a sudden, we realize that we are out of soap. We realize the meal is giving out. We thought we had plenty.

And you know, God can change the wind, and it can blow in the opposite direction before we know what has happened. And let me tell you, it is going to happen, I believe very seriously, it is going to happen. Here we have been boasting about the richest nation producing so much we do not know what to do with it. If history tells me anything, if the Lord Jesus tarries, we are going to see the opposite side of that story right here in this country. God knows how to work those things out.

There is not any bright star on the world scene. But "The LORD will not suffer the soul of the righteous to famish . . . . " It does not matter if the world is burning down around you, inside you, your soul and your spirit can be aglow. Thank God for the Christian faith. Thank God for that which He puts inside you when He saves you. Though Heaven and earth pass away, this does not have to pass away. So He will not suffer the righteous to famish or the soul of the righteous.

"He becometh poor that dealeth with a slack hand: but the

hand of the diligent maketh rich." Now wait a minute. Apply that to your own situation. He has poor grades who deals with his studies with a slack hand. He makes poor grades. He who does not practice his piano, flunks. He who does not practice voice, flunks. He who does not study his lessons is tempted to cheat on examination to try to get by. "He that dealeth with a slack hand becometh poor, but the hand of the diligent maketh rich." The fellow who studies his lessons goes singing a tune to the examination. A real tune. Not one of these "passing the cemetery at night" type tunes, but he can really sing because he has spent his time wisely. He has bought up the hours, the opportunities. He does not mind the test, and he is not tempted to cheat on examination because he knows the answer.

"He that gathereth in summer is a wise son: but he that sleepeth in harvest is a son that causeth shame." We had a fellow around here that we could not wake up. We never could wake him up. All he knew how to do was sleep and eat. Sleeping gave him an appetite. And he slept all the time. By the way, that fellow is in the army now, and it makes me a little uneasy that our defense rests upon such fellows as that because he is asleep somewhere. I do not know where he is, but he is asleep.

"He that gathereth in summer is a wise son: but he that sleepeth in harvest is a son that causeth shame." You can apply this same thing. "Blessings are upon the head of the just: but violence covereth the mouth of the wicked. The memory of the just is blessed: but the name of the wicked shall rot."

Oh, yes, we talk about George Washington. I read today that this famous train that made its last run yesterday, the Dixie Flyer—it used to be a real train; I remember it. Then it got to be called the Dixie Creeper. It lost its glory. They finally took it off yesterday. This conductor who has been riding the train for about fifty years—they tell me that a trainman gets attached to his trains like a man gets attached to his dog or to his horse—and he feels that it is *his* train. He was broken-hearted when he made his last run on the Dixie Flyer yesterday. He was talking about the famous people that used to ride that train: senators, congress-men, and other people that he mentioned. And then he said, one very infamous person rode that train once—Al Capone, from Chicago to Atlanta, to the federal prison in Atlanta.

"The memory of the just is blessed." You do not name your children "Al Capone." You do not name them "Nero." Those names are associated with something that is shady. "The memory of the . . . blessed [the good, the righteous, is blessed]: but the name of the wicked shall rot."

"The wise in heart will receive commandments: but a prating fool shall fall. He that walketh uprightly walketh surely: but he that perverteth his ways shall be known."

He that walketh upright can look you in the eye. That is what it means. The fellow who has nothing to hide. When he shakes your hand, he looks at you and says, How do you do, sir. But the fellow who cannot look at you, cannot look you in the eye, has something to hide—something down inside, he is afraid that you may know, afraid that you may find out. You know it is a wonderful thing to live so that when somebody knocks at your door, you do not have to send the children to open the door; you go yourself. If you have your bills all paid and somebody knocks at the door, *you* go to the door. If you have not paid your bills, you send somebody else to the door while you go out the back door. You do not want to face them.

You go downtown, you can look every businessman in the eye. But if you have not paid your bills, you are afraid you are going to meet him on the sidewalk. You dodge around. You are uneasy. You are always looking over your shoulder. Driving down the highway, you are driving within the speed limit, you hear a siren, you say, I wonder who that fellow is after. But if you are driving over the speed limit, your heart beats faster. Now listen, you can apply this to anything. Oh, the joy! The dividends of living right!

"He that walketh uprightly walketh surely . . . ." He walks with his head up. He looks people in the eye. But the fellow who

16

lives a shady life; it shows in his eyes. "He that winketh with the eye causeth sorrow . . . ." "Step off to one side here and talk with me." I am always afraid of these nods of the head at the National Association. It would be a wonderful thing to have a National Association where there were no nods of the head or the wink of the eye. You know.

"He that winketh with the eye causeth sorrow: but a prating fool shall fall." I would advise you to read the Book of Proverbs carefully and prayerfully.

Shall we stand.

PRAYER

We thank Thee, our Father, for the wisdom of Thy Word. Help us that we may apply the truths of it to today's situations. In Jesus' Name. Amen.

3

January 25, 1966
Scripture: Matthew 13:18-23
Subject: Sower, Seed and Soil

SEEING YOURSELF IN A PARABLE

In the 13th chapter of Matthew, there is a story, a parable. We are all familiar with it, and I just want to call your attention to the first part of it and then get on over into the 18th verse where an explanation is given. Every Christian fits into this parable somewhere. Look at it honestly and see where you are and who you are in this parable. It is the parable of the fellow who went to sow seed. Some fell by the wayside, some fell on stony ground, and you know the story. Some fell among thorns, but other fell on good ground. Now that is the first part of the parable.

In the explanation of it, found beginning in verse 18, "Hear ye therefore the parable of the sower. When any one heareth the word of the kingdom, and understandeth it not, then cometh the wicked one, and catcheth away that which was sown in his heart. This is he which received seed by the way side."

In other words, as you sow the seed of the Word, much of it is going to be wasted. It will fall by the wayside. The people who hear it will not understand it. They do not know what you are talking about. You may wonder why they do not. You may say, "Oh, well, he just does not want to listen." Satan may have that mind and heart of that one so blinded that he actually thinks it is the most foolish thing he ever heard. He does not grasp any of it. So those are the seed that fall by the wayside, and many of them fall there. Men are so preoccupied. Their hearts and minds are so filled with other things, they do not grasp what you are saying at all. Now you have them in your audience every Sunday morning. There they are. They are looking right at you. Some of them are asleep. Some are looking at the bulletin, or they are doing something else. They are not hearing what you are saying. All right, that is one group.

Now verse 20, "But he that received the seed into stony places, the same is he that heareth the word, and anon with joy receiveth it." Now this fellow sits up and listens. He responds and he reacts. When you tell him something, you can see a smile come across his face. He is the fellow who gets all worked up. He is easily moved. He is the fellow who is looking for something sensational, something new; and when he hears it, he tells it all over the community. He is the fellow who thinks he gets saved over again every time you have a revival meeting.

He gets all worked up and goes out with a Bible under his arm the first Sunday morning after the revival. He talks to everybody he meets down the street, and he talks loudly; he wants everybody to hear him and everybody to see him. He is really on top of things. With joy he has received the Word. He will drive 100 miles to hear his favorite evangelist, but he will not drive 3 blocks to hear his pastor on Wednesday night prayer meeting. In fact, there is something wrong with his pastor, anyway, come to think of it. He is not spiritual enough. So he gets the family in the car and drives a hundred miles to hear his favorite evangelist. He follows him all over the country; that is after he got saved again in that last revival.

All right: "Yet hath he not root in himself, but dureth for a while: for when tribulation or persecution ariseth because of the word, by and by he is offended." You can see him, like a tire with a slow leak. He is gradually going down. Now that is this fellow.

He cannot take routine. He cannot stand the same pastor to preach to him on Sunday morning, Sunday night, and Wednesday evening. He has got to have something new. Really he is not interested in the Word. He is interested in being made to feel good. He is a fellow who goes by feeling. I think this word "joy" is a significant word to describe this fellow. He " . . . with joy receiveth it." He nods his head and says, "Amen," but after a while when routine comes, he has to go back to work, and the evangelist is gone. Now I am not blaming the evangelist here, do not misunderstand me. The evangelist is gone out of reach, and he has to settle down to routine. "Anon," by and by, he becomes offended. That is, he just fades out.

Now, you have this group of people in every community. Most every church has this element in it, and they are a heartbreak for the pastor. He gets encouraged and then he is discouraged. He watches them as they go up, and then he watches them as they go down. He is always trying to stablize them but never able to. We have them coming to school here like this. We have them who figure that this is going to be one big camp meeting. Well, I am not opposing the camp-meeting spirit, but they cannot settle down to study Greek, Ancient History, Bible Survey, and Bible Doctrine—that destroys their spirituality. That takes all the joy out of being a Christian, and they begin to fade out. They say God is leading me away. You know, that is an insult. It really is. I would not say that God was leading me, even if I felt that He was; I would not say it. So the Lord leads them somewhere else.

All right, now there is another group. "He also that received seed among the thorns is he that heareth the word; and the care of this world, and the deceitfulness of riches . . . ." Now notice, " . . . the deceitfulness of riches, choke the word, and he becometh unfruitful." I certainly know some people like that. I believe I know some who fit into this category perfectly. Some of my friends, some of the fellows I used to look up to, they had ability. They had fervor, they had a message, they had zeal, and they had dedication. Some of them have dropped out, almost out, of the ministry, just staying in enough to be counted, but their time and their interests have faded away. Their interest is in other things.

I am thinking of some right now, some heartbreaks. Some who ought to be leaders in the Free Will Baptist denomination, could be, and at one time, they were. Today they are in business, they are in secular work, and they are just preaching a little on the side. Some of them have ceased preaching entirely.

Now what happened? All right, they received the Word. The thorns, the cares of this world got them. Some of them let their education get the best of them. Some of them went so high in education until they could not find a place of service in the Free Will Baptist denomination, so they reasoned. They had to get out or either waste their talents which they acquired through education.

Well, now, their education could be used. They are deceived at that point, but they feel that way about it. "There is no place in my church for my talents, for my abilities," they say. So they educated themselves out of the ministry as far as Free Will Baptists are concerned.

What happened? The cares, the thorns, of this world choked the Word out of their hearts. I tell you it is a serious thing when a man stands up and announces that he has been called to preach the gospel and has given himself to it and has gone so far as to prepare for it. Some of the fellows I have in mind, prepared; they sat right where you are sitting now. They studied, they got the message, and they could preach the message. They had great ability. But some way, the cares of this world got hold of them, and the Word was choked out of them. They are not preaching it today. They are doing other things.

Well, God understands. I am not the judge, but I will tell you, I fear for those men. I fear for anybody who allows the Word to be choked out by "the cares . . . and the deceitfulness of riches . . . ."

I want to point out one or two things. I am thinking right now of four men. I am thinking of four men I know, and I know their wives. In every instance, the four instances that I am thinking about, the wife is an ambitious, hard-driving person, who cannot be satisfied with the ordinary necessities of life. She is behind her husband goading, prodding, and driving him. Now I do not know whether she is to blame; it may be a team. But the four people that I am thinking of right now (and I could call their names), in each instance, the wife has so much pride that she could not live on a preacher's salary and be satisfied. Now I am not trying to shift all this blame to the wife, but I want to say this to you fellows. You marry a preacher's wife. Be sure that she is a preacher's wife. Do not take somebody else's now, but you get a preacher's wife when you get married.

You tell her about what she can expect. Tell her just a little under what she might expect so she will be pleasantly surprised. A preacher had better not marry a banker's wife. She can ruin you. Now I know a few men that I take my hat off to for staying in the ministry and staying married to the one they have. I do not see how they have done it. It can affect your ministry.

"But he that received seed into the good ground is he that heareth the word, and understandeth it; which also beareth fruit, and bringeth forth, some an hundredfold, some sixty, some thirty."

Now this is the kind that we like. The fellow who hears the Word. He understands the Word. He understands the cost, and he is not one of these up-and-downers. Now he may have joy and express it, or he may be the quiet kind. You do not need to go around sticking thermometers in people's mouths all the time taking their spiritual temperature. The fellow who is quiet may be the best Christian. The fellow who jumps the highest and shouts the loudest may not be be the fellow who will stick. There are other ways to judge and to test spirituality.

Here is a fellow who understands the message. It fell upon good ground, and he bears fruit in the sunshine and in the rain. He is faithful, he is loyal, and he is true. He does not register everything that happens, as far as you can tell. He is just the same. You preach a good sermon; he sits there and listens. He does not say anything, but he goes out the door and shakes your hand. He may not be the fellow who tells you that he enjoyed the sermon. He is the fellow who is just there. Thank God for them. Every church has a few of that kind. They are the backbone of the church. They are the people who make this institution possible. They are the ones. We know that when we have a need here, we know certain people who are going to respond to that need. There are those stable people who are fixed, and they stay put and they are the ones who will come to your rescue when you need them. Thank God for them.

I hope you are one of them. I hope you are not one of those who receives joy and then goes out, grows cold, and loses his fervor. I hope that you are not one who receives it and then permits the cares of this world to choke it out. I hope you are the good kind. Let us all be. Shall we stand, please.

PRAYER

Our Father, we thank Thee for Thy Word. Help us to see ourselves in it, to be rebuked by it, to be instructed by it, to be encouraged by its message. Bless us throughout this day. In Jesus' Name, Amen.

February 3, 1966
Scripture: Hosea 2:18-23
Subject: Hosea and Gomer

4

A DOOR OF HOPE

Ray Lee: Dr. Johnson, will you come to the pulpit, please? I would like to read this document. "Dr. L. C. Johnson, President, Free Will Baptist Bible College, on this your 52nd birthday, we the student body of 1965-66 wish to express our most sincere appreciation for your faithful dedication to our college and to hereby pledge to you our continued loyalty in years to come.

Ray Lee, President
Donna Watson, Secretary"

We know that you will remember us by this, but we also realize that as our president, it takes a lot of clothes. You have to dress up every day of the week, we know. So I know you believe in "ear-marked" money, don't you? We are ear-marking this one-hundred dollar check for you to buy a new suit.
(Editor's Note)
Ray Lee died suddenly on March 4, 1966, of a cerebral hemorrhage during an intra-society basketball game at Free Will Baptist Bible College, Nashville, Tennessee.

I am finishing, as far as I know now, the messages that I will be bringing from the Book of Hosea, with the latter verses of chapter 2. I want to say again, study Israel's place in God's program whether you believe she is to have a place in the future or not. Whether you believe there is only a spiritual Israel, you must formulate a policy or a position concerning Israel. I have my views, as I said. On the basis of my views, I am able to have a systematic, theological position concerning Israel, past and future. So much is said in the Word of God, even in the New Testament, concerning Israel that you must have a position. So this is one of the main emphases that I want to make. Do not ignore Israel. You cannot. There will be too many loose ends of Scripture that you cannot tie together if you do so.

Now, I want to just review since this will be the last message, for the time being at least, that I will bring on this book. Remember that God is using this unusual union that He commanded to teach a lesson concerning His people Israel. He told Hosea, His servant, to join himself to this woman Gomer who had a bad reputation. She proved to be untrue and unfaithful to him. He did this in order to teach a lesson concerning the relationship existing between Himself and His people. What Gomer did to Hosea, Israel had done to God. She broke the heart of Hosea, her husband. Israel had broken the heart of God. Israel had joined herself to other lovers and so did Gomer. God was using this to teach a lesson. I do not know why He was causing Hosea to suffer so much in order to teach this lesson, but that is God's business, and that is the way God did it. So we find then that Gomer was untrue and unfaithful. Finally she decided that when she lived with her husband it was better with her than it was before so she said, "I will return."

In order for her to return, something had to be done. She just could not walk in and take up her place in the home without doing certain things. So it was said that the valley of Achor would be a door of hope. That little statement in Scripture would have no meaning at all unless you could find out what the valley of Achor and the door of hope was.

You find that in Joshua chapter 7, when Achan had sinned. He had taken those things from the spoil of the fallen city of Jericho and had put them in his tent. Because of this sin, God had withdrawn His blessings, His power, and His protection from the people of Israel. They went out to battle and were defeated and driven back. The sin of Achan caused the loss of thirty lives in that one little skirmish, trying to take the city of Ai.

As I pointed out yesterday, I want to emphasize again, your sin is not an isolated, personal thing altogether. It touches other lives. You may be the pastor of a church. You may fail to live like you ought. You may say, "Nobody knows. I am not hurting anybody." But you are. If you are not living the kind of life you ought to be, then you *are* hurting somebody else. You are causing the downfall of others just as Achan caused the loss of life of thirty men when they went out to battle because God could not be with them. Those thirty men lay in their graves, not because of *their* sin, but because of Achan's sin.

You never know how many lives are destroyed and ruined by your own careless behavior. You may think it is only personal, nobody's business but yours. But it is not so. God not only holds you responsible for the sin that you commit, but He holds you responsible for the lives that you ruin or destroy. This is a serious business.

So they took Achan out into the valley of Achor. They burned the goods of his household, and they stoned him and his family. Only then was the judgment of God lifted and the blessings of God returned to Israel. The valley of Achor was a place of judgment. It was a place where the wrong was made right, the valley of Achor, a door of hope. It is the only door of hope there is for you to get back into favor with God. In order for you to be taken back into that proper relationship with Him, you must repent. You must be judged. That which is causing the trouble must be destroyed, forgiven. You must repent. It is the only valley; it is the only door of hope. You cannot do it by raising your church budget; you cannot do it by increasing your visitation program; you cannot do it by spending more time reading your Bible and praying. You cannot do it by sacrificially giving to good causes. You cannot restore the favor of God if there is sin in your life.

Now that is the cheap, easy approach. That is the Catholic approach. That is the way of penance, giving God a tip, buying God off. God will not have any of it. The only door of hope for you is the door of repentance, confessing your sins and forsaking them. Having them covered by the blood is the only door of hope for you to be taken back into favor with God. Do not kid yourself, you cannot work your way into it. You cannot sacrifice your way into it. The only way is repentance, the forsaking of sin. So the valley of Achor is a door of hope.

Hosea said to Gomer, "Now listen, I want to take you back." Trying to allure her, he had been making love to her. He had been speaking comfortably unto her. He was alluring or enticing her. Now he said, "In order for you to come back, you are going to have to repent. You are going to have to really be sorry before I can take you back, as much as I love you." The only way God can take us back, as much as He loves us is for us to confess and forsake our sins.

So we got through that yesterday. Now, closing out with these last verses, verse 18: "And in that day will I make a covenant for them with the beasts of the field . . . ." That is, he is talking about Israel when they have been taken back. When they have passed through that door of hope, the valley of Achor, where their sins have been judged and done away with, then God said, " . . . I will make a covenant for them with the beasts of the field. . . ." They will lose their ferociousness. They will cease to be the enemy of man. I am reminded what Isaiah said in chapter 11 of his book, "The wolf also shall dwell with the lamb, and the leopard shall lie down with the kid; and the calf and the young lion and the fatling together; and a little child shall lead them."

In other words, in that day when judgment has been lifted and Israel has been restored to favor with God, then, He said, I will make a covenant with the beasts of the field, and they will not be ferocious any more. They will become tame and gentle, and a friend of man. Isaiah describes that day in chapter 11. What a day! What a day! When fear has been lifted from the world. The animals do not fear man, and man does not fear the animals. Peace reigning and ruling. That is when they come back to the door of hope, the valley of Achor, where their sins were burned and judged.

" . . . And with the fowls of heaven, and with the creeping things of the ground: and I will break the bow and the sword and the battle out of the earth . . . ." There will be no more war. There will be peace, and of that time we read in chapter 11. Peace will cover the earth " . . . as the waters cover the sea."

" . . . And will make them to lie down safely. And I will betroth thee unto me for ever. . . ." That is God talking to Israel. There will be no more divorces. You know, God spoke by the naming of these children. He said, I will name this one Lo-ammi, and the other one Lo-ruhamah, meaning, "I will not have mercy any longer" and "I will not be your God any more, and you are not my people any more." There was a divorce: God separating Himself from His people. Now He says, " . . . I will betroth thee unto me forever . . . ." There will be no more divorces. " . . . I will betroth thee unto me in righteousness, and in judgment, and in loving-kindness, and in mercies. I will even betroth thee unto me in faithfulness: and . . . ." In other words, Gomer will not break the heart of Hosea any more.

Israel will not break God's heart any more. She will be faithful. She has been very unfaithful. Israel spit in the face of the Son of God, the Messiah. She disowned Him. "Let him be crucified . . ." and " . . . [let] his blood be on us, and our children," she said. And that is true. God said, "Let it be so." The blood still remains, and the judgment is still resting upon the heads of the children of those who said, "Let it be so." God said, "All right." But then that will be lifted.

"I will even betroth thee unto me in faithfulness: and thou shalt know the LORD. And it shall come to pass in that day, I will hear, saith the LORD, and I will hear the heavens, and they shall hear the earth."

In other words, as it is in Heaven, so will it be here. Heaven and earth will get together. You know, there is peace in Heaven, but you have to go to Heaven to find it. You cannot find it down here. Men are trying to find it. They are trying to establish peace. They cannot do it.

You know, it is an awful feeling to work at something that you know cannot be brought to pass, a feeling of futility. Now maybe it is a good thing that our president—I do not know whether he knows this or not—thinks he can bring peace. Now the only reason he would think that, is that he does not know the Bible. Maybe he is just pretending. Maybe that is the way he has to talk, he is president. But if he goes home at night and opens the Book and reads from the Word of God, he will learn that you cannot bring peace to this old world. Maybe it is a good thing he does not know it. He would get awfully confused and frustrated. No, it would be better. But he will never bring peace.

All right. " . . . I will hear the heavens, and they shall hear the earth; And the earth shall hear the corn, and the wine, and the oil; and they shall hear Jezreel. And I will sow her unto me in the earth; and I will have mercy upon her that had not obtained mercy; and I will say to them which were not my people, Thou art my people; and they shall say, Thou art my God."

What a wonderful time. What a wonderful reunion! What happened to Gomer and Hosea is depicting this scene which is going to happen to God's people when they return. Where God had said, I will not have mercy. Where God had said, Thou art *not* My people, now when He has taken them back and He has betrothed them unto Himself forever, then it shall be said, Thou art My people. You have obtained mercy. And they shall answer back and say, Thou art my God. I have accepted Your Son. See, He can never be their God until Jesus becomes their Messiah. But they will recognize Him. As long as they say, "I will not have Your Son," God will say, "I will not have you." But when they accept God's Son, God will accept them. That is the way He does with us. God will not accept us until we accept His Son. He thinks a lot of His Son and when man accepts His Son, He accepts us as sons.

Shall we stand, please.

PRAYER

Bless Thy Word to our hearts, our Father. We thank Thee for the blessings of this day. Watch over and care for us throughout the day. In Jesus' Name. Amen.

5

February 3, 1966
Scripture: Psalm 112
Subject: Fear of the Lord

THE FEAR OF THE LORD

We are glad to have Mrs. Welch with us. Those of us who were here during those years when she was—in fact, she was here longer than most of us—and we are glad to have you, Mrs. Welch.

If you would like, turn in your Bibles to Psalm 112. It is one of my favorite Psalms: "Praise ye the LORD. Blessed is the man that feareth the LORD, that delighteth greatly in his commandments."

Let us pause there for just a moment and notice what these three verses say before we read any more. First of all, a note of praise, then a statement. "Blessed is the man that feareth the LORD, that delighteth greatly in his commandments." I have heard all sorts of definitions for this word "fear" or "feareth" in the Bible. Some say that it does not mean fear; it means "awe." Maybe that is right. Maybe there is just a narrow line that separates the two, a shade of difference in meaning. But, nonetheless, fear is a wholesome thing. I do not think that we need to try to explain away fear. Fear is essential. It is good to be afraid of certain things.

In a sense, I was afraid of my father. Now I have heard some men say that in a derogatory way, but I do not mean it that way at all. There was that respect. I did not get overly familiar with my father. That does not mean that I did not love my father, but I did not get "buddy-buddy" with my father. As a result, he did not have to discipline me nearly as much as he would have had he not kept that distance. I respected my father. As I say, there was some fear that I had. I suppose you would call it fear. I think it was a wholesome thing. I held him in higher regard than I did most other people. So I think that it is a good thing to fear the Lord and nothing to be said against it at all. The beginning of wisdom is to fear the Lord. Notice what he says:

" . . . Blessed is the man that feareth the LORD . . . ." I am afraid to do wrong. I am a coward when it comes to doing wrong. I am afraid of the consequences. I was afraid of my father in that sense. He left a job for me to do, a field for me to plow, a chore for me to perform, and he went off. If he returned and I had not done it, I was afraid.

First of all, I was embarrassed; and then I knew that he would be displeased. Not that he would always punish, but there was that fear. I am afraid of sin, and it is a wholesome thing to be afraid of sin. So if you have some sin in your life, you are trying to serve God, and you are trying to get your prayers answered, you have every reason to be afraid of sin. Sin is that which hinders your prayers being answered. Sin is that which hinders the joy that you get out of being a Christian. I believe that it is part of being a Christian to fear sin. If you lose your fear of sin, you are in bad condition. So, " . . . Blessed is the man that feareth the LORD . . . ." He has the proper respect for what God's Word says. He believes it and when it talks about judgment for sin, he believes that there will be judgment for sin and that he cannot escape it.

Then the next thing, " . . . Blessed is the man . . . that delighteth greatly in his [the Lord's] commandments." One writer put it, "His commandments are not grievous to those who love the Lord." It is no real chore for a Christian to keep the commandments of the Lord. Now in moments of weakness, you may break the commandments of God; but your attitude or your purpose is to keep the commandments of the Lord in everything.

Now you know, examination time is upon us. If you have a proper respect for God's Law, God's Word, God's command-ments, why, every teacher could put his examination on the blackboard and walk out, and there would be no dishonesty whatever. But in moments of weakness we forget. We get into a tight situation and because we are weak we yield to certain

34

pressures. But I say again, if we had proper regard for the commandments of God and feared God as we ought, there would never be any dishonesty on examinations. We could always leave our billfold on our dresser, and it would be there when we returned if everybody had proper regard for the commandments of the Lord and feared the Lord. It is a wonderful thing to fear God. It is that which keeps men right, and to delight in keeping God's commandments.

Now we have some rules and regulations around here, and I hear people who do not understand them sometimes criticizing them, "Oh, those rules are terrible!" They are not to the man who wants to do right. The Law is despised by the man who wants to do evil.

The Law gets in the way of the violator, not the man who wants to do right. The man who wants to drive 80 miles an hour in a 50 miles speed zone, gets irritated with the speed laws, not the man who wants to drive within it. And so, the student who wants to do right around here, he fears God, and he delights in keeping the commandments of God. To him, rules are not problems. He does not chafe under them at all.

I have noticed young people come to school; they get along very well; they are happy. Sometimes they fall in love and start dating, and then they get as cantankerous as they can be. They get to hating and despising the dating rules. They do not want a chaperone anywhere around. Now why? Well, you say, I just do not like anybody around. Nobody is going to bother you when you are dating if you want to behave yourself. Nobody gets close enough to hear those silly things that you talk about. Nobody wants to hear it anyway. It would make you sick. Only people in love can stand such. That is not made for normal people. But seriously, I have noted that a student gets to despising the rules when he wants to violate them. As long as everything is going along and the rule does not touch him, he does not care how many rules you have. In fact, he is glad for them. He is glad you have got one for the other fellow. But when he wants to violate one, he despises them, and he starts griping about it.

Now you know the commandments of God are the same way. There are a lot of people who are just raving mad at God and will not admit it. They are living in sin and disobedience to the commandments of God, and they do not want to admit that is their trouble. They take it out on somebody else.

Now notice something else. First of all it says, " . . . Blessed is the man that feareth the LORD, that delighteth greatly in his commandments. His seed shall be mighty upon the earth . . . ." You have heard a lot about preachers' kids and how bad they are. On the whole, their batting average is mighty good. Somebody ran a survey not too long ago, and I was very interested in reading it. More ministers' children have become outstanding than any other professional group, if you call it a professional group. More have been governors of states, more have been presidents, and you find it true right on down the line. This man who keeps the laws of God and delights in keeping them and fears God, his seed shall be mighty upon the earth. Thank God for ministers' children, those who have been reared in godly homes. They do not all turn out bad.

" . . . The generation of the upright shall be blessed. Wealth and riches shall be in his house . . . ." The man who fears and delights in keeping the commandments of God has wealth and riches. You say, "Oh, boy, I am going to start keeping the commandments. I will get rich." Yes, you will be rich. There is no doubt about it. There has never been a man yet that kept the commandments of God that did not get rich. It never fails. Every out-and-out Christian is wealthy. You say, "Well, this is a bunch of backslidden Free Will Baptists around here. Something is wrong with us. We had better join something else." No, you are rich. You are rich if you are a godly person.

Now listen, would you trade places with a rich sinner? I mean a man who had all the money that he could handle? No, you would not. You would not swap places with a sinner that is filthy rich. I would not, if we just had to swap places. For me to take his bank account and for me to take his spiritual condition and swap, I would not do it. You would not either. I am richer than he. Any wealthy millionaire oil man out of Texas who is a sinner, I have got it over him. I am richer than he. I have got something that he cannot buy with all his money. Now he could have what I have if he wanted it.

So the man who fears God, keeps His commandments, and takes pleasure in keeping His commandments is rich. Thank God for this faith that you have. It is not on the market; you cannot call up the stock exchange and buy shares in it. It is a gift. You receive it when you receive Jesus Christ. So you have something. Do not feel sorry for yourself. Do not feel sorry for yourself. You may have to ride the bus while the other fellow drives a Cadillac. You may have to walk where you go; but while you walk, there is something down in your soul that money cannot buy. So, " . . . Wealth and riches shall be in his house: and his righteousness endureth for ever."

I will tell you what is keeping America and making it what it is today: It is the godly heritage that we have. Our forefathers who feared God came to these shores, destitute as far as worldly things go. In their hearts, they had a fear of God, and they wanted to keep His commandments. They passed on to us a wonderful heritage, and it has made America the greatest nation in all the world. We have never lost a war. The last few years we have stopped winning them, but we have not lost one. But that has made America great.

Now what are you going to pass on to America to keep her great? Where is that sterling character, the faith in God that we used to know, that our forefathers passed on to their sons? Are we going to pass it on? We are going to pass on a TV generation of softies with no convictions. People who do not react with disgust at sin and evil. Thank God for the man who can register disgust when he sees sin. We are coddling a generation of young people that are sitting before the TV and instead of registering disgust at that filth, trash, and immorality that you see on the screen, they delight in it. We are not going to have a generation that will register disgust.

Every time I pass a liquor store I register disgust. It still makes me mad. I saw just this morning, I believe, a whole strip down one side of the newspaper. "Yellow Stone," I suppose is whiskey, I do not know. I would not even look at it. It made me angry. I wish I could tear that paper up. I wish somebody would put out a paper that we would not have to look at that stuff. I would subscribe to it. I was brought up in a day when you did not have to look at neon lights, liquor stores, and beer taverns, and I never have gotten used to it.

You came up later, and maybe that is all you have ever known. Perhaps you do not register disgust because you have never known anything different. I pity you. This generation will never know how to register disgust at those sordid love scenes on TV because that is all they have ever known. I get up and turn my TV off in disgust. That is the only way I know to register it. If it would do any good, I would throw it out the back door. All you have got to do is look in through the window at your neighbor's , and you cannot get away from it.

"Wealth and riches shall be in his house: and his righteousness endureth for ever. Unto the upright there ariseth light in the darkness: he is gracious, and full of compassion, and righteous." You have never seen a real godly man that was not tender, gentle, and kind. I was thinking of that this morning. I do not know what caused me to think of it. I was thinking of a man just recently who was careless in the way he talked to a waitress. He was not thinking. The waitress came and graciously took our order, and he was a bit short. We were in conversation, and without thinking he answered her rather curtly. He did not intend it that way, but I was sitting there listening and I said, "How many times have I answered somebody in that fashion without thinking?" Maybe many, many times. But in his heart and soul, every good man is a tender, gentle, thoughtful, compassionate man, and does not want to hurt anybody.

I know a man who has always been known as a rough-and-ready type fellow. He would kick you out of the office at the drop of the hat. He would fight. That has been the image that people had of him, and that is what I thought about him until I had to borrow some money from him one day. Why, I was scared to death. I was desperate; I had to have it. I went in to see him. You know, when you borrow money from a man, he wants you to pay him back, and he is very nice to you until you get it paid back at least. But any way, I found this man to be a very gentle, tender, considerate fellow. He was a gentleman in every sense of the word in his personal dealings with you, a real Christian. I have found every good man to be that kind of person. It is the little men who will rule you. The little man who has got to bolster his ego. He does not really have it, but he has got to pretend that he has it. He is the fellow who is hard to get along with. But the good person is always compassionate, thoughtful, a gentleman, or a lady.

"Unto the upright there ariseth light in the darkness. . . ." I have preached on that several times here. That is one of the greatest thrills to me in all the world. In the darkness, there is always a light! You know, they had this blackout up there in the northeast a few weeks ago. One hotel up there bought 30,000 candles. I think I will go into the candle business and get located up there and hope for another blackout. They said that the candles sold at extortionate prices.

It was a total blackout. Airplanes flying along, and I read a report that one pilot was speaking over the loudspeaker system and said to the passengers, "I would like to call to your attention that we are now passing over Boston," and there was a glow of lights there. If you have ever taken a plane ride, you know how it looks. He was pointing out Boston when all of a sudden, no Boston. You can imagine how you would feel up there with everything going black all of a sudden.

There was total darkness. Listen, you know God might have been trying to say something to America. He might have been saying that is the way you are as you are pushing Me out the door. You are getting to be like this. No light. That reference fits every person who is not a Christian: total darkness, total eclipse. But not to the upright. There is always light. There is never a blackout. *Never* a blackout in the Christian's life. There is always that light. You always know where you are going. You do not have to stumble. "Unto the upright there ariseth light in the darkness . . . ." There are dark places in life. You will go through the valley of the shadow, but there is a light in your heart and soul if you are living for Jesus Christ.

Shall we stand, please.

PRAYER

Bless O Lord, this day to us and us to the day, and the responsibilities that are ours. Help us to be faithful and true to them. We thank Thee for Thy Word. May we hide a portion of it in our hearts today that we may not sin against Thee. In Jesus' Name, we pray. Amen.

6

September 21, 1971
Scripture: Jeremiah 5:25
Subject: "Sin Withholds Good Things from the Lord"

SIN WITHHOLDS GOD'S BLESSINGS

I want to say just a word concerning the message Sunday evening. You heard Mr. Forlines speak on Sunday evening, and it was a great message. I hope you recognized it as a great message, a great truth. I want to point up these things to you because sometimes we can come into a service and take for granted, well, this is just like it always is. I will just settle down here and go through the routine of the service, and you never do enter into it in thought or in spirit. It is very easy to do. All of us are guilty of it at times. From this platform time to time you hear various speakers. Some of them are visiting speakers, and some of them from our own men here on this platform. You hear some of the greatest messages you will ever hear. I hope the commonplace things, the routine, will not blind us from these facts, that you will stay alert and that you will drink in every bit that you can because you need it. All of us need it.

The main thought of the message was that if you say you are a Christian and remain indifferent as a way of life, you just stay indifferent about spiritual things, then you are not a Christian. I think the Bible amply verifies this. We speak of worldly Christians. I guess I have said that, but I never have liked it. I did not like it when I said it. Worldly Christians. I just wanted to point this out to you because you have heard some great messages already this year. I have heard them as I sat here on this platform. The preaching is as good as you will hear anywhere, and let us benefit from it.

It is always a danger when you meet here day after day, at the same time. The same bell starts, the same bell stops you. We have to do things the same way, the same time to meet our schedule. There is always this danger of settling down and letting many good things pass over and never benefiting us.

Now I want to call your attention to a verse of Scripture found in Jeremiah, chapter 5, verse 25. "Your iniquities have turned away these things, and your sins have withholden good things from you."

"Your sins have withholden good things from you", I said somewhat jestingly to a friend of mine not long ago. He was commenting on something, and I said, "I see that you still have some of the old Adamic nature left over." His reply was, "Yes, I have enough of the old Adamic nature just to enjoy living." Now that was said in jest, but I got to thinking about it. I meant that back in our minds all of us have this idea that I do not want to get too good. I do not want to get so good until I cannot enjoy living. The devil prompts this attitude. He will tell you not to be too spiritual, or you will not have any fun. I think this is a pitch that he makes for young people especially. I do not want to get too holy or I will be an oddball.

Spirituality does not make you an oddball. It makes you what God intended you should be. Now a wrong idea about spirituality will make you an oddball, but getting close to God never hurt anybody. The nearer you get to God, the better you are, the more normal you are, measured by God's standards. The further away from God you are, the more abnormal you are. Now you may be more normal measured by the world's standards. If you wanted to be a normal businessman, you would stop by a liquor store this afternoon on your way home. So many of them do. They have had a hard day at the office. They say, "I am tense; I need to relax. I will get a bottle of whiskey, go home, and drink it." That happens all the time. That would be according to the world's standards. But that is not according to God's standards.

The devil has been telling people all through the ages that you cannot enjoy living if you are godly and live righteously. He first approached Eve with that same philosophy in the Garden of Eden. Now he said, "Eve, God is withholding something good from you, and if you will only eat of this fruit, then you can have the good thing that God is withholding," and Eve bought it. She said, "That must be right." She ate it, her eyes were opened, and she beheld good and evil. It was the first time that her eyes had ever seen evil. Everything that she had ever looked at before was good. She saw no sin in anything. There was no guilt. There were pangs of conscience as she realized she had done evil. She had never felt that before.

Adam and Eve, living in the garden, did not have to have clothing because they saw no evil. They knew no evil. When she sinned, she saw evil for the first time. She had seen good before. They wanted to put on clothing immediately because they realized that they were naked, and they had a guilt feeling. They sewed fig leaves together to make them aprons to hide themselves because of a guilty conscience. For the first time they saw sin in things. The devil had played a trick on them. The devil is still playing that trick. He is telling people all the time, "You just cannot live by the standard of the Word of God and get along in this world."

A business man said to me, "You cannot live according to the teachings of this Bible and stay in business in today's business world." Now he is supposed to be a good Christian. But he said it would not work. You cannot be prosperous; you will go broke. See, the devil had pulled a trick on him. He said, in other words, "God's standards will not work. You have got to cheat a little." So the Bible says here, " . . . Your sins have withholden good things from you."

Now the devil has always been a liar. Jesus called him the father of lies. He lied from the beginning, Jesus said. So he is just an old, wicked, filthy liar when he tells you that if you are too holy and too good, you cannot enjoy living.

Many sinners have a feeling of pity for Christians. I heard a person say not too long ago, "But what do you do?" In other words, what do you do with yourself? Do you just sit? Now he did not say this, but this was implied. You cannot do this, you cannot do that, you cannot do the other. What do you do, just sit and twiddle your thumbs? He does not see what there is to the Christian life.

What are some of the good things that Satan withholds from you? Well, he withholds everything that is good. Just think of anything that is good, and sin will withhold it from you eventually. But let us just name a few. First of all, sin will withhold from you the favor of God. You cannot have the favor of God if you are living in sin. You cannot see the smile of God. I think when David sinned, there was a shadow that came between David and God; and David could not see God's face, and he was troubled and concerned. Let me say this. This is a sign of being a Christian. If you are troubled when you sin, this is a good sign that you are a Christian. But if you can sin and not be troubled by it, I would be troubled. I would not even claim to be a Christian. If I could go on and enjoy my sin and not be troubled, I think I would have every reason in the world to feel that I was not a Christian at all.

You may stumble and you may fall, but you will want to get up. You will not want to wallow in the quagmire of sin. No child of God gets a kick out of sin. And let me say this to you. You do not get a thrill by going back and reliving the past sins of your life. I sometimes hear preachers preach, and they recite the sinful story of their lives over and over again. Sometimes you can use it to illustrate and it is all right. But if you keep digging up the past and dragging it up, you give the impresion that you may be proud of your past sins and get a kick out of reliving them.

If, down deep in your heart, you are proud of your conquest in the field of sin and you get a kick out of it, there is something wrong with your heart. It is not a holy heart. It is a sinful heart. You cannot be proud of your past sins, and you cannot enjoy your present sins either. There is a sickening feeling at heart when a child of God sins.

Read the 32nd Psalm. There David is describing the pleasure, the attitude of his heart, during the time when he sinned and when he repented. Evidently it must have been quite a long time because David tells us some of his experiences during that period. He says, "When I kept silence, my bones waxed old through my roaring all the day long. For day and night thy hand was heavy upon me: my moisture is turned into the drought of summer."

He goes on and describes his barren heart during that period of time. That barren soul dried up within him and his conscience bore down upon him. God's hand was heavy upon him. He could not get away from a guilty conscience. He felt like his bones were drying up.

God was merciful in sending Nathan to him one day. He said, "Thou art the man, David." David then had to unclothe his sin and say, "Yes, I am." As long as he tried to hide those sins, he said God's hand was heavy upon me and the very moisture of my soul dried up. Whosoever sinneth shall not prosper. Whoso covereth his sins shall not profit. David had been covering his sin, and his heart and soul were giving him trouble.

If there is sin in your life and you are a child of God, there is trouble and you cannot enjoy life. You have either got to get completely away from God and let your conscience die, or else you have got to get right with God. You cannot go on being a child of God and enjoy living if you are living in sin. Sin withholds the favor of God.

It is a wonderful thing to be able to get in touch with God when you need Him. Sin separates. That is another verse of Scripture. Your sins have separated you from God. You cannot have this favor. You cannot see His face, and you cannot have the power of God. Your sins withhold the power of God. God's power is not there. Any man who has known the power of God upon his life misses it when it is gone. He is not happy. It is fruitless to get up and beat the air, to try to serve God with an empty heart. It is just words, sounding brass, tinkling cymbals, when the meaning is gone. When the anointing is gone, there is barrenness; there is emptiness. The power is withheld when you sin. You cannot live in sin, pretend to serve God, and have any fruit. God will not allow it. God will not anoint you. Not only that but the joy is gone. One of the fruits of the spirit that Paul talks about in Galatians 5 is joy. You know, it takes joy to keep going in the Christian life. There are heartaches, self-denials, but there is some joy too. This is what the world does not understand. This is the reason the world says, "What in the world do you do?"

A person asked me one time what we did here on campus to enjoy living. Some think this is a monastery, a monastic life. They evidently think that we go inside the wall, sit, and never smile. This is not a monastery. This is a place where happiness and joy are if you are right with God. Now listen, this could be the most miserable place in the world for you if you are not right with God.

I would advise a person who is not right with God not to come here. He would be dissatisfied. Not only would he cause us trouble, but he would be troubling himself. This is no place for a person who is not interested in Christian things. But if you are interested in Christian things and you want to do right and you want to live for God, there is a lot of fun around here. There is joy, and I think we have more happiness and joy on this campus than any campus I know anywhere.

There is joy even without bands. Oh, I hear a little horn blowing once in awhile, but we do not have to have marching bands. You do not have to have Saturday night dances. You do not have to have drums. You do not have to have beards. You do not have to have immorality. Just clean, decent living and enjoy it.

You know if you are not right with God, everything goes out of focus. Nothing is right. Once in a while in your church, you find a church member who has known the power and the favor of God, the joys of the Lord, and then he gets into sin and dries up. He gets out of whack and causes trouble because he is troubled on the inside. Listen, if you are troubled on the inside, you are going to cause trouble around you. If you are right on the inside, you are going to make things right around you too. You will be easy to live with because you are at peace with yourself when you are right with God. But sin withholds the joy of the Lord, and it makes you sorry that you are a Christian.

You pity yourself, the poor Christian. "I cannot smoke, I cannot chew, and I cannot run with folks who do," you know, that sort of philosophy.

If you are where you ought to be in the sight of God, you are not sorry you are a Christian. You are rejoicing that you have been saved from the ravages of sin. You get up every day thanking God that He has made you a child of His, He has cleaned you up on the inside, and your life is not being ruined by sin. Many of you are trophies of God's grace. Your life would be ruined, it would be completely wrecked had God not entered in and intervened. So sin withholds favor from the Lord.

Oh, there are many things sin withholds. It withholds that deep-settled peace, when the storm clouds of trouble come, and they are going to come to all of us. No use to talk to you when you are young. Some of you do not know trouble yet. Some of you have, but most of you have not. Down the road, there are storm clouds that trouble, periods of darkness, loneliness, and heartache that every man has to experience or will experience if he lives very long. But down deep underneath all of that, there is a deep-settled peace. There is a bedrock that holds you steady. God plants that indescribable something in the soul of His children, when the storms are raging. You know all is well when you experience that calm, when everything else about you is being shattered and torn; when sands are shifting under your feet. Sin will withhold that from you.

Sin will withhold a good name. You cannot have a good name very long if you live in sin. It ruins a good name. It takes away your reputation. Sin withholds a good name. It withholds a good conscience. You know you cannot buy a good conscience with popularity. You cannot buy a good conscience with fame. You cannot purchase a good conscience with scholarships. You cannot purchase a good conscience with wealth. A good conscience comes to men who know God and are right with

God. Sometimes you are lonely. You have to walk alone along a lonely path. But I will tell you to walk straight, to look yourself in the eye and say, "I have done right." That is what counts, that good clean conscience. You can smile while people throw stones at you. You can stand up under all kinds of opposition. You are not playing to the grandstand, you are not listening to the applause of men. You are listening to that inner voice of conscience that has as its foundation this eternal truth of God. When you have found it, you have taken your stand. Your conscience is clear. That is the reason those men of old could stand and be stoned and pray for those who stoned them. They were seeing the face of God, and their consciences were clear, clean.

I would rather have a good conscience than anything I know. It worries me when I feel that I have done wrong, when I have compromised. I have sold out for expediency. I feel dirty. I feel cheap when I have not done right. I have not stood for principle. I feel like what I am, just cheap, common. Oh, but those times when God has given me the courage to stand even though others did not understand, I have felt so good and decent. I have wondered why I did not do that all the time.

When you have said *no* to the pressures of sin, go home at night and say, "I am mighty glad I said *no*. I am mighty glad I took my stand. I am mighty glad I did not yield." I feel so decent. I feel respectable. You get up in the morning and look in the mirror as you shave and you say, "You know, there is a decent man." But to look in that mirror and say, "There is a compromiser, there is a weakling. There is a person who let passion overcome him. He did the common thing, the cheap thing. He has no character." I know of nothing that would drain the spirit out of a man anymore than that sort of feeling. You walk with downcast eyes, you cannot look yourself in the eye, neither can you look the world in the eye.

You may put on a big front, but down inside you know you are a compromiser. Sin withholds that from you. You cannot feel decent and clean with a guilty conscience. It takes something out of you.

So sin hurts you every way it touches you. There is not any of you any better off from any sin that you have ever committed. Now you know something that you would not have known. Eve knew something that she did not know after she had sinned. There are thousands of things that you would be better off if you did not know.

Some of us walk through life with chains around our feet and around our necks. We hobble along through life with the shackles of sin, memories that we wish we could forget. We will never soar as high as we would have if we could forget them. Every sin that you commit in some way becomes a millstone around your neck. Now God forgives it. We ought to forgive ourselves. I know that. We ought to try to forget them, but you are not any better off through the knowledge you have gained through sin. You are worse off. The one who has sinned least in this audience this morning is better off than anybody else.

Thank God for the grace of God that can make us all the same in the sight of God. Sin withholdeth good things from us. Do not dabble in sin. I wish I could make you scared of sin.

If there were a rattlesnake here in this building this morning and you had never seen a rattlesnake and did not know what it was, you know what I would do? I would lecture to all of you of the danger of a rattlesnake. I know what rattlesnakes will do. They are very common where I came from. I do not enjoy going into the woods because of rattlesnakes. If there was a rattlesnake loose, I would lecture you and tell you, do not get near it. It will coil and it will strike and it will put poison in your body and kill you. It is dangerous. Do not get near a rattlesnake. I would try to make you just as afraid of a rattlesnake as I could. I would paint as horrible a picture as I could about a rattlesnake, and I would tell you about it. I wish some way I could do that about sin. I wish I could paint the horrors of sin as they are and get everyone of you afraid of sin. Some of you have dabbled with it so much, and petted it so much, you would say, "It is not dangerous. It will not harm you." The devil has you deceived if you think that way. It is horrible; it will harm you.

PRAYER

Our Father, help us to feel as Jeremiah felt when he said sin would withhold good things from us. Give us that attitude. If we have that attitude, we will have the attitude and the spirit of the Lord. If there are any of us who are proud of our sins, who love our sins, Lord, pity us and have mercy. Convict us so that these can be dealt with in our lives so that the good things of the Lord will not be withheld from us. In Jesus' Name. Amen.

7

November 21, 1972
Scripture: Titus 2
Subject: "God's Advice to the Young and Aged"

GOD'S ADVICE TO THE YOUNG AND AGED

I want to read from Titus, chapter 2. The epistles, as you know, are given primarily to practical Christian living. Telling Christians, those who have been saved by the grace of God, how they should live. They are very practical instructions for Christian behavior which is so very important. The practical aspect of Christian living is emphasized around here a great deal. It is emphasized in chapel perhaps more than any other one truth. No doubt it is proper that we do this because you are studying your doctrine, your theology, and other areas. I believe one emphasis that has characterized Free Will Baptist Bible College and its students over the years is the conduct of our students.

This is one thing that is mentioned to me more often in this city than any other. I have so many people say to me statements like this, "I know your students. I see your students. They are nicely-dressed, well-behaved, courteous, and refined." They make so many nice comments. I believe our emphasis on Christian behavior in chapel and other places is largely responsible for this. This is the way it ought to be. A Christian institution should be characterized by Christian behavior. The only theology some of these people will ever know who travel West End Avenue will be what they see in your behavior. That is all they will ever know about Christianity. They may not be saved. Many of them are not, of course. But they know that good conduct should go along with the Christian profession, and it should. This is what is emphasized in many of these epistles. That is what is emphasized in this chapter this morning, some very practical things.

"But speak thou the things which become sound doctrine." This is the way he begins. In other words, if your doctrine is sound, then there are certain things that are becoming to it. It is not becoming for the person to have sound doctrine and be careless in his behavior. Now many people have sound doctrine, but they are careless in their behavior. They are not sound in their Christian living. The two should go together. To have sound doctrine, you ought to have a good life because sound doctrine begets sound living, proper conduct. So he is talking about things that become sound doctrine.

It is more proper if you are going to live careless to have the theology that reflects your living. The two will go together. You would expect someone who is a liberal to be off on his behavior. You would not expect a person who has a sound doctrine and who can recite all the fundamentals of faith to be off on his pattern of living. So he is talking about faith that becomes sound doctrine. Now he talks to four groups of people. He is talking to the old men, the old women, the young men, and the young ladies; and he gives a message to each. Now he says to the aged men, "be sober"; that is, be serious. You say, I expect old men to be serious. They are getting toward the evening of life, and they do not get excited about the pleasures of this world anymore. Naturally, they are rather morbid. He is not talking about being morbid. He is talking about being serious because this matter of Christian living is serious.

I want to recommend to you an article in *Contact,* this month's issue. Mr. Forlines talks about the place recreation has in the church. I think it is excellent. I hope that it is read seriously across our denomination because this matter of recreation can bring a levity into the church. It can get out of control. It can leave the impression that Christianity is a game of hopscotch. I do not see anybody playing it anymore. Maybe you do not know what I am talking about. But you can very easily leave the impression that Christianity is just a game through emphasizing recreation, having fun. It is something to be taken lightly.

Paul is emphasizing here another side of this thing. He is saying, Tell the old men to be sober, that is, to be serious. You do not have to be the life of every party. You do not need to be known as the best story teller. You do not need to be known as the best joke teller in the community. You do not need to be known as the best golfer in the community. If you play enough golf to be the best golf player in town, you play too much golf. If you are known as the best fisherman in the whole country, you fish too much. So you need to be careful. It is all right to fish, and it is all right to play golf; but you do not need to spend too much time at it. You do not need to be characterized with these things. And you do not need to be characterized by being the life of every party, even though Christianity is not morbid. It is serious.

He is saying to these old men, " . . . be sober, grave, temperate . . ." that is, have control of yourselves, be sound in faith. He puts the behavior along with his faith. He says these things go along with sound faith. He also adds, " . . . in charity, in patience . . . ."

Next he talks to the older women. He says, " . . . likewise, that they be in behaviour as becometh holiness, not false accusers . . . ." Now he knew some weaknesses of women even back in those days: talking a little too much. Men talk too much. I do not know why he listed this under the advice to women, but he did. Aged women are not to be given to much wine but teachers of good things. He is giving advice to the older women that they may teach the young women to be sober; that is, serious minded. If they are going to teach it, they are going to have to be a good example themselves. So he is giving the same advice to the older women that he gave to the older men. Then he tells the older women, " . . . Teach the young women to be sober, to love their husbands . . . ."

Now I do not know just how they should go about that, but let me say this to you young people. Many of you are going to get married soon after you get out of college. You are at the age that you are thinking of getting married, and it is only normal and proper. But you are going to have to learn to love one another after you get married.

Now you think that you are in love when you get married, and as far as you know, you are in love. But I want to tell you something. It is just puppy love until the true love develops that you will know after 30 or 40 years. You are going to have to learn to love one another. It is going to grow. I know what you think. You think that old people who do not sit close together when they drive down the highway have fallen out of love. No, they have just fallen in love, and they do not have to prove anything. The closer you sit when you drive down the highway, the harder you have to prove that you love one another. After you really fall in love, you do not have to prove it anymore. She sits where she wants to, and you sit where you want to.

I am serious about this. Most of love is learned after you get married. The trials of life, the tears, the disappointments, the sickness of your children, and the heartaches: They bring you together and melt your lives into one life. Most of this is learned after you marry. So you are just starting to school when you get married. Do not get impatient. That is where divorce comes in. You get impatient. You think, "Well, I thought I loved him." But you get up and look at him with his face covered with a beard. You say, "This fellow does not look good to me." These long-bearded fellows, I still do not see how any woman tolerates it. But you look at him unkempt. You say, "Is that the fellow I married?" He looks at you the same way with curlers in your hair and housecoat on.

Let me tell you this. You always get up and get dressed, comb your hair, go to the kitchen, and cook a good breakfast, and you will never have any problems with your man. That is right. If I had to look at some of these things that I see seven days a week, I might get a divorce too. I could not stand it. But if you will take care of the little things in your marriage, the big things will take care of themselves. If you will take care of the little things, you will never have any problems.

It takes discipline. You have to feel that it is worth it. You ought to go to a little trouble to please your husband just like you

54

went to the trouble to please your boyfriend. If you will practice a little of that through life, everything will work all right. But you are going to have to learn to love one another after you get married; give it time. Do not get impatient. This is what he is saying to these older women: Teach the young women to love their husbands.

Teach them " . . . to love their children . . . ." This has always sounded strange to me. Do you have to teach mothers to love their children? Let me tell you this: You have to practice taking care of your children and develop an interest in them. If you will do it, your love will grow. There are many mothers who are irritated by their children. Their children are in their way. They hinder them. They have to change their pattern of living when children come in the home and they do not want to. They want to be carefree. So you have to practice these things. Love does not come automatically. It does not come in a package all wrapped up. You have to practice and cultivate it and it will come. He tells the older women to do this for the sake of the younger women.

Now he talks to the young women: " . . . Be discreet, chaste [that is, pure], keepers at home . . . ." Keep the home together. Listen, there is not anything more important than keeping that home together, and it is a job. I will tell you, I would hate to keep a home together. Wives make all these appointments for their children to get their teeth taken care of. When they are sick, they make appointments with the doctor and see that the medicine is taken. They see that their clothes are in shape, that everything is in readiness, that the meals are prepared, and the right kind of meals day in and day out. I will tell you that is one of the biggest jobs. It would kill the average man if he had to do it.

You want to take off some weight? Most of you are not married, but if you want to take off some weight, just take over your wife's work for a week or two. It will take inches off of you in a hurry if it does not kill you. And my, what it is to have a good environment at home. It is pleasant to come home after you have had a hard day and find everything is good, the fire is going, the house is warm, the meal is cooked, and everything is fine. I will tell you, you will have no problem keeping a home together if you will make a good home. This is why God, no doubt, said man needs a helpmate. Man cannot do that. His fingers are too blunt, too big. He just does not fit. You talk about liberation for women. They are not slaves. They are queens in the home. They are homemakers. They keep the home together. What a great thing it is, " . . . Keepers at home . . . ."

I am saying this to the younger women. Now some of this sounds a little strange today. " . . . Obedient to their own husbands . . . ." How do you like that? Some say, "I do not believe that. I believe in 50-50." I do not. I believe in 100-100. In other words, it is a hundred-hundred deal. You giving all and she giving all. This 50-50 deal does not work in marriage. Give yourself 100 percent to your husband and feel that he is the greatest man in all the world. If you feel that way toward him, he is going to feel that way toward you. But if you just have a 50-50 feeling toward him, it will reduce to a 25-25. After a while, it will all be gone.

Marry the kind of man that you can be glad to obey. I think this is what it means: that you will want to please him. You know, when you want to please someone, it is not hard at all to obey. If you know what he wants, that is what you do. If you know what he likes to eat, that is what you prepare if it is good for him. You know how to please him and that is what you do. If you are pleasing him, then you are happy. Then he wants to please you, and this makes a wonderful home. So he says here to the young women, be obedient to your own husband. Do not marry the kind of man that you cannot respect. If you cannot respect him, you cannot love him. If you respect him, you will want to do what he wants you to do. It is not a pain. It is a pleasure. This is God's order.

With the liberation movement some of the women are trying to push, I am so glad to see so many women speaking out against this thing. The woman out there in the man's world is chained. She is in bondage, but the woman who is serving as God intended is the one who is liberated. " . . . Obedient to their own husbands, that the word of God be not blasphemed." It does not say in order to please yourselves, but it says that you may have a good testimony as Christians.

Now he speaks to the young men. " . . . Likewise exhort to be sober minded." You mean even young people? Yes. College age people? Yes. Before we get married? Yes. You mean all the fun is going to go out of life? No. But remember that being a Christian is serious business. I am concerned with the levity and the lightness that I see in the Christian movement today. I see it in the kind of songs that we sing. I am not happy with these little meaningless jingles that have a light, lively tempo and a little bit of harmony thrown in. There is a lightness of message, a lack of depth.

I want to say to any of you who sing, analyze the song. I am 100 percent disgusted with this semi-rock stuff. Those great majestic hymns. Where are they? Who knows them? Who sings them? They have gone out the window and some little light, frivilous something that makes you want to jump up and down a little bit has replaced them. It has some kind of a Christian message to it, you say. It is lacking in depth. The songs that fail to magnify, glorify, and exalt the Lord Jesus Christ are not worthy.

You know songs can be man-centered, or they can be God-centered. Our songs do not need to be centered around man. They need to be centered in God, a God of glory and majesty. I would like to see us get back to the seriousness in all of these areas that the Bible talks about. So much of this music appeals to the flesh. We use it to gather people around us. Music attracts people, yes, but what are people attracted to? Some frivilous melody or jingle that is thrown together will attract the flesh, and it can be very deceptive. So we need to be serious.

I want to say just a word, skipping over here, "For the grace of God that bringeth salvation hath appeared to all men, Teaching us . . . ." Listen, if you know the grace of God, if you know Jesus Christ, you have already been taught that you ought to deny ungodliness. When you get saved, you get a set of convictions. Nobody has to teach you. You know it is wrong to be immoral if you are a good Christian. You know it is wrong to be dishonest if you are a Christian. If you know the grace of God, you know what is right and wrong. You do not have to be told by anybody. The grace of God has taught us that we are to deny ungodliness. If you do not know that, you are not saved. If you are always trying to go as far into sin as you can go without getting in trouble, there is something wrong in your heart. You are not right with God.

PRAYER

Thank you for thy Word, our Father. How we need it daily. Help us to hide it in our hearts. Thank You for the way some were listening. Some were not listening. We all have to answer for every opportunity we have had. Be with us throughout the day. In Jesus' Name. Amen.

8

August 29, 1973
Scripture: 1 Peter 2:7-9
Subject: Jesus Is Precious

JESUS CHRIST IS PRECIOUS

There are always quite a few meetings and loose ends that we have to get together at the beginning, so I am not going to keep you long. The weather is unusually warm too, so chapel will be rather brief today. You remember the announcements that pertain to you. Now we have plenty of seats for the ones who are standing. We are not going to ask you to come now, but tomorrow let us all find our seats and be seated because there are plenty of seats. I think it will be full if we have the ones standing seated tomorrow. So find your places until we get seats designated. It will be a little confusing, but we can find our places.

In 1 Peter, chapter 2, verses 7 through 9 - "Unto you therefore which believe he is precious: but unto them which be disobedient, the stone which the builders disallowed, the same is made the head of the corner,

And a stone of stumbling, and a rock of offence, even to them which stumble at the word, being disobedient: whereunto also they were appointed.

But ye are a chosen generation, a royal priesthood, an holy nation, a peculiar people; that ye should shew forth the praises of him who hath called you out of darkness into his marvellous light."

This verse 7, "Unto you therefore which believe he is precious . . . ." I wonder what our attitudes this morning are concerning the Lord Jesus Christ? What are our feelings toward Him? Is He just another person to us? Is He just a person we have heard preached about all of our lives, and we have made some kind of profession concerning Him as our Savior? Or is He a living reality in your life? What experiences have you had with the Lord Jesus Christ that have developed your attitude toward Him?

Well, first of all if you are a Christian, there has been the experience of salvation. Jesus Christ is precious to us. We could go back and say that He is precious because of who He is, His own person. He is a person without sin. Never was there an evil thought that flickered across His mind. Can you imagine a person like that? It is hard for us to imagine that Jesus Christ never entertained an evil thought. Jesus Christ never entertained hatred. There was never jealousy in His heart. He held no grudges. There was no deceit at any time in His life. Was He deceitful? He was always honest with everyone, honest with Himself.

Jesus Christ was the sinless One. He is precious because of that. Now it is hard for us to appreciate a sinless person. Most of the time we would be uncomfortable around a sinless person, but we are not uncomfortable around Jesus. Perhaps you have met a few people that pretended to be perfect. They thought they were sinless. I have met a few people like that. I was always uncomfortable around them. First of all, I did not have respect for them because I thought that they were deceiving. They were deceiving themselves but not so of Jesus. Jesus Christ was the sinless Son of God. He was precious and is precious in His person. He loves people. He loves you. He has your best interest at heart.

So then He is precious because of what He has done. He died in your place and mine at Calvary. The unselfish One, the One who loved us so much that He gave Himself as a sacrifice in your place and in my place at Calvary. He is precious because of Calvary. Then He is precious because I have come to know Him as my Savior. He is the One who spoke forgiveness to my soul one day, when my soul was troubled because of sin. I tried so many ways to get rid of my sin. I tried being good. That would not work. I tried good works and that did not work. There still was the burden of guilt of sin upon my heart and soul. I struggled with it. I had to live with it. It caused me to lose sleep. Now I do not know what your experience has been, but when you met Jesus

Christ, there should have been a great burden lifted from your soul and your mind, a tortured mind, perhaps. All the sins of our past were gone, and we felt clean and decent to stand before God for the first time. He is precious because of what He did in my heart and in my life.

Notice the way that Peter puts it here. He says, "Unto you therefore which believe . . . ." See, this is something special for those who believe, not for everyone. Jesus Christ is not precious to everyone. He is precious to a special group of people. He is precious unto the ones who believe.

He is precious not only for that reason, what He did for me when I confessed my sins, but He is precious as you think of Him as your High Priest. You know, the continued ministry of the Lord Jesus Christ is something that is not emphasized nearly as much as it ought to be. We think of Jesus as having gone back to Heaven and sitting at the right hand of the Father. We tend to think He is sort of idle there, waiting until the time comes for Him to return to this earth, but that is not true at all. Jesus is continuing His ministry on your behalf. He is pleading your cause up there at the right hand of God the Father. He is your High Priest, the covering of His blood was for our sins. He is interceding for you and me. He is active on our behalf. His continued ministry, I am glad for that. I would have fallen beside the wayside long ago had it not been for the continued ministry of the Lord Jesus Christ. In my moments of weakness, He has interceded. Whenever I sinned, I went to Him and confessed my sins, and He took my case up with God the Father. He went between, and He has satisfied God because I have confessed my sins. He is faithful and just to forgive us our sins. I am glad I have such a High Priest, such a representative in Heaven today as the Lord Jesus Christ.

He is precious because He answers our prayers. I wonder if you could look back in your past experience and put your finger on some definite answers to prayer? What a wonderful thing it is to look back and say, "I know that Jesus Christ heard and answered my prayer concerning this particular, specific matter." Oh, what a wonderful thing when our hearts are burdened. We come to Him and He lifts the burden, casting all our cares upon Him because He careth for us. So He is precious; any way you look at Him, He is precious.

You can think of many other ways. I could think of many other ways that Jesus Christ is precious. If you are a preacher, you ought to make a sermon on this. You could just go on and on and on and name things and ways in which He is precious.

But now notice, there is another side to it. He is not precious to the ones who do not believe; He becomes a stumblingstone. He gets in the way of the sinner. The sinner is trying to have peace. The sinner is trying to do the things that he wants to do in life, and Jesus Christ gets in his way. Jesus Christ is a problem to the sinner.

Ah, listen, Jesus Christ is trying to cause that sinner to stumble and turn to God, but the sinner will not. He keeps stumbling on in his blindness. He is a rock of stumbling to the ones who do not believe. He is a great bother to the one out of the will of God.

You know, I have seen a few students here that Jesus Christ bothered. He will bother you if you get into sin. He will trouble your heart, your mind, and your soul. You cannot have peace because God has said in His Word, "There is no peace," to the wicked. God will not let you have peace. God will not let you have true happiness. Oh, the devil will give you some sensations that we call happiness now and then. He will stir up our senses, and we will laugh and we think we are having fun for a while. There is a big difference between having real deep peace, deep peace of the soul, mind, and heart that only God can give, and the "peace" that the devil gives. God said, "You cannot have peace." If you are fighting against Jesus, you are stumbling over a stumblingstone, and He is causing you all kinds of problems. Until you find the will of God for your life and submit to the will of God, you are going to continue to be frustrated and have problems. He is a stone of stumbling for those who do not believe. He is precious to those who do believe. This sense of believing means that we have yielded ourselves unto Him. "Unto you therefore which believe he is precious . . . ." I trust He is a precious Savior to you.

May we stand.

PRAYER

Our Father, in these days of getting registered and adjusted, sometimes our emotions are so stirred that we lose sight of Jesus. But in the midst of our activities and in the midst of emotional upheavals, we pray that we might not lose sight of Jesus. May we let Him be precious to us today, in meeting all the needs of our lives. In Jesus' Name. Amen.

9

October 9, 1973
Scripture: Galatians 1; Titus 2; 2 Peter 1
Subject: Apostasy, Etc.

THE GRACE OF GOD TEACHES US

We will read from three places this morning: Galatians, chapter 1; Titus, chapter 2; and 2 Peter, chapter 1. You may want to turn there, or you may want to just listen while I read.

One of the distinctive doctrines of Free Will Baptists is the doctrine of the possibility of apostasy or apostatizing. That means the possibility to be lost after you have once been saved. I would like to just say a word about this. I will not go into it in detail. You will have this discussed in various Bible courses, but we believe that it is possible for a person to lose his faith. We believe that you are saved " . . . by grace . . . through faith; and that not of yourselves . . . not of works, lest any man should boast." We do not believe in a work salvation.

Now many people think that you have to believe in a work salvation if you believe in the possibility of apostasy. To me that is not true at all. We believe in salvation by grace through faith, but we do believe it is through faith. We believe that a person's faith can be weakened and be lost. Now we do believe, or personally I believe, that a person's behavior has a bearing on his faith. This is the only way that your behavior will affect your salvation, but behavior will affect your faith.

For instance, if you fail to go to church, to read your Bible, and to pray, then after awhile you will begin to weaken in your faith. You get out and start living in sin, and your faith will be affected. It will be weakened. There is a danger in letting your faith weaken. It can get to the point where your faith will be lost. You can make shipwreck of faith. But since you are saved by grace through faith, you have to shipwreck in faith in order to lose your salvation. We do not believe it is works that saves you or keeps you saved. It is your faith, but works as I said may have, and I think will definitely have a bearing on your faith. So it is very important the way you live.

It is very important to be faithful to the Lord because your faith can weaken and it can be lost. You can make shipwreck of your faith. Now this is one of the cardinal, distinctive doctrines of the Free Will Baptist denomination. Other Baptist groups and many other groups, of course, do not believe that after you are once saved, you can lose your faith. They believe you are saved no matter what, and you are going to be saved for all eternity. I think when it talks about eternal life that it is not talking about duration of time necessarily. I think it is talking about quality of life. In other words, when you have Jesus Christ in your heart, you have eternal life because He is eternal life. But I do not think it is talking about duration. I think it is talking about the quality of life, the kind of life that you have. And your faith, we believe, puts you in touch with this life.

There has been a change I think in the Free Will Baptist denomination in its emphasis of this truth in recent years. There are still people who believe if you sin, you are lost. Well, this brings you into all kinds of problems. They believe that your works determine your salvation. They believe that you are saved by grace through faith initially, and then after this, it is up to you. Your behavior, not your faith necessarily, but your behavior determines whether you continue as a Christian or not.

Now there is quite a difference at this point. We will not labor the point here this morning. I want to say this to you, to you young preachers and you who go out to teach: I would not get deeply involved in a discussion of this kind until I had studied and had it well in hand. You can do great harm. I would stay away from certain of these difficult problems. I would stay with the simpler things. You know you are saved; give your testimony. Preach the things that you are sure of. But I would stay out of these deep theological waters. You are not ready to wade there yet. I know that it is fascinating. I know that you get great delight in arguing this in the dormitory, but confine the arguments to the dormitory. Do not let it get out here in the churches where people can be confused by your own confusion. So I would just warn you at this point.

Some of these things belong later on down the road. Do not get too anxious to get into them and set the world straight on them because you may not be as sure of just what you believe at this point as you think you are when you once get to discussing it. But I want to raise a warning. Even though we believe in salvation " . . . by grace . . . through faith . . . Not of works, lest any man should boast," it is not license, whatsoever, for careless living. Absolutely not. We repudiate this 100 percent. People who think that they can be saved by grace through faith, not of works, and go out and live any way they please and take that sort of attitude, as far as I discern, they have not been saved. Your attitude was changed when you were saved. You are not looking for a license to sin when you have been saved. A child of God is wanting to live right. Now he may have weaknesses, and those weaknesses may overcome him along the way; but the pattern, listen, the pattern, the general behavior of a child of God, is to do right. If that is not the general pattern of his life, there is something wrong.

Now you can have a false faith and a false hope. You can believe that you are saved and not be saved. The Bible says, "There is a way which seemeth right unto a man, but the end thereof are the ways of death." Just because you feel saved sometimes does not mean that you are. You had better look at the pattern of your life. The general pattern of your life ought to be right. The desires of your heart, soul, and mind should be to live right. When you are overcome of a sin or a weakness, the attitude of a child of God when he is overcome is to have a broken heart. If you can get up from sin and smack your lips and enjoy it and delight in it, there is something wrong. There is something wrong. If you can go back in your memory and relive your sins with pleasant delights and fantasies, then you are committing that sin all over again in spirit. There is something wrong.

I say again, the child of God wants to live right, and sin is horrible to a holy heart where God lives. Remember that you have received a Holy Spirit, the spirit of God, and God's Spirit living in you is a Holy Spirit. He gives you a holy attitude. The spirit of your heart and life, if God dwells there and reigns and controls it, is a holy attitude, a holy desire. The Holy Spirit lives in your heart, and this is the spirit of your life if God is in control. Now there is the flesh that you still have to contend with, but you have these two natures, these two spirits. A child of God has the Holy Spirit that makes him want to be holy. So with that in mind, I want to read these verses.

Verse 4, chapter 1, Galatians: "Who gave himself [talking about Jesus Christ, of course] for our sins . . . ." Now we know that in this we have redemption; we have salvation. He gave Himself for our sins, but notice now the purpose of it: that He might deliver us from this present evil world according to the will of God and our Father. It is the will of God and the will of our Father that we be delivered from this present evil world. Now I am not going to get theological here. I understand we have the theological commission here. I ought not to be preaching on theology today. They are meeting here today. Where are these men? Oh, they are here. Well, anyway we are glad to have them. I want to get them theologically straightened out anyway.

You could say, "Well, this applies to our ultimate salvation when we are taken out of this world and given a new body." Well, let that be as it may. God wants us to live right here and now. It is God's will that we be delivered from this present evil world in our walk and in our behavior. God does not expect us to continue to walk in the old sins that we walked in before we were saved. Sometimes Christians get involved in sins after they are saved that they never got involved in before they were saved. What a shame.

God does not want you to walk in the flesh. God wants to deliver us from this present evil world. Now notice, this is an evil world. We have got to learn how to live righteously and holy and godly in an evil world. There is nothing in this world that makes it easy for us to live right. Everything is against you. Everything is against you. Radio is against you. You do not hear much decent on the radio; some, it is against you. Television is against you. Billboards are against you. Magazine racks are against you. Your peers that you lived with out in the world, they were against you, most of them. Not many of them were Christians. Society is in general against you. Everything is against you. It is an evil world.

Yet He says Jesus Christ gave Himself for us that He might deliver us from it, that He might save us from it. God expects us to be saved from this evil world. If the kind of clothes you wear are suggestive, put on the right kind. We are not to be controlled by the pattern and the fashions of a godless society. Why in the world Christians get sucked into this, I do not know. Why we do not use our head and our senses, why we just go along, I do not understand it. The pressure of this world, we conform to it. Somebody said that the only thing different about Christians is we are just about ten years behind. We finally come around to adopting the standards of this present world. We are just a little slower. We are reluctant to be immodest, but eventually, if we are not careful, we will be dressing immodestly. God help us not to be influenced by this evil world. God wants to deliver us from it.

You know a lot of times in courtship, Christian young people will do the same things that they did before they were saved. They are doing the same things that unchristian young people are doing. They just salve it over with a little prayer at the end of it, a little pious talk, or maybe they will read a portion out of the Bible and then go on and behave in courtship just like the world. God forbid. They stir their passions up to a boiling point and then hope to escape sin. It does not make sense.

God wants to deliver us from this present evil world because it says this is the will of God our Father. God does not want us to behave like sinners after we have been saved. We are His children. We represent holiness, righteousness, and purity. Oh, God forbid that we take this matter of being Christians lightly and be influenced by people to behave according to the flesh and ruin our testimony.

Listen, you can ruin your testimony with yourself. Before you ever hurt your testimony with anybody else, you are going to hurt your testimony with yourself. You have got to have a good testimony with yourself. The first person that you have got to live with, and the most important person that you have to live with, is yourself. Listen, if you cannot have confidence in yourself as a Christian, you need not go out and try to persuade people down the street. If you have got a guilty heart and a downcast look and you cannot respect yourself, you have already lost your testimony with yourself and you have lost it with others.

Keep a good testimony with yourself. Know within your heart that you are clean and pure and right with God. You do not have to say too much about it to other people. Did you know it? It just leaks out. If you have got a good testimony with yourself, you can look yourself in the eye and know that you are clean and decent and that you have got character to resist and withstand temptation. You have got self-respect. But if you wilt under the force of evil impulses and passion and you succumb to it, you have got a downcast look in your soul. You do not have a testimony with yourself. God wants us to live righteously in this present evil world.

Now Titus, chapter 2, verse 11: "For the grace of God that bringeth salvation hath appeared to all men." This is saying basically the same thing that was said in chapter 1, verse 4, of Galatians. Now notice it says, " . . . the grace of God that bringeth salvation hath appeared to all men . . . ." Now what does it do? It teaches us, and one of the translations is: It has trained us to reject and to renounce all ungodliness. Listen, when you are saved, you get a college and seminary education, all in one. Now you do not learn all the theology. You do not learn all the books of the Bible, but you get something that only God can give you when you get saved. You know what this is? You are taught by the grace of God that you ought to renounce all unrighteousness and ungodliness. It says here, The grace of God that hath appeared teaches us. Teaches us what? To deny ungodliness and worldly lust.

Any born-again child of God knows that it is wrong to morally sin. Now he may not know whether he ought to go here or there. There may be some things that he does not know, but listen, God puts in your heart something that tells you that it is wrong to sin. No child of God believes that it is right to lie. Be thankful for the grace of God that saves and teaches them it is wrong to lie. Whether he is a Christian in darkest Africa or whether he is a student at Free Will Baptist Bible College, no professor, Greek, Hebrew, or anybody else has to give him a theology course to teach him that it is wrong to lie. God puts that there when the grace of God has appeared. He gets it in his salvation experience.

Nobody has to tell a man that it is wrong to steal. I believe God puts that in his heart when the grace of God appears. Because remember, the Holy Spirit has come if he is saved. The Holy Spirit has come and He tells him. He flashes a red light and says it is wrong to lie, it is wrong to steal. God puts it in his heart.

No young person has to be told that it is wrong to commit adultery. God puts that knowledge in his heart when he is saved. You do not have to go to college to learn. He does not have to ask his roommates on that question. He knows. He knows. He knows. Because the grace of God has appeared and it teaches us that we are to deny ungodliness and wordly lust. And what else? That we should live soberly, righteously, and godly in this present world.

Listen, the grace of God does not teach you that you have a license to sin. No, the very opposite is true. It teaches you that you do not have a right to sin. More than that, it teaches you about what sin is in great measure. There is no excuse. There is no excuse for us misbehaving.

You can put the lowest, the most uncultured person on this campus; but if he is saved, he is right with God, and wants to live right, he will not give the dormitory supervisor any trouble. Oh, he may not know how to read the clock to tell that it is ten o'clock. He may be that ignorant. But I will tell you he will ask some of his roommates to tell him when it is ten. He cannot read the clock. He will want to go to bed if he is supposed to, if he wants to live right.

You see, we do not sin out of ignorance. We do not sin out of ignorance. We sin because we are trying to find some excuse to sin. We want to be persuaded. We look up somebody who will persuade us to do what we want to do anyway. You can always find those people around. Then, we will point a finger at them and say, "He made me sin." It is just like I said the other day about this little sign, "The Devil Made Me Do It." Instead of "the devil making me do it," it is my "roommate talked me into it." No! No! No! No! No! You wanted to. You found a roommate that would agree with you, and it eased your conscience to say your roommate persuaded you. It takes some of the burden off of you, makes you feel a little more respected. No, your roommate did not do it. Can the roommate persuade you better than the grace of God? Then the grace of God is not much in your life. The grace of God teaches you, not your roommate, not your roommate.

The grace of God teaches you that " . . . denying [all] ungodliness and worldly lusts . . . [that you are to] live soberly, righteously, and godly, in this present world." This is the duty and the responsibility of a Christian.

You may say, "My date persuaded me. I knew I ought not to get married, but my date persuaded me." Do not let your date persuade you. Listen, if you have a boyfriend that tries to overpersuade you to get married against your better judgment, you give him up. Let me tell you, fellows, if you have a girlfriend that is too anxious to get married, take to the woods as fast as you can. That is right. That is right.

There are some things that you fight, and there are some things you win in flight. You know the Bible did not say for you to fight youthful lust. You know what it said? It said to run from it. If you stand around and try to fight youthful lust, you will lose the battle. It says to flee youthful lust. Get away from it. Do not hang around it. If you have a boyfriend or a girlfriend that is too big of a temptation to you, do not go back to see them again. Let me tell you, there have been more Josephs than that one recorded in Genesis 2. There have been a lot of Josephs that have had to flee, and had the sense to flee, when the going got rough. Flee the lust; get away from it. If you just keep hanging around it, after a while you will talk yourself into sin. You can work with your conscience.

Listen, I want to give you a little saying. I am going to try to remember it. Riding along the other day, I had my wife to write it down. You know one thing about it: You cannot travel on these interstates and think very much, but I try. I "snuck" in a little bit of it. If you bring up a long settled conviction for review, that is the first step toward compromise in sin. If you hold a conviction that this thing is wrong and it is settled in your soul, then be unyielding. Somebody will begin to talk about it, and you will begin to think about it and say, "Well, maybe, I ought to rethink this thing." That is the first step toward compromise in sin. Do not let anybody talk you out of those settled convictions! God put them there. God put them there. Do not bring it up for review. Say, "No, I am not going to do it. I have already settled it in my heart, and I am not going to let anybody talk me out of it."

That is the kind of character that God can use, people who get fixed, not always floating around subject to the whims and the ideas of the current market. You will not amount to anything for God if you are unsettled. You will always be digging yourself out of trouble if you are like that. You ought to put that one down. That one is good. You may not recognize it, but you ought to put it down. You ought to think about it when somebody is bombarding you with new ideas. Do not give it up lightly.

I am just going to read this one. I will not have time to talk about it. "Whereby are given unto us exceeding great and precious promises: that by these ye might be partakers of the divine nature, having escaped the corruption that is in the world through lust" (2 Peter 1:4).

Thank God, I got saved. I am so glad that I do not know about some sins. I do not have to live with them. I know there are weaknesses, and there are temptations for all of us; but I am glad that I do not have a repertoire of sins that I can dangle from my lapel and count. I do not need them. God knew that I was too weak, I suppose. I am glad that I do not have to live with certain memories or certain sins. I do not want to. I can be better off without them. God help me that I should not delight in any sin that I have committed. We have all sinned, yes. But the fewer sins that you have to think about in your old age that you committed in your youth, the better off you are.

You know, we make heroes out of these people with trophies of sin. They go around and dangle them and say, "Look here. Look here. Look here what God saved me from." I am glad that God saved me, yes. But I am glad that I do not have certain trophies of sin to dangle in my memory. It does not help you appreciate the grace of God anymore.

Listen, the grace of God and the mercy of God should be exalted for keeping you from sin more than saving you from sin. See, the grace of God teaches us to live in such a way that we will not sin. We ought to magnify that side of the grace of God. We make too big heroes of these people who have lived in the gutter. Let us exalt the fellow who is saved and has escaped the corruption that is in the world.

You may not appreciate it now so much, young people, but I will tell you one thing: The older you get and the nearer home you get, the prouder you will be of the fewer sins you have committed in your youth. It takes on a new significance the longer you live, the longer you live. While you are young you are trying to brag about it, and you are under the pressure of telling people about your sins, too. Everybody is sort of gloating over them. But after you get older and grow in the Lord, every time a memory of sin comes, a tear in your heart comes. You are not proud of it. You escaped the corruptions in the world. May we stand.

PRAYER

Our Father, be with us this day. Bless these young people. Help them to live pure, clean, holy, godly lives in this present world by Your grace and power. And by the conviction and the determination of their hearts, give them character. In Jesus' Name. Amen.

10

December 18, 1973
Scripture: Proverbs 31
Subject: "Counsel of a Mother"

LOOK FOR A VIRTUOUS WOMAN

Now I am just going to read some verses and say very little, but I want to read from Proverbs 31. This is the advice, the counsel of a mother, a good mother, to her son. Nobody can give counsel to children like a mother, and this was a good mother. She must have been a good mother, a wise mother, and she had a deep interest in her son. Here is the advice that she gave him.

"The words of king Lemuel, the prophecy that his mother taught him." See, these are things his mother taught him. "What, my son? and what, the son of my womb? and what, the son of my vows?" In other words, seemingly, this mother is saying, "When God gave you to me, I made certain vows. I gave you back to Him. I told God that He could have my son." Now a Christian mother will do that.

"Give not thy strength unto women, nor thy ways to that which destroyeth kings." Then he tells what destroys kings: "It is not for kings, O Lemuel, it is not for kings to drink wine; nor for princes strong drink." In other words, drinking wine and strong drink will destroy kings.

"Lest they drink, and forget the law, and pervert the judgment of any of the afflicted." In other words, they cannot make right decisions regarding their people, their subjects, if they are under the influence of drink. Oh, how many politicians and leaders have this weakness. Their minds are befuddled because of strong drink. One of the great leaders of this state just a few years ago was killed in an automobile accident. He was a brilliant man, a brilliant man, and could have done so much! But he got ensnared by strong drink.

"Give strong drink unto him that is ready to perish, and wine unto those that be of heavy hearts." In other words, use strong drink for medicinal purposes, as a medicine; that is all right. You take alcohol once in a while; the doctor perscribes it as a medicine. He says to drink some wine when you have a heavy heart. That would take the place of our tranquilizers today. There is not anything wrong if it is necessary to take a tranquilizer. I think we take them when we could go to other sources for our help. But nonetheless, only drink these things as a medicine.

"Let him drink, and forget his poverty, and remember his misery no more."

There is a time when the burdens of life overwhelm you, the problems, the cares. So for some temporary relief, why, he is saying that these things are all right.

"Open thy mouth for the dumb in the cause of all such as are appointed to destruction." In other words, take up for the poor, for those who cannot defend themselves. This is good advice. You have heard and you have read, so many times on television and in your newspaper, of people who have been murdered, of a woman being molested, and people not stopping to help. Now he is saying, If you have honor, son, do not do this. Help those who are in need.

"Open thy mouth, judge righteously, and plead the cause of the poor and needy. Who can find a virtuous woman? for her price is far above rubies." In other words, she is saying to her son, Now one of these days you are going to want to get married, and when you do, you look out for the right kind of a wife. Now she is going to describe the kind of a wife that he should look for.

So he says, "Who can find a virtuous woman . . . ?" Another translation puts it, as a woman of strong character, a woman of strong character and a virtuous woman, for her price is far above rubies.

"The heart of her husband doth safely trust in her, so that he shall have no need of spoil." In other words, marry the kind of woman that you can trust. You have complete confidence in her integrity and in her purity so that you will have no need of unjust spoil.

"She shall do him good and not evil all the days of her life." Another translation adds some words there that they thought should be added: that a good wife will encourage and boost the spirit of her husband. I think this is one reason the Lord saw that man needed a helpmeet. Man can take a whole lot, but he gets discouraged and down and out sometimes. He needs somebody to boost him up. Oh, pity these men who have wives who nag them all the time and destroy their spirits and add a burden to them instead of lifting a burden from their shoulders. But a good wife, a good wife will do her husband good.

She is saying to her son: You look for this kind of woman who will do you good and not evil. This kind of woman, this virtuous woman, "She seeketh wool, and flax, and worketh willingly with her hands." She is not lazy. She is not a loafer. "She is like the merchants' ships; she bringeth her food from afar. She riseth also while it is yet night, and giveth meat to her household, and a portion to her maidens. She considereth a field, and buyeth it: with the fruit of her hands she planteth a vineyard." This all speaks of industriousness.

"She girdeth her loins with strength, and strengtheneth her arms." In other words, she is doing those things that builds her character. She is not sitting before the television and watching all these soap operas all day long and tearing her character down instead of building it up. She is strengthening her character, reading good literature, perhaps. She is listening to good music. Listen, I get awfully disturbed at the kind of music that you have to listen to if you listen to music that is piped out to the general public. You have to be selective. Music is a tremendous force. I get concerned that this little cheap, beat-type music gets into churches and into the religious service. That little foot-patting kind, you know, that is just the same beat over and over again. It is not worth 2¢ on the music market. But it is easy, it is cheap, people can sing it, and it is what people like so we fall into the trap of singing it because anybody who can read a single note can sing it. It appeals to the flesh and it is popular. God forbid that we should fall into that trap.

So she does that which builds her character, strengthens her arms. Listen, you have to work at building character. It does not come easy. You have to discipline your thought life. You have to choose the kind of music that you listen to, the kind of literature that you read. You have to work at this business of building character. It does not come automatically. So she strengthens her arms.

"She perceiveth that her merchandise is good: her candle goeth not out by night." In other words, when calamity comes she does not fall to pieces. She is not the fainting kind when problems arise. She measures up to the situation. That is the test of a person's character. What does he do in the critical moments? What does he do when everybody else is falling apart? What does he do when the pressure is on him? Can he keep his head, his cool? Can he withstand temptation? Does the best within him come out when the pressure is greater? That is a person of character. Why most anybody can operate smoothly when there is no pressure. Most everybody can think clearly when there is no pressure. But when the pressure is turned on, what does it reveal about you? Well, I will tell you; it will reveal what you have been becoming all these years. That is when what you are comes out.

So, this woman, " . . . her candle goeth not out by night." In other words, the darker it gets, the brighter the light. She is not subdued by the darkness around her .Her candle is not put out by the darkness; it shines the brighter. We live in a dark world and your candle can give a glowing light the darker the night. But you know so many of us wring our hands and say, "Oh, my, everybody else is doing it," and we fall right in line. God pity. This woman does not do that. So this mother is saying to her son, You find this kind of woman for your wife.

"She layeth her hands to the spindle . . . . She stretcheth out her hand to the poor . . . ." She is generous. She is tenderhearted.

"She is not afraid of the snow for their household: for all her household are clothed with scarlet." In other words, she has been busy. She has been getting ready for the snow. You know a lot of us are not ready for the snow when it comes. We do not have the right kind of clothing. We say, "Oh, well, it is cold is it not?"

Listen, you had better be preparing for the emergencies of life. They are out there, students. You are going to face some of them when you go home Christmas. You are going to face some of those testings. If you have not been preparing for them, you will meet them unprepared. You had better look for the winter snow. You had better look for the August heat, too. You had better get ready for the emergencies of life. Do not let them catch you unaware. One of these days you are going to act out what you are. Somebody said something; I read it. I wish I could remember just how it was stated. It is something like this: Your thoughts are rehearsals for your acts. You think about it. You are just rehearsing now what you are going to do later on. If you are building good, strong character, you are going to stand when the night sets in, when the snow comes. If you are not, you are going to fall. You are going to be caught unprepared.

"Her husband is known in the gates . . . ." In other words, he is Mrs. So-and-So's husband. That does not sound very good to us, does it? But listen, a good woman can make just a mediocre man into something that is worthwhile. A good woman. Man needs a good woman. In Proverbs, another place, in the 18th chapter, I think, it says, "Whoso findeth a wife findeth a good thing . . . ." I do not think he left anything out there intentionally, but he who finds a good wife finds a good thing. But if you find the wrong kind, you have not found a good thing; you have found a terror.

Her husband is known in the gates. " . . . He sitteth among the elders of the land," and so on. I wish I had time to read all of this. "Her children rise up, and call her blessed . . . ." May we stand, please.

PRAYER

Our Father, be with us this day. We thank Thee for these months together. Bless us in these closing days of this semester. In Jesus' Name. Amen.

11

January 18, 1974
Scripture: Romans 1
Subject: "Is God Becoming Less?"

IS GOD BECOMING LESS?

I am reading from Romans, chapter 1, this morning, beginning with verse 16. "For I am not ashamed of the gospel of Christ: for it is the power of God unto salvation to every one that believeth; to the Jew first, and also to the Greek." I am just pausing there a moment.

The gospel is the power of God unto salvation to everyone that believeth. There has to be faith. There has to be the believing for that power to become effective in your heart and life. But it is the power of God; it changes. It changed your life if you are a Christian.

"For therein [that is in the gospel] is the righteousness of God revealed . . . ." We would not know too much about the righteousness of God if we did not have the gospel. But in the gospel we have God's righteousness revealed and also revealed how we can be made righteous.

"For [in the gospel] therein is the righteousness of God revealed from faith to faith: as it is written, The just shall live by faith." Another thing is revealed in verse 18: "For the wrath of God is revealed from heaven . . . ."

Notice the two things that are revealed. The righteousness of God is revealed in the gospel, but the wrath of God is also revealed. It is revealed from Heaven against all ungodliness and unrighteousness of men who hold the truth in unrighteousness. So you have two things revealed: the righteousness of God and the wrath of God. Now some men preach through righteousness and the love of God but say very little about the wrath of God. Both are revealed, and you will not be true to the gospel unless you preach both because the gospel contains both. His Word contains both the righteousness of God which has been revealed and the wrath of God which has also been revealed. These two things are evident: that God is a God of righteousness and that He is a God of wrath. So we need to keep these two things in mind.

Now notice, the wrath of God is revealed from Heaven. It did not come through the reasoning of man's mind. It came from Heaven. God revealed it. It is written in nature. You do not have to be smart to understand that there is a penalty for sin. So this has been revealed from Heaven that God is a God of wrath against all ungodliness and unrighteousness.

Now whatever is unrighteous in your heart and life God is against it. God is opposed to it and there is a penalty that is attached to every act of unrighteousness. I think that every impure thought carries with it a penalty. It is doing something to us. We may not realize it, but it is. Every act of sin carries its penalty. " . . . The wrath of God is revealed . . . against all ungodliness [notice, all ungodliness] and unrighteousness of men . . . ."

Then verse 19: "Because that which may be known of God is manifest in them; for God hath shewed it unto them. For the invisible things of him from the creation of the world are clearly seen . . . ."

Now God is invisible; we cannot see God. "For the invisible things of him from the creation of the world are clearly seen . . . ." Now how are they seen? He tells us. Being seen or understood by the things that are made, this physical world, the world about you, tells you about the invisible God. The physical, tangible world tells you about the invisible God. You say, What does it tell us?

Well, it tells us much. You read Psalm 19 for instance. "The heavens declare the glory of God . . . ." This physical world does not tell you how to be saved, but it tells you about the glory of God, God's glory. This physical world tells you that God is great, that God is righteous, that God is good, and it reveals His glory. Let us notice what it says about this a little later on.

84

So the invisible things of Him from the creation of the world are clearly (now underscore that word clearly) seen, not dimly seen. It is not something that you have to grope for and search for. It is evident to anyone who wants to see it. The invisible God is telling us about Himself in great measure by the physical world that He created. We can understand much about the invisible God by looking at the physical world, the physical world that He created. It tells us about His glory.

"The heavens declare the glory of God; and the firmament sheweth his handywork." It is clearly being understood by the things that are made, even His eternal power and Godhead. So you look at the physical world, and you say, "Whoever made this has great power." Take the physical body, for instance. Wise scientists have studied it all through the years, and it is still a mystery to them. The doctor will be the first to admit that he knows so little about the physical body. It is a mystery. God made it. Yet so many of the doctors will not give God the credit and the glory for making it. They have the idea that it just fell together some way, evolved through some process. Man cannot understand all that God made. It is so wonderful and we look at it and we say it took a powerful person to make this world and to create man and so on. So we understand His eternal power, and we understand His Godhead. It leads us to the conclusion that this world did not just fall together. It is not just a happened-so. God is back of it. So the physical world tells us of God's eternal power and Godhead.

That is a pretty good course in theology. If you will open your eyes and be honest, you can see all of this, this physical world that He has made. Because God has told us so much about Himself through this physical world that He has made, He says we are without excuse. We cannot go around and say, "Oh, well, I did not know." Now this is the first thing that we want to do when we get in trouble. "I did not know." "Why did you not tell me?" "Why did somebody not inform me?" "I would not have done this."

Listen! The people who sin do not sin in most instances because they are ignorant. Some doctors who operate on people for lung cancer have been seen with a cigarette hanging out of the corner of their mouth. That is right. You go into your doctor's office. You know that they know what cigarettes will do to the human body, yet they are smoking. They say to their patient, "You put up those cigarettes," and all the time they are lighting one. It is not because they do not know. They know. The man who drinks, he has had too many object lessons in what liquor will do to the human body. He knows. He does not sin in ignorance. The person who is immoral. He does not have to have anybody tell him the fruits of immorality. He has had too many object lessons. He does not sin in ignorance.

God said, I have told you so much about Myself that if you sin, you are without excuse. You are without excuse. God has written these eternal truths into the heart, into the very fiber of man's nature. If man wants to live right, he can live right. The trouble is, he has a depraved heart. He doesn't want to see these truths. Now He says, "Because that, when they knew God . . ."; in other words, this suggests that there was a time when they knew God. They knew about His Godhead. They knew about His power. They knew more about God maybe than we know. "Because . . . when they knew [Him], they glorified him not as God . . . ." Now it says that the heavens declared the glory of God, His glory, His majesty, His power. This is what the physical world tells us about God. But He says when they knew this, they would not glorify Him as God. They would not honor Him. They pulled God down to a lower level.

Let me tell you again. I emphasized this yesterday. I am going to emphasize it again to all who preach. In your preaching and in your teaching, make much of the majesty and the glory of God. Lift Him up as a glorious Being. Do not talk about the sinner and man's sins all the time. Talk about the majesty and the glory of God. We need more songs about the glory of God. Our singing needs to be more God-centered, and our preaching needs to be more God-centered than man-centered. If we will do that, I believe there will be a difference. Our own concept of God will change. It will do something to us.

So the first thing they did, they did not glorify Him as God. They made Him something less than God. They reduced Him to maybe just a super-human being. You know some of the songs that go around, they lend themselves to that philosophy. They make God a buddy, just a little above us, a little better than us, but they do not give Him the glory that He deserves. So this is the first step. They made God less than He was. They had a poor concept of God. God was becoming less than He was.

If God became less than He was, they became less of what they ought to be, and that will be true in your life. As God becomes less than what He is to you, you will be less than what you are supposed to be. It is important that we have the right concept of the majesty and the glory of God. God is a God of righteousness which has been revealed. God is a God of wrath which has been revealed from Heaven also. If we will keep these things in mind, it will help us to give God the glory and the adoration that He deserves. We need to have a great God to worship and to serve. The first step here was, He became less than great to them. When He became less than great, they said He does not deserve our glory. He does not deserve our respect.

After God became less than what He was in their eyes, and they would not give Him glory, then they were unthankful. This was the next step. Neither were they thankful. Notice the process: God was less to them than He really was. He had come down to their level, and now they were not grateful for what God did. They became, they were becoming, their own gods. You know you are not thankful if no one does anything for you, if you do it all yourself, if you are your own god. If you supply all your needs, you have nobody to thank but yourself. You just pat yourself on the back. You give yourself the glory. God is becoming less; you are becoming greater. Humanism. This was the process.

Now the next step. They are ready for it. They became vain in their imaginations. They got the wrong concept of themselves. First of all, they had the wrong concept of God. They did not give Him glory, and they were not thankful. Now they had the wrong concept of themselves. They were vain in their imaginations. Do you know one of the major things wrong in our educational system in this country is that it has deified man and humanized God? It has made man think more of himself than he should and less of God than he should. Humanism, developing the resources within man so that man could conquer and become the master of the universe. Through psychological maneuvering, he could maneuver other men to do what he wanted to do and have his way. He became the master. This has been the velocity and great part of modern education.

I want to say here, there is a danger; education is the most dangerous tool you can pick up. It is the most wonderful tool, but it is the most dangerous tool. It is charged with danger. You know Satan always takes that which is most wonderful and turns it into instruments of great destruction. He does not play around with a peripheral thing. Studying here in this institution, you can get the wrong idea of yourself. You know you have to hold education up one day as something that you must have, and the next day you have to knock it down and say that it is no good, to keep it in its place.

Some people are going to get the wrong idea. They will think that since they came to Free Will Baptist Bible College that they ought to have a big church. They may be called to one down in the forks of a creek somewhere and then turn up their nose at it. They may say, "Why look, I have a degree and I know a little Greek." Let me tell you this: If you ever know any Greek, do not tell anybody about it.

Anyway, ". . . they . . . became vain in their imaginations." Vain in their imagination. They thought too highly of themselves. They were not taking the place that God should have had in their hearts and lives. When you begin to think too highly of yourself, you are getting prepared to do other things. It does not always stay up here. It feeds out into all of our activities of life. When God becomes less than He is, a God of righteousness and a God of wrath with eternal power, and you become more than you are, you begin to think of yourself as important, and you ought to have what you want. You are getting ready to commit sins of most any kind. This is what they were getting ready to do.

I looked up the word *vain*. I thought I knew what it meant. It meant a whole lot more than I thought. But one of the things was empty; empty, fruitless, meaningless. So they became empty or foolish in their thinking, exalting themselves, vain in their imaginations.

Now their hearts were darkened. They thought along these lines so long until now they could not feel. They became insensitive to the workings of God. God could not get through to them to move them. Their hearts were darkened. They could not think straight. They could not feel right. They had a different attitude. It seems that they were now being confirmed in this. Darkness had settled. Ah, listen, before you can sin, a measure of darkness has to settle over your mind and you have to think wrong. If you are thinking right, you will not sin. Sin comes through a thought process, rationalizing, preparing yourself to do what the flesh wants to do. After a while, you say, "Well, it is all right." When you start out thinking, you say, "Oh, horrors, no. That is not right." Then you keep thinking and tomorrow you say, "Well, wait a minute. Let us think about it some more."

I go back to a statement I made to you earlier this year. If you bring up for review a long held conviction, it is the first step toward sin. This is wrong. I know it is wrong. Now you say, "Well, maybe I ought to rethink it. Maybe I ought to rethink it. Everybody else is doing it. Maybe I ought to get in on it." This is the way sin begins. After a while you approve that which before you did not approve. That means that your heart has been darkened, or you could not think that way. Sin does it. So this is what was happening to them.

Listen, students, you had better watch this process of thought and this process of sin. It can get to you. You had better watch it. Check yourself when you start thinking along these lines. So their hearts were darkened. Now they were professing themselves to be wise. They were their own boss now. They were wise. But He said they were fools. As they thought they were becoming wise, God said, "You are becoming fools." Think on it. Think on it. They were so deceived. Is it not pitiful that as they thought they were getting wise and sophisticated, they were becoming fools? We have had students here from time to time who walked up and down the dormitory halls talking about their exploits in sin as if they were wise. They thought, "I know the ropes, I have been there, I know all about it." Knowledgeable. Why, God says, "You are fools." Man's evaluation is that he is wise. God's evaluation is that he is a fool. Anybody who tampers with sin is a fool because he has been made to think wrong, to feel wrong, and to like wrong. The wrath of God has been revealed against all unrighteousness, but he is ignoring it. He is saying that he can outsmart it because he has made God less than God is. So he is playing the game of sin because God is not who He is to him, and he can outsmart God. So therefore he goes out to enjoy sin and God says, "You are not outsmarting me. You are a fool."

You know we have enough evidence of this that we could see it if we wanted. There might be somebody sitting here this morning who is arguing with this as I preach it. In your heart you do not believe it. You do not believe it. You are vain in your imagination. Your foolish heart has been darkened, and you are professing yourself to be wise enough to outsmart God, to enjoy sin, without the penalty of judgment. You can only think that way if your heart has been darkened. If you are professing yourself to be wise, God is saying, "You are a fool."

They " . . . changed the glory of the uncorruptible God . . . ." Now they were changing God. First of all, they pulled Him down to less than what He was. Now they said, "We want another kind of God. We do not want that God of wrath that we have been told about, the One we used to fear and dread. We dreaded it so much that we could not enjoy sin, and now we have made Him less than He is, and we have tasted sin and we like it. Now we do not want the kind of God who is always threatening us with judgment and with wrath." So they said, "Let us make us another kind of God." So now they did not say, "Let us not have a God." They said, "Let us just make us a different kind of God, a God of love that always loves and excuses and winks at sin and will not punish." He lets us get away with it. So they ". . . changed the glory of the uncorruptible God into an image made like the corruptible man . . . ." See they made God like man, one of them.

" . . . And to birds and fourfooted beasts, and creeping things." This kind of God was not going to hurt them when they sinned. This kind of God would not be angry when they sinned. No judgment from Heaven; a very convenient God. Listen, you can have a convenient God. Make God less than He is to accommodate your sins if you want. Men do that so they can enjoy the fruits of their sins and still have a God. But God says you are fools because it has already been revealed from Heaven; the wrath of God has already been revealed from Heaven against all unrighteousness and ungodliness.

But they said, "We do not want that kind of God," so they made them one of convenience. "Wherefore God also gave them up [He says, All right, go ahead] to uncleanness through the lusts of their own hearts, to dishonour their own bodies between themselves." Now they really could enjoy their sins, dishonoring their bodies. God gave you this body. He made man and breathed into him the breath of life. He thinks so much of this body of yours that He is going to raise it up in resurrection power one day. He is going to call it from the dust of the earth. God not only redeemed our souls; He has redeemed our bodies. Now here they are taking those instruments that God had made, that God had glorified, and they were dishonoring their bodies, making them instruments of lust. Here again is an area of life. In the marriage relationship, there is no relationship like it in all the world; God made it that way. The devil enters into this area of man's life, and he desecrates it. He gets man to use that which enobles the dearest of relationships and to use that illicitly. It brings the severest judgment of God of any sin in the Bible talked about. It is the sin that bothers more people and that leaves its ugly mark on more lives than any sin. It is a peculiar sin that brings forth the peculiar wrath of God because it is the most enobling experience that man can know in human relationships when it is within the bounds that God placed. The devil works more vigorously at this point to mar more lives than any other point in man's life because he knows that it is an enobling relationship within the framework of God's will. The devil tries to get it out of the framework of God's will to destroy lives. They are dishonoring their bodies. Young people, do not dishonor your body. Do not dishonor your body in lustful practices or immorality. Do not do it. Do not do it. There is a penalty. There is a mark that it will leave on you that no other sin will. Keep yourself pure. Save this relationship for the framework within which God put it. Do not let the devil tempt you to destroy the glory of that relationship, desecrate it, dishonor your body.

Listen young men, do not be ashamed to say that you have kept yourself pure. You know some fellows are ashamed to admit it. They think, well he is a sissy. He does not know much. Listen, you know enough to keep yourself clean and pure. You are smarter than anybody else. Do not follow the crowd. You are living in a day that everywhere you turn, everywhere you turn, there is a suggestion to leave the old paths. Do not do it. Do not do it. Do not dishonor your body. Keep it pure and clean by the grace of God. This is some of the progress of their sins. May we stand please.

PRAYER

Our Father, be with us throughout this day. Bless these students. We thank Thee for them. Save them for Thyself, Thy glory, to work out Thy will in their lives. In Jesus' Name, Amen.

12

September 4, 1974
Scripture: Psalm 1
Subject: "Blessed is the man that walketh not in the counsel of
the ungodly."

THE BLESSED MAN

We have good professors, but sometimes things float
around in the dormitory that prejudice people this way and that.
Do not listen to that. You do what you ought to do; get your
counsel from somebody who can counsel you about what you
ought to do regarding your course work.

Psalm 1, a very practical, familiar psalm . . .

> Blessed is the man that walketh not in the counsel of
> the ungodly, nor standeth in the way of sinners, nor
> sitteth in the seat of the scornful. But his delight is in
> the law of the LORD; and in his law doth he meditate
> day and night.

Let us pause there to notice this contrast which is so obvious.
Blessed is the man that does not get his advice, his instruction,
from ungodly people. It gets you in trouble every time. Whether it
is somebody in the Bible College or whether it is somebody out
away from here, do not get your advice, your counsel, from a
person who is not living right. Now, you may find somebody
around here who gripes about everything. Nothing is right, and
nothing is like it ought to be. Do not listen to that person. I hope
we do not have one this year, but so many times in a group this
size you will have somebody who is a griper or a complainer, and
that person could influence you. Do not identify yourself with
such a person.

"Blessed is the man that walketh not in the counsel of the
ungodly . . . ." Think back in your experiences to the times that
you have gotten in trouble, the times that you did things that you

have regretted since then. Mostly, you did it because you were influenced by somebody who was not right. Now you think about it. The boy who takes up the habit of smoking. He was influenced by somebody, see, some little friend of his. Or maybe it was his dad. But perhaps it was some peer who said, "You ought to try one." And he started smoking not intending to have lung cancer forty years from then, but perhaps he did. See, he got his advice from the wrong source.

Now, you just think back to the time that you have gotten in trouble. Remember when you have done things you should not have done, and think of somebody who might have influenced you to do that. You see, you would have been better off not to have known that person, to have never listened to that person, to have never been a friend to that person.

So, happy is the man that walketh not in the counsel of a person who is not living right. Oh, you say, "Everybody here is a Christian." But did you know a Christian can give you bad advice sometimes if he is backslidden and not living close to the Lord? A backslider is a dangerous person. We think of the drunkard as being dangerous, the harlot as being dangerous; but listen, a backslider is dangerous because he is trying to justify his own spiritual condition. He would like for somebody else to walk with him. You know, it is lonely to walk in sin alone. You want somebody to give you fellowship. So, blessed is the man that does not listen to the ungodly advice from whatever source it is given. You have to make up your own mind about some things.

Nor does he stand in the way of sinners; that is, he is not identified with sinners. And do not get the idea that I think we have a group of outlaws around here, except Dr. Outlaw. We only have one! I am talking about the other kind of outlaw, though. We do not have an underworld gang around here, but I want to warn you: You can get identified with the wrong crowd even in a Bible college, if there is a wrong crowd. I have said this to you before and I want to emphasize it: Do not be disarmed by thinking everybody in a Bible college is just like he ought to be.

Do not listen to the advice of everybody who comes along, even in a dormitory owned and operated by a Bible college. You are going to have to have your own personal set of convictions. Every man ought to anyway, whether in a Bible college, in pastoring a church, or wherever you are. You ought to have a personal set of convictions, things that you have settled within your own soul, heart, and mind: There are some things I am not going to do; there are some things I am going to do; there are things I believe in. And you ought to live by these standards. Be true to yourself, and you will not be identified with the wrong crowd. Blessed is the man, happy is the man, that does not walk in the counsel of the ungodly or stand with the ungodly or identify with him.

Now notice, "But his delight is in the law of the LORD; and in his law doth he meditate day and night." He meditates, thinks about, the Word of God. He measures every decision that he has to make where a moral issue is involved. He measures it by the Word of God instead of the advice he gets from the ungodly. He meditates in it; he thinks things over in the light of what God's Word teaches. When it comes to a temptation to fudge a little on a term paper or an examination, or whether it is involving moral things in dating or courtship, he will think things over in the light of the Word of God in which he meditates day and night. A fellow who does that is not going to go wrong. He is not going wrong.

So he meditates in the Word of God; he delights in it. Now notice, it is the fellow who meditates in it who delights in it. See, if you do not meditate in it, you will not delight in it. If you do not think about it, you will not delight in it. This can be the driest book in all literature. It can be the most meaningless book in all literature. It will be the hardest book to read in all literature if your heart is not right. Sin will keep you away from the Word of God.

But if your heart is right (if you are living for God), this can be the most precious book. You will delight in it. The Word of God, the law of God, is not a boring thing; it is a delightful thing. You will want to do the will of God when you meditate in it, when you measure issues by it. Oh, listen to me, students. We are living in a day when you cannot listen to many people. There used to be a time when you could listen to most anybody and they would give you good advice. People had right and wrong sharply defined. Not any more; not any more.

So you are going to have to measure things yourself by the Word of God, or you will be walking in the counsel of the backslider or the ungodly. You will get your life mixed up and messed up, and you will live to regret it. Oh, you say, "He is a friend," or "She is a friend." Do not go by that. You can have a friend who will give you ungodly advice and influence you to do the wrong thing. People who are not our friends have little influence with us.

So, blessed is the man that does not listen to ungodly advice and is not identified with sinners. But he meditates in the Word of God, and he measures issues by the Word of God. He delights in the Word of God more than he delights in the advice from his friends, from his roommate, from his classmate. He would rather do the will of God than to please friends or anybody else because he delights in it.

Oh, listen, that will make a real Christian out of you; that will give you a testimony. Notice what it says down here about that: "And he shall be like a tree planted by the rivers of water, that bringeth forth his fruit in his season . . . . " The fellow who meditates in the Word of God, who delights in the law of God, brings forth fruit. Listen, students, the man who is living for God is bringing forth fruit. You cannot help it. You cannot help it. If you are meditating in the Word of God, you are delighting in it. You are not taking advice from the ungodly; you are producing fruit.

So, if you want to be a fruit-bearing Christian, just get in the Word of God. Live by what it teaches. You will be like a tree planted by the rivers of water. You will have a freshness. There will be new buds; there will be fruit. You do not have to worry about bearing fruit; you just be the right kind of tree, and you will bear fruit.

96

" . . . His leaf also shall not wither . . . ." That is, when the winds of adversity come, the leaf on that kind of tree stays green and fresh and does not wither under the bombardment of winds of adversity. You cannot stop a Christian like that. You cannot put his light out. You cannot keep the freshness from being there. But you can lose your freshness if you do not stay in the Word of God and if you take counsel from everybody that comes by. You may get in trouble.

" . . . His leaf also shall not wither; and whatsoever he doeth shall prosper." God will even turn adversity into prosperity for you. "The ungodly are not so . . . ." They are fakes. They cannot back up what they say. Look at his life. Where is it going to lead him? To a fellow who gives you bad advice, you just say, "Now, what is going to be the end result of this? Where is he headed? What kind of spiritual person is he? Is he a safe guide?" Analyze it.

"The ungodly are not so: but are like the chaff which the wind driveth away. Therefore the ungodly shall not stand in the judgment . . . ." There is coming a judgment when the deeds of men's lives are going to be tested. Would I like to stand in judgment doing what this ungodly person is advising me to do? The thing I am tempted to do, how am I going to feel about this in the judgment? There is a judgment, you know. And that thing you did in secret is going to be brought to light in the judgment. How am I going to justify it there? How am I going to like to stand there in the judgment and have the deeds of my life revealed? See, there is a judgment. The ungodly, the man who lives in sin, is not going to stand in the judgment. When judgment day comes, he cannot take it. His life cannot endure.

" . . . Nor sinners in the congregation of the righteous." There is going to be a weeding out one day. Sinners will not stand in the congregation of the righteous. They will not be there.

"For the LORD knoweth the way of the righteous: but the way of the ungodly shall perish." He knows the way of the righteous. He knows the way of the ungodly. He can separate them. There is coming a judgment. I ought to live today in the light of the judgment and do those things that I will not be ashamed of in the judgment day. That will keep us living right, students. There is nothing that keeps us living right more, perhaps, than to know that what I do today is going to be tried at the judgment. I will have to answer for it.

May we stand:

PRAYER

How precious is thy Word, our Father. We thank Thee so much that Thou hast given it to us. How we need it. Give us hearts to delight in it. May we meditate in it. May we weigh issues by it, judge our decisions by it. May it guide our lives. In Jesus' Name we pray. Amen.

13

September 6, 1974
Scripture: Genesis 13:12
Subject: Lot . . . pitched his tent toward Sodom

SHALLOW CONVICTIONS BREED SORROW

If you would like to turn to the Scripture reading, it will be a brief reading. I will call your attention to several verses, however, as we move along in the message. It is Genesis, chapter 13. Genesis, chapter 13, concerns Lot and Abram (or Abraham). I am going to read one verse from this chapter 13, verse 12.

Abram dwelled in the land of Canaan, and Lot dwelled in the cities of the plain, and pitched his tent toward Sodom.

I want to talk to you today about this man, Lot. He is an interesting character. He represents so many people that you know. In fact, he may represent many characteristics of your own life. We can see ourselves in these Bible characters. Some of the characteristics of Abraham maybe we see and like, but we may see some of the characteristics of Lot, and we do not like what we see.

Anyway, Lot had an opportunity, but he missed the opportunity. He did not take advantage of it; he was not made out of the same character as his Uncle Abraham. I want you to note several things about Lot. You know the story: Lot and Abraham had prospered; they had great herds. They were both wealthy. They were living in a land dominated or inhabited by the enemies of the Lord. Abraham's herdsmen and Lot's herdsmen could not get along very well because of their work and the interest each had for his master.

So Abraham very wisely suggested that it was time to separate. "We are going to have trouble. And it will not be a good testimony for us to be feuding, fighting, and fussing among godless, heathen people. We will be acting just like they are acting." You know, that always hurts the cause of Christ when God's people act like the world around them. So Abraham did not want that to happen. It was time for separation.

The fact of the matter is, this was the first time Abraham had fully obeyed God at this point. God had spoken to him, you remember, back in chapter 12 and told him to leave his country and kindred. Well, he left his country, but he did not leave all of his kindred. He took his father and his nephew with him. I do not know why. He partially obeyed. You know, so many times we do that. We only partially obey. And as long as we do that, that which we do not surrender in full becomes a millstone around our neck. It hinders us.

After Abraham and Lot had separated, you recall God spoke to Abraham and gave him a vision of the land and some promises that He had not given him heretofore. Here was the complete separation that God had required long ago but was just now being realized.

So, Abraham said to Lot, "You look over the land. You make a choice." Verse 9:

> Is not the whole land before thee? separate thyself, I
> pray thee, from me: if thou wilt take the left hand, then I
> will go to the right; or if thou depart to the right hand,
> then I will go to the left.

In other words, here was a time of choice for Lot. It was going to reveal the kind of character he was. I want to say this to you: I believe that in every Christian's experience there is a time of testing. I do not think that any Christian is exempt. There comes a special time of testing.

It is not that God needs to know what you are or what you will do; He already knows. But God wants us to know. It is important for you to know what you are. It is important for the world around you to know what you are. God already knows. But it is important for you to know, and it is important for those around us to know.

I want to say again, I am convinced that in the life of every

Christian there comes a special test. Some men pass the test; some men flunk the test.

Jesus Christ was tested. There came that supreme test immediately after His baptism. He was led of the Holy Spirit into the wilderness to be tempted of the devil. So, even the Son of God was not spared that period of testing! He came through. He did not yield. There was no flaw in His character. There was no weak point there. " . . . In all points tempted like as we are . . . ." Every conceivable point of His character was tested. There was no weakness, no flaw.

Others have been tested. Simon Peter was tested. You know what happened in his case; he failed the test. He did not know the weaknesses of his own character. Happy is the man, blessed is the man who knows the weak points so he can fortify himself. Peter was very boastful. He said, "I will stand for you. I will die with you." And Jesus told him, "Before the cock crows, you will have denied me three times." You see, commitment was not supported by dedication.

You can overcommit yourself. Your maturity or your dedication may not be sufficient to support the promises that you make to God. Now, His grace is sufficient, but in the instance of Simon Peter, he was not as strong as he thought he was. You may not be as strong as you think you are. In a moment of ecstasy, in a moment of spiritual victory, you may make some boasts or some promises to God that you will not keep.

But, nonetheless, I believe every man is tested. You had better get ready for the test. You had better be aware that it is coming. It may have already come. Some of you, since you became a Christian, may have done things that shocked you. You may have already been on your face before God pouring out your heart, having disobeyed, and having fallen into some grievous sin that you thought that you would never fall into. You may have been trapped by the devil. In this moment of testing, you may have failed. There may have been weaknesses of your character that you did not know were there. You may have cried out and said, "Why did I do it? Why did I do it? I did not think that I would ever do such a thing." Men are tested.

I have noticed how God singles out and uses those men who come through the test, who have grace and character, and they say, "No! No! I will not yield." You had better get your mind made up. If you wait until you are under the pressure of temptation to make up your mind, you are in trouble. I want to say that again. If you wait until you are under the pressure of temptation to make up your mind about moral issues, you are in trouble. You had better get it fixed: "There are some things I am not going to do, by God's help and by God's grace. My mind is made up. This is right. This is wrong. I am going to stand for right, come what may."

I think that is what the Bible means when it says about a certain character, "My heart is fixed." "My heart is fixed." You should settle the issue before you go on a date. You should determine the kind of person you are going to be. "My mind is made up," I am not going to wait until I get on some shadowy lane somewhere in a parked automobile to make up my mind. It is too late then. I am going to be decent; I am going to be pure because God expects it of His children.

You know, some people get their minds made up, they think, but then they bring things up for review. They start debating. That is what Lot did. Look in verse 10: "Lot lifted up his eyes, and beheld all the plain of Jordan . . . ." In other words, he said, "Well, I will think this thing over." See, Abraham had his mind made up. He said, "Now, it does not matter to me." He did not have a selfish spirit about him. "You take the right or left; I will take what is left." See, his mind was made up.

Lot's mind was not made up. He said, "I will think this thing over. How much time, Uncle Abraham, do I have to think this over?" "Well, take a couple of days." "All right, that is good." And he lifted up his eyes and he looked. Listen, if your mind is made up, you do not debate; you have already got the answers when the test comes.

You go into an examination; your mind is made up; you are

not going to be dishonest. You go and write a term paper; you are not going to copy something that is not your own without giving proper credit. See, your mind is made up. You do not debate it. But now, wait a minute. If you say, "Well, now, let me think this thing over," and you start debating it: "Should I, or should I not?"

Lot got in trouble; he lifted up his eyes; he did not have his mind made up. Young people, we want you to make up your mind to live clean and pure and live for God. Cut out this suggestive music that stirs the baser part of nature. Turn off the television programs that excite the lower nature. Throw away the filthy literature that stimulates the flesh. Avoid all suggestive conversation that leaves your mind dirty. Stay out of those situations where the flesh will overpower you. Do not be persuaded by somebody's smooth talking to do things that you know you ought not to do.

Maybe I can recall a little phrase that I coined last year. *You have got certain fixed convictions when you get saved.* I believe every man's heart has to be right with God at the time he is saved or he cannot be saved. I believe there is full yieldedness to God at the time you are saved. There is a desire to live clean and pure and godly when you are saved, or you are not saved. God puts that in your heart. No matter what your weaknesses, at the time you are saved. You have a full desire and intentions to live clean and pure and holy.

Now, do not leave that. That is the best moment of your life, when you have such intentions. *But whenever you bring up long-held convictions for review, you are headed for trouble.* In other words, "I do not think it is right to be impure. That is settled in my heart." But then somebody begins to talk around you, and you read literature that suggests it is all right to sacrifice your purity. In fact, you are not even sacrificing your purity. It is sort of the noble thing. And you begin to review it. You say, "Now, my mother told me that it was wrong. I know it is wrong. I have always thought it was wrong, but maybe it is not wrong." And you start reviewing it. See, you are lifting up your eyes. You do not have your mind really fixed. You begin to debate the issue.

When you get into a debate with the devil, he will always win. I want you to nail that down. Whenever you get to debating with the devil, he will always get you just like he did Eve. He has convinced many a boy that he ought to do things that the boy knew he ought not to do. He was convinced by the devil because he lifted up his eyes. Many a girl has lost her purity when she said she would never do it because she reviewed her past stand and somebody convinced her that breaking it was not so bad.

You had better not bring up for review those long-held convictions that God put in your heart and start looking toward the well-watered plain. You had better get your heart fixed, settled on some issues: "I am going to tell the truth; I am going to be honest; I am going to be pure." You had better not start debating it and reviewing it.

Lifting up his eyes, Lot said, "All right, Uncle Abraham, I have my mind made up." "You do?" "Yes, I believe I will move down toward Sodom, if you do not mind, Uncle Abraham." Uncle Abraham said, "Any way, son, any way, I am not concerned."

Listen, young people, do you have your mind made up? What kind of person do you want to be? What kind of person are you going to be? You will save yourself a lot of frustration when you come out and take your stand for God and for decency and let everyone know it. They will not be pestering you all the time. Let your stand be known.

So, he chose. He lifted up his eyes. He chose the well-watered plain. He looked. Notice verse 10: *he looked, he chose, he journeyed.* You know, that is interesting. If there had never been a look toward Sodom, he would never have journeyed toward Sodom. The look, the gaze, led to the journey and it led to ruin. He looked; he chose. He chose the well-watered plain. Then he journeyed; he separated himself from Abraham, too. He got out from under the influence of his Uncle Abraham.

You know, he changed crowds that day; he changed his

companions that day. You know, when you take a step into sin you always change companions. He had to throw off the restraints of a godly uncle. As far as I know, you never read in this record where Lot built any altars. You read time after time where Abraham built an altar. Not Lot; he was just a casual observer. He agreed with it all right. He did not protest. He may have brought the stones and piled them up at the direction of Uncle Abraham, I do not know. But he never built any.

The Christian who never builds any altars always ends up in Sodom and Gomorrah with no testimony. Along your pathway of life, young friend, there ought to be a lot of altars that you have built, things that separate you, points of dedication, points of separation from the world, recommitment, getting things straightened up again. You are going to need to do it right here in Free Will Baptist Bible College. We cannot build your altars for you. Every man has to build his own altars; it is a personal thing. I cannot consecrate myself for you; you cannot for me. I have to build my own altar, and I have to worship from my own altar. And so will you.

So, he looked; he chose; he journeyed. You had better not look, or you are going to take a journey in the wrong direction. He separated himself from Uncle Abraham.

Now, notice in chapter 14, verse 12: He was persecuted; he got in jail; he was a prisoner of war. At first, they did not want him. Listen, the world does not want you. You have disowned the world, and they have disowned you. You go back there, and it will not be as friendly to you as you thought it would. At first they disowned him. But you know, after a while he got so identified until, instead of disowning him, they honored him. They took him in. You stay out there long enough in the world, and after a while they will take you in. You become identified, you make enough compromises, and they will take you in after a while. In chapter 19:

> And there came two angels to Sodom at even; and Lot
> sat in the gate of Sodom . . . .

Now he was the mayor. Now they have taken him in. Oh, listen, this old world will flatter you after a while if you will identify enough. If you will compromise enough, it will put its crown of honor on you.

I am thinking of some students that sat where you are sitting now. They got out there in the world, and at first the world, some of the academic world, would not pay any attention to them. "Where did you go to school?" And they would hem and haw and mutter out, "Free Will Baptist Bible College" under their breath. So they had the name and the stigma of this institution erased from their record, and they put the stamp of some great university on their record. Now they no longer say to anybody, "I went to Free Will Baptist Bible College, but I went to University So-and-so." I know some of them today that the academic world has taken in and crowned with honor, but what price did they pay? The price of their testimony, and the price of their ministry.

Some of them said God called them to preach. I doubt that they would tell anybody, unless they already knew, that they were preachers. They are Professor So-and-so. But as far as their testimony, it is gone, gone. The world has honored them, yes. The world honored Lot; the world honored Lot, made him mayor, Sodom did. But what a price.

His sons-in-law laughed at him when he tried to give a testimony. It sounded so strange coming from Lot. They laughed and mocked. You know, we find Lot compromising all the way. God told him, "I am going to destroy this city." The wicked men came down there to take the men, angels, the heavenly representatives who came to Lot's house; and Lot said, "Do not take them. I will give you my daughters instead." He was a negotiator; he was a modern-day politician. He was willing—he was willing to negotiate the virtue of his daughters. Lot should have stood in the face of those men and said, "You will not enter here."

Listen, I want to say a little something to you: A man of God should never choose the lesser of two evils. You never are called on to choose the lesser of two evils. You are never justified in choosing the lesser of two evils. Lot said, "I will choose the lesser of two evils. I will protect these heavenly representatives from these degenerates, but I will sacrifice my daughters' purity." A lot of young people choose the lesser of two evils. You do not have to do it. You stand four-square for God and say, "No evil at all; no evil at all. I will die before I sacrifice these men or before I sacrifice my daughters." God had to work a miracle to save the situation. He blinded their eyes.

Lot was trying to save the situation through compromise and negotiation. That is the way of the world. God will save His cause through miracles. We do not have to say that we compromise and negotiate. Stand for God! Pull up! He had to be snatched out. Thank God for His mercy and grace. Lot is due no credit at all, not at all. He was a man who failed every test.

You may have failed some of yours. So you had better get back where God can use you.

May we stand.

PRAYER

Dear Lord, be with us today. Put character, put Thy grace in us. Give us determination, give us commitment. In Jesus' Name, Amen.

14

October 4, 1974
Scripture: Psalm 8
Subject: Man is made in the image of God

LIVING IN THE LIGHT OF HIS MAJESTY

One of the very familiar Psalms is Psalm 8. We will read that Psalm this morning.

O LORD our Lord, how excellent is thy name in all the earth! who has set thy glory above the heavens. Out of the mouth of babes and sucklings hast thou ordained strength because of thine enemies, that thou mightest still the enemy and the avenger. When I consider thy heavens, the work of thy fingers, the moon and the stars, which thou hast ordained; What is man, that thou art mindful of him? and the son of man, that thou visitest him? For thou hast made him a little lower than the angels [or as one translation puts it, Thou hast made him a little lower than God or the heavenly beings], and hast crowned him with glory and honour. Thou madest him to have dominion over the works of thy hands: thou hast put all things under his feet: All sheep and oxen, yea, and the beasts of the field; The fowl of the air, and the fish of the sea, and whatsoever passeth through the paths of the seas. O LORD our Lord, how excellent is thy name in all the earth!

That is, as I said, a very familiar Psalm. I do not know just why David was inspired, or what he was thinking about or perhaps seeing to cause him to write this Psalm. Of course he was inspired of the Lord. Perhaps he was out at night looking at the heavens; I do not know.

The majesty of God seized him. That is a mighty good thing to happen in our lives. That has been impressed here for at least two occasions recently. It was emphasized by one of our visiting speakers, and also in last Sunday evening's service: the majesty of God. Isaiah saw God in His glory and in His majesty, and it changed his life.

Somewhere along the way we need to see more than our sinfulness. We do need to see God in His glory, in His majesty. In this Psalm, David saw this; he realized it. He looked at the heavens, and maybe that suggested to him the glory of God. He said, "You are bigger than the heavens." I am sure that you read from time to time—there was an article recently in *Reader's Digest* about astronomy, about the greatness of this universe. Man cannot comprehend it. So many billions of light years away a star sends forth its light. It takes billions of years to travel within our sight with light traveling at the tremendous speed of 186,000 miles per second. That is more than man can comprehend.

But David looking at the heavens said, "The heavens declare your glory. They are the works of your fingers, the moon and the stars which you made. In comparison, what is man? He is so small. Yet he is so great. The thing that makes him great is that God made him just a little lower than Himself." That is, He made him just a little lower than the heavenly beings. I do not know whether that translation is right or not that says, "Thou hast made him a little lower than God." But we do know that man was made in the image and likeness of God. Whatever that means, it means that man is important. No other part of God's creation did He say that He made in His image. When it came to man, He made man in His image, in His likeness. We are important beings.

There is an eternity about you and about us that no other part of God's creation has. Some people talk about animals: Do they have souls? Why, no, they do not have souls like we have. It is not wrong for us to go out and kill an animal and slaughter it and dress it and eat it. Animals do not have souls like we have notwithstanding all the emphasis that is placed on animals, dogs, and cats. Drive along the highway, and you will see these memorial gardens to dogs. You see them burying dogs in costly caskets and all of this stuff. You know, that is not having natural affection. That is unnatural affection.

I like dogs. I grew up with them. I wish I could have one now. I like to have a dog you can kick. You know, you need somebody to kick. You cannot kick your wife. You need some outlet for your frustrations.

Nonetheless, man is a distinct part of God's creation. I do not like to classify man as an animal. I do not classify him as an animal. He is more than that. When God crowned man with honor and glory, His glory, His honor, God stamped something within man's being that makes him distinct. It lifts him above any other part of His creation, notwithstanding the biology that you may have been taught in high school.

Some of you were brainwashed; you were confused by some smart professor that does not have sense enough to believe in God. But he can look at the heavens; he can look at this universe, and he has to be mighty dumb to come to the conclusion that there is not a supreme Being. God has given enough evidence of His being that when we look at the heavens they declare His glory. There is no language where His message does not go out through the heavens. And yet, some of these smart aleck professors deny His existence or question it. They confuse a lot of sincere, young, immature people and send them out in life with all kinds of doubts and confusion that they may never get over. If they do, it will take a long time.

Here we are told that God made him a little lower than Himself, in His image, in His likeness. He put this stamp upon man, this image, this glory that lifts man above all the other parts of His creation and makes him distinct. Man is a wonderful being. He has wonderful capabilities. This world that we live in is a wonderful world in so many ways.

There in the early part of the Book of Genesis we read about the people who came to a certain place, and they said, "We want to stay here. Let us build us a tower that it may reach the heavens. Let us make us a name that we will not be scattered abroad." God did not like that. He came down and confused their language, their speech, so they could not understand one another. God is the greatest segregator that you have. God segregated man according to language.

Now you will not get along very well if you have to live with somebody you cannot understand. You will just saunter off and find your crowd that you can talk to. God knew this would happen. So He segregated society at this point by giving them confusion of speech and understanding. This little group went this way who could understand one another, and the other went the other way, and so on. God did not want man to pool his depravity. He knew that man was capable of doing some things that evidently God did not want him to do.

Man has tremendous power to do things. He is just a little lower than God. We have the power within our bodies of procreation. God never did create but two people, as far as I know. Then He turned procreation over to man. Now, I do not know what your theology professors tell you, but I am telling you right. Man has the power to beget life within his body. He is that much in the image and likeness of God.

So we need to understand our worth. We are important. But along with that goes a responsibility. We are responsible to God. God created us; He is our Maker. This verse tells us that: "Thou hast made him a little lower than . . . " Himself. Along with that dignity and that power that God gave to us goes responsibility. Now, if you do not know who you are, you are going to go through life confused. A lot of people do not know who they are. You take the atheist, the communist who do not believe in God. They have one concept of man. We have another concept of man. They look upon man as an animal.

When you look upon yourself as an animal, you are going to act like an animal, you are going to behave as an animal, you are going to follow your impulse, and you are going to do what you are urged to do by your emotions. That is the reason we see so many people today living like animals. They are simply following

112

the inner urge of their depraved nature, and they are throwing off all restraints, doing as they please. Anything they are urged to do by their depravity, they do it because they have been taught that there is no God; or if there is some supreme Being out there, they are not accountable to Him. So they are living for the here and now. Eat, drink, and be merry for tomorrow you may die. Get out of life what you can, while you can. Enjoy it to the fullest.

I would live like that too, perhaps, if I did not believe in God and know that I was responsible to God. I might. The philosophy would be very logical, in a sense. A lot of people have been brainwashed along this line, and we are seeing the results of it. But man is more than an animal. Man was put here by God, he has a God-ordained purpose for being here, and he is going to give an account to God at the end of the way. Now, when you live in the light of these three truths, it will do something to your behavior. God put me here, I have an ordained purpose, and I am going to have to give an account for my behavior at the judgment.

Now, what is man? Well, man is created with a living soul. As I said, there is an eternity about you. Today's activities, what you do today, what you have done up until this hour, and what you will do the rest of this day, will have to be reported at the judgment. The Word of God says that for every word, every idle word, we will have to give an account at the judgment. Whether the deeds have been good, or whether they have been bad, we will have to give an account at the judgment.

You know, it is an interesting thing to be able to pick up broadcast music that is being played at this moment in London or in Europe somewhere, or across the world. Scientists have given us something that we take for granted. You turn a little knob and hear a symphony that is being played in London, England. You hear it at the very time that it is being played there. I cannot comprehend that. There is music all around us right now. We cannot hear it, can we? But if you will take a radio and turn it on, you can turn to stations all over this country and around the world if you had the right instrument. You could pick up music that is in this auditorium right now that we cannot hear. Great symphonies are being played; I wish I could tune in on them. I wish I could tune out some of this stuff that we hear in Nashville.

But here it is. Well, I do not know but what everything you say and everything you do is being recorded some way in this universe. It is going to be played at the judgment as we stand there. God will turn a little knob, and He will pick up the tape of our lives. There it is. We will listen to it. I do not know how it will be done. But I know that we are going to have to listen; we are going to have to face what we do here in this world when we stand before God.

There is an eternity about us. With this dignity and this glory that God has placed upon us come responsibility. Students, we need to learn to live in the light of eternity, not in the light of what I can get away with here and now, but in the light of eternity.

So man is an eternal being. Now as I said, the communists do not take that into account. They elbow their way through life. They will run over countries and take them into captivity. They will kill you or anything else to promote communism because there is no God; there is no judgment. When they die, they die—that ends it all. There is not a Hell for them. They really have it made; do they not? Anything that they can do to get by, that is all right, or whatever society approves.

A lot of us have been influenced by this situation ethics, the changing society. And it is a changing society. Things that were wrong ten years ago are not wrong any longer. You would be amused if I told you some things that were wrong for Christians to do when I was a young Christian. Did you know it was considered wrong to drink *Coca Cola* when I was a young Christian, in my part of the country? Did you know it was considered wrong to drink iced tea? Why, it was considered sinful.

Now, I think that was absurd. Personally, I think that was an extreme. But a lot of people felt that way. Did you know it was considered wrong to go bowling? Well, I am not too sold on it yet.

There is a little hangover on some of these things for me that bothers me. I have not quite gotten free from it. I have nothing against bowling if you do not have to watch beer guzzlers and all this stuff around. I guess maybe you just have to decide that for yourself. But I am just telling you.

Can you remember the time that it was wrong to go to picture shows? "Well," you say, "it is still wrong around here." Well, not going to picture shows is no guarantee that you are going to Heaven. We know that. But we cannot understand, for the life of us, why you have to pay your good money to go down there and have your mind soiled with the filth of Hollywood. Some of those people have been divorced and remarried many times, others of those people are living on drugs, many are living in immorality of every kind imaginable. Why in the world Christian people want to subject themselves to the influences of these people, I cannot understand; I cannot understand.

Anyway, all of these things used to be considered wrong. We have changed a lot. Did you know it was wrong—and you realize this now—that we thought it was wrong to dance? I heard somebody tell the other day that some Free Will Baptist church had a dance. I hope it was wrong. But I will tell you what: When these recreational centers that we have built all across our denomination are there to be used, there is going to be some worldly-minded person one of these days who is going to suggest that it is better to have a properly-chaperoned dance in the recreational center than to let our young people go out here to these places.

It is coming if we do not have some good strong preaching. It will catch up with us. It has with other denominations. It will come to us. We had better keep some of our convictions sharpened and honed up, or we will gradually slip into these things. Now if you do not believe there is a judgment, if you do not believe you are accountable, if you lose sight of eternity, we are going to slip into some of these things.

Christianity is more than doing and going and giving.

Christianity is a way of life. It has a set of convictions; it has a set of values built in. We need to understand it.

So, what is man? He is made in the image and likeness of God. He is here for an ordained purpose. Have you ever seriously considered why you are living and why you are here; what you are doing here? Ah, but if we could get a hold of this fact that what I am doing here is very important, it would change some of our lives. Then, as I said, that we are going to have to give an account to God for the way we lived.

> Thou madest him to have dominion over the works of
> thy hands; thou hast put all things under his feet.

This authority that God gave to man makes man important, and it also makes man responsible. How are you living? Who are you? Who are you? Is there a question mark that is hanging over from high school that some professor put in your mind, and it is not quite clear who you are?

I am surprised sometimes when I learn that some young people are confused at this point. We take it for granted that you have already settled all these questions. But that is not always true. I want to say again, your estimation of yourself will determine your behavior to a great degree.

May we stand, please.

PRAYER

Our Father, wilt Thou clear our minds of the confusion that this world plants within them. Help us to turn to Thy Word to find out who we are and what we are doing here and that we will have to stand before You one day to give an account. Bless every student, every one of us, throughout this day to live in the light of eternity. In Jesus' Name. Amen.

15

October 8, 1974
Scripture: 2 Corinthians 3:18
Subject: "Changed from glory into glory"

CHANGE ME LORD, FOR GOOD

. . . A practical hint to you. Train yourself. Discipline yourself to participate in the service. Now you do not have to sing. Many times I do not sing. I am singing in my heart. For various reasons, maybe I will not sing. But I am participating, nonetheless, in the spirit of singing. Now you can fall into the habit of just throwing your mind out of gear when you come into a service, and you will not benefit very much. But I think everyone is participating; I watch you as you sing and it is encouraging and it is also a contribution to the service.

Just this other word: It is a thrill to observe you on this campus day after day, coming into chapel, and in chapel. Most of you listen, or at least you appear to be listening. It is an inspiration. I have made a note in years past when I pastored, and I remember some dear people to this very day who were good listeners. Now, the reason I remember them is that they stood out in contrast to rest of the audience. If everybody had listened I would not have noticed these particular ones. But what an inspiration.

I think of two dear ladies right now, well I think of three in particular. One of them was maybe 80 years old, but she listened. She drank in every word. I was just a boy preacher you might say, but she would tell me that was the greatest sermon that she ever heard. But now, the thing about it is that she meant it. It was to her. Because at 80 years of age she could not remember the last one! Well, anyway, at 80 years of age, she was a good listener, and it was an inspiration to me, a real inspiration.

I remember two other ladies. They were not as elderly, but they were mature Christian ladies. Now, I do not know why I remember the ladies. Maybe they looked better, I do not know.

But nonetheless, they listened. Oh, they just pulled everything out of you that possibly could be pulled out in the way of preaching. They were good listeners; they participated by listening.

Now, you know, you can be a real contribution to this service. You come in, you say, "Well, I am not to preach today so I do not have anything to do." Yes you do. You make a tremendous contribution. And I have noticed this year in particular, it seems to me that you listen better than most years.

Now, once in a while a fellow will get his head turned to one side and his eyes half open. That kind of fellow I wish I could just pull a veil around him and cut him out because he puts a damper on the service. But most of you listen, and that is a mighty good thing.

Look in 2 Corinthians, chapter 3, the last verse in this chapter, verse 18:

> But we all, with open face beholding as in a glass the
> glory of the Lord, are changed into the same image
> from glory to glory, even as by the Spirit of the Lord.

Now, let us just notice what this says before we start talking about it. "But we all, with open face beholding as in a glass . . . ." Now the glass here could be the Word of God. " . . . The glory of the Lord, are changed . . . ." You could put a period right there, and you could preach a sermon from that point. "Beholding . . . the glory of the Lord, [we] are changed . . . " see. " . . . Into the same image . . ." that is, you look into the glass, you look into the Word, and you see the glory of the Lord. You are changed into the image, the same image." . . . From glory to glory . . ." there is the process. It is something that goes on and on and on. The longer you look, the more you are changed. The more of His glory you see. But you have to look and it says we are all changed when we look. The thing keeps up, and the process goes on and on, " . . . from glory to glory, even as by the Spirit of [God]." The

118

Spirit of God working in us, enabling us to see as we look into this glass. We see something that changes us, and it is from glory to glory.

That is wonderful. That is the reason you are here in this school. That is the important point of being here. You might as well be in a state university somewhere. We cannot teach you English, literature, or history any better than anybody else. A rank sinner can teach you what a verb is. I understand some people around here have never learned what a verb or a noun is. You are not responsible; the school system of this country is responsible for not having taught you.

But anyway, I want to talk about this matter of change. I was going to bring a little quote that I read from a magazine, but I think I can give the gist of it to you. Oliver Wendell Holmes said something like this: "When the mind is stretched to a new idea, it never returns to its original dimensions." I want to say that again; I think that is just about the quote. "When the mind is stretched to a new idea, it never returns to its original dimensions." Something has happened to it; it expands. Your mind having been stretched to new ideas never does become as small again. It has expanded and it stays expanded. It has to make room for new truth and new ideas. Day by day, the things you learn stack up and stack up, and your mind is expanding. You are being changed by these ideas, what you learn, the experiences you have.

You could add a little saying to that: You are not the same today that you were yesterday. You are not the same person. Oh, you say, "Yes, I am. I got up and looked in the mirror this morning. I had the same warts and the same blemishes. I am the same." Oh, no! The warts may be there, the blemishes may be there, but you are changed. You are not the same as you were yesterday. Tomorrow you will be a different person in some ways. We are all undergoing a change as we have new experiences.

Now, I want to say this: Let us make a distinction. We are

not going to fall into the trap of the communists and the liberals who say that there is no law that sticks except the law that everything changes. I do not go for that. There are some things that are immutable. Principle never changes. It has always been wrong to lie. It is wrong today; it will be wrong tomorrow. It will always be wrong to lie. It has always been wrong to be dishonest. It is today, and it will be tomorrow. It has always been wrong to be immoral. It is today, it will be tomorrow, and there are no circumstances when it is right to be immoral, no circumstances. These things are fixed, and they do not change. God does not change, but we change.

The reason God does not change is that He is holy and He is perfect. There is nothing that can be added to God. That is not true of us. We are depraved, sinful people. Even after we are saved, we need to undergo a change. I think this is what this verse of Scripture is talking about.

But there has always been the desire to go back to the old and to be like we were. Now you listen to some of us older people talk around here, and we are talking about olden times and how it was in the good old days. But none of us wants to go back to those good old days. We imagine how perfect it was. Why, you do not want to go back really if you get down and analyze it. We would get up in the morning and the water would be frozen and there was no heating system. You had to go out to an old well or a pump and bring in the water. You do not want to go back to that. We forget all of that, though.

I have a painting in the office of my home where I was reared. My daughter painted it this last summer. I sit there and become nostalgic as I look at that and remember. But you know, the strange thing is I have added some things to that house that did not use to be there. A bathroom and running water are there now. I used to have to run the water.

But, nonetheless, you know, you can look back to the good old days, but we do not really want to go back there. The Children of Israel, after they had left Egypt and they got out into the wilderness, said, "We are going to die out here. We do not have anything but manna and quail to eat, and water from the rock. We want to go back to the leeks, the garlic, and the onions of Egypt." But you know, if God had let them go back, they could not have enjoyed the onions, the garlic, and the leeks of Egypt, having eaten the manna from Heaven. The most miserable people in the world are those people who have once tasted of the heavenly things, the heavenly manna, and then think that they want to go back to the garlic and the onions of Egypt. They go back and they think that it will taste like it used to taste, but it does not any more. They remember the thrills of their sins. They do not remember that their nature has been changed. They cannot enjoy now the past sin that they enjoyed. Then they were depraved in nature and knew nothing of the grace of God.

I say again, the most miserable, frustrated people are those people that are out there, neither in Egypt, neither in the Promised Land, but wandering around in the wilderness of sin. There are a lot of people who live in the wilderness all their life. They left through redemption; they left Egypt. They crossed the Red Sea through the miraculous new birth, but they never were willing to go on into the Promised Land, into all the fullness that God had provided. They are afraid to go back, but they are unwilling to make the surrender to go into the land and possess the good things that God has provided. Many Christians spend their lives going in circles unwilling to move away completely. They want to look back across the Red Sea and long for Egypt.

There are some of you who talk up and down the halls of these dormitories about your past exploits into sin. You claim to have been redeemed and put on the other side of the Red Sea, separating you from the old life. But you stand on the banks of the Red Sea on the other side and look back over and talk about the good times that you had when you lived in sin. Shame on you! You are frustrated. You do not love the land you are in. You do not want to go back to the old, but you stand there and wish for it and daydream about it. In fantasy, you relive the old life and try to enjoy the fruits of sin without actually participating in them. You cannot enjoy the things of God.

If you have been redeemed from your past sins, you had better shut them out of your mind. If you have a sanctified heart, there will be no longing for Egypt and the garlic and fleshpots of Egypt. You had better have your mind changed. Anybody who talks about his past sin is glorying in his past sin. There is no reason to talk every day about them and open up that old ugly, filthy package. You have a dirty, sinful heart if you can do that.

You will not glory in your past sin when Jesus comes on the throne of your heart. Any memory of them, you will detest. You do not like to relive the things that you detest. So there has been a change.

Oh, sometimes you hear people say, "That will not change me." I hear it said in regard to school. Somebody wants to take off to one of the universities or liberal schools, and they say, "Oh, I can go there; it will not change me." Do not fool yourself. Let me tell you; if we do not change you, you might as well pack up and go back home. I want to put you on notice now, that what we are here for is to change you. It would be a mighty poor institution that could not make some impact on your life. It will be a mighty poor teacher that cannot make some impression upon you. Your dormitory friends are making an impression.

We are in the business of changing people. We make no bones about it. These institutions are just lies when they say, "We are all broadminded. We are here to consider truth. We do not know what it is. We are not going to tell you what we think it is lest we prejudice you. We are just going to hold up a lot of options." They are as dishonest as they can be. They are trying to change you in a subtle way. They are trying to disarm you and to make you think that you are not being changed while they are changing you all the time.

Yes, we are in the business of change. You need to be changed; I need to be changed. But you hear them say, "Oh, that will not change me. I can go with that unsaved boy, and he will not change me. I can go with that unsaved girl, and it will not change me. I can hobknob with the wrong crowd; they will not change me. I can be a missionary."

You know, we have had a few students that came here, who felt called to minister to the intellectual. A freshman boy will come in and say (we have had a few over the years), "I feel called to the intellectual group." They take off to Vanderbilt and get in an argument with a PhD candidate. They say, "I am called to this ministry. They cannot change me." He has already been changed, or he would not have such an attitude. It is all right to witness to the elite, the so-called intellectual, but let me tell you, some of these folks called intellectuals do not have sense enough to get out of the rain. They are not as intellectual as they think they are. They are so dumb that they laugh at God. "The fool hath said in his heart, There is no God . . . . "

But anyway, we are being changed. Every human experience changes us. Listen now, listen to me—every experience that you have today will change you. Every conversation that you engage in will change you. Every time you listen to music, it gets inside you and does something to you.

We are changed by human experience.

It is like taking a rose and touching it. Did you know that when you touch a rose it is changed? There is a little bruise there. It may be invisible to the eye, but your fingerprints are left there and that little rose has undergone a change. If you touch it very heavily, there is a little bruise that is left. That little rose will carry through its life the touch of your hand. Every human experience leaves its mark upon your mind and upon your life. You are being changed by it. When you read a book, you have to evaluate what you are reading. You are being changed as you evaluate. You do not always have to approve in order to be changed.

Then another thing, time changes us. Human experience changes us. Listen, now, all change is not for good. You think back upon your life, and you remember people that you have met along the pathway of life that had you not met, you would have been a better person. There are some people who have put marks upon your life that will never be erased. They put a bruise there that you will carry to your grave. Even divine grace will never erase the touch of those people upon your life. You may be a bruised rose. On the petal of your life, there will be that bruise that will be there. Even though divine grace has forgiven the sin, the bruise, the change that was wrought in your mind and in your experiences is indelible. It will not go away even with the washing of Calvary.

That is the reason we ought to be careful, young people; we ought to be careful about these human experiences that we have. They are doing something to us, doing something to us. I do not know that I go with that quote that says, "A bird with a broken pinion will never soar as high again." Divine grace . . . I do not know how to appropriate Divine grace or how to apply it in these cases. But I know one thing: Sin never leaves you the same. You will never be the same after sin. It never helps anybody.

This philosophy that I have got to go out and experience things in order to learn is a damnable philosophy. You do not have to burn yourself on the stove of experience to learn. You do not have to come out and become a drunkard to know the sin of drink. No! But experience changes you.

And time changes you .I want to tell you something. (You will remember it 30 years from now; some of you will remember it 20 years from now.) You will not think like you do today when you get 50. Is that going to be a surprise to you? Oh, you say, "Horrors! You mean I am going to think like those old folks walking around here?" Yes, sir. I can tell you that you are going to think just like them or a little more so. You may be worse than we are.

Now, I do not want to discourage you, but you are going to undergo a change. You are going to think differently. Time is going to bring about some change. When you get to be a parent and you have teenage children, you are not going to be nearly as hard on us then as you are now. You are going to undergo a change. Not that you are going to approve different things, but you are just going to see life in a different way. Time changes you. Either for good or for bad, time changes you.

You know, the Apostle Peter wanted to go back to his nets. He said, "Let us go fishing. Let us go back to our old nets." You know, that was one of the most miserable experiences that Peter ever had in his life. "Oh," you say, "the night he denied the Lord . . . ." Yes, that was a sad night. But it was a sad time when he picked up his old nets and thought he would get the same thrill that he used to get when he would cast them and pull in the catch.

You know, he got those old nets out, but he had lost the art of the thing. It just would not fall right. When it did fall, he did not feel the tug of the fish. He had lost the touch. The old world was not the same any more; he had walked on new ground. Now as he went back to the old way, it was not the same. Let me tell you, young people, around here on these grounds you have walked on new ground. Now you may go back to the old nets, but it will not be the same when you get back there. You have changed; you have changed more than you know it, more than you know it.

I said awhile ago all change is not good. I think of some people, some characters in the Word of God, their change was not for the good. I am just going to to mention one. I have thought of several, but I will mention one as an illustration.

David changed one time. He had an experience that left an ugly mark on his heart and life. He was never the same after his great sin.

There was a weakness that showed up in his life, in his family, and in his administrative responsibilities. He was never as strong. David had reached his highest point before he committed that sin. There was a weakness; there was a deterioration until it got to the point that his own son thought that he could take on his old dad. His own godless son recognized the weakness in his daddy, and he exploited that weakness. The weak, feeble sort of way that he dealt with his son who molested his daughter showed that he did not have that inner conviction, that inner courage, that a man of God ought to have. It had been eaten away, eroded by sin.

Listen, young people, I think of friends of mine that I have watched over the years. Sin has eroded their convictions and washed them away. Now they are only the hull of men that they could have been. The heart is gone out, the fire, the conviction, the character. Saved by the grace of God, yes, but feeble in their conviction. God pity them.

I never tell the Lord when to take me home to glory. I am going to leave that to God. But there is one thing for sure: I do not want to be around here until I get feeble and weak in my convictions. I want to go out strong if God will permit it. Therefore, I had better not dabble around and play with sin.

May we stand.

PRAYER

Dear Lord, be with us this day. Bless these students. We thank You for them. Meet every need in all of our lives. In Jesus' Name. Amen.

16

October 24, 1974
Scripture: Psalm 23
Subject: The Lord is my Shepherd

I SHALL NOT WANT

This morning I am reading one of the most familiar passages in the Bible. That is Psalm 23. We are delighted to have these brethren visit with us today. Had I known they were going to come, I would have asked one of them to have spoken. And yet, as I thought of it being 9-weeks exams, it is hardly fair to any visiting speaker. I do not know that you listen during examination time, but we go through the routine anyway. No, I hope that even during exams when we open the Word of God that we feel a responsibility to listen. It is not man talking when we read God's Word; it is God speaking to us, and He has a message for us. This is a timeless message.

It is a wonderful thing to read the Word of God and to find new things in those passages that you have memorized, that you have heard all your life. Yet there is a depth there that you never do exhaust, a supply, an inexhaustible supply. I hope that you are training yourselves to see things when you read the Word of God. I think so many people read that do not see; they do not meditate. It takes time to let God speak to you out of His Word, but He always will.

The LORD is my shepherd; I shall not want.

Now, those are familiar words: " . . . I shall not want." It is wonderful to know that we have a God who supplies our needs. "I shall not want." You cannot have anything better than that. There is no insurance policy that you can buy that can provide this for you. There is nothing in this world that you can lay hold of that is as wonderful as this statement. " . . . I shall not want" in this world of want, in this world of uncertainty and confusion. God is saying, "I will not let you want anything."

Your life can be so harmonized with God that you will only

want what God provides. The further away from God you get, the more wants you will have. That is one trouble with the world today. We have more than we have ever had, but we have more wants than we have ever had. Is that not strange? We live in better homes, drive better automobiles, eat better food, and wear better clothing. We can go places and see things and do things that we never could do before. We thought that would satisfy, but it will not. The reason the world is so confused and restless is that we are away from God.

But you can bring your life into such harmony with His will that you will be satisfied. "Delight thyself also in the Lord; and He shall give thee the desires of thine heart." In other words, line your life up with God's will, and then you will have the desires of your heart. I do not know whether anybody has fully tested this or not. I do not know whether you have; I do not know whether I have, whether we have put this to the test or not. These are such familiar words; we read them and think we believe them. But do we?

Now what are the wants of your life today? Well, you say, "I want money. I do not have money. I am insecure. I do not know where I am going to get money to pay my bills" or "I want this" or "I want that." Just think of your wants; now just make a want list. Every housewife, I suppose, has a want list. You go through the week and make a list of things you are out of. You say, "We will go to the store a certain day and get this," and you make a want list.

Well, all of us carry a want list in our heart: things we would like to have, things we would like to do. But here it says, "The LORD is my shepherd; I shall not want. He maketh me to lie down in green pastures . . . ." Oh, you say, "I like that part about lying down." He does not say, "Get out and start hustling." He says, first of all, "He maketh me to lie down...." That is, He gets me quiet so that my soul is not agitated so He can speak to me.

This is a busy world. Now, David himself was quite a busy fellow when you follow his life. He did a few things, killed a few bears, wild animals—to start off with. If you follow his life

128

through, you will see that he did not stay under a shade tree all the time. But when God spoke to him and he penned these words, he said, "The Lord maketh me to lie down in green pastures . . . ."

I suppose green is one of the most restful colors that we have. If you went through the buildings in the city of Nashville today, you would find more green walls than any other kind. There is something about it that rests you. So he uses the green pastures to symbolize restfulness, quietness. Is your soul calm and quiet and resting today, or are you agitated? Is your life like a smooth-flowing brook, or is it turbulent?

Did you wake up today and start worrying? Do you have a boyfriend on this campus who is not paying as much attention to you as you would like? Let him go; he is not the one for you anyway. God will have a better one for you. Oh, you say, "No, he is the only one." How do you know? God might bring a better one by. It could be a girlfriend.

Or maybe it is your classwork. You are not passing like you would like. But are you studying? Do not expect to pass if you are not studying. But if you are doing your best, then take it easy. Let the teacher worry. See? But if you are doing your best, then that is all God expects. You are making an A with God and an F with your teacher. Your teacher does not know as much as God.

Listen, are you worried and fretted? You cannot have a good testimony if you are worried and fretted. You cannot do it. If you are too busy to stand still to talk to people when they have problems, you are just too busy. I see pastors who are so busy they cannot give you but 5-minute appointments. I do not like to to go a doctor that is too busy. When he walks in the room and starts thumping me, I want to be the only one that is on his mind. I do not want him thinking of somebody down the hall in another room. I want him to give me his undivided attention, think about my problem. If you have problems, you are not going to talk to people who are too worried, too fretted, and too busy to listen. Oh, how we need to be calm in this troubled world.

I have said so many times, and I think it is so true: Some of us cannot preach very good sermons, but we can live good sermons. That is the only way we will ever do much preaching, some of us, by the way we live. If we can rest in the Lord, and people can see that rest, and it is reflected in our countenance, I will tell you, people will beat a path to our door to want to know where we found such rest. They will want to know the secret of it, and we can tell them.

But, "He maketh me to lie down in green pastures . . . ." How wonderful. Notice something else, " . . . he leadeth me beside the still waters." He uses that word, "leadeth" twice here in these verses. We will get to the other one in just a moment. "He leadeth me beside the still waters," another figure of speech suggesting quietness, serenity, calmness, and composure as you go about your duties. You are quiet, collected, not worried.

"He restoreth my soul . . . ." He renews us. We get frazzled, tired, and worn. This old world gives us a beating. We need some quiet place to have our souls restored, the inner man, the inner spirit. God keeps it fresh. The Bible talks about being renewed like the eagle, about running and not being weary. These old bones get creaky. They get arthritis, and we cannot move about, but the inner man can stay young and fresh. God wants us to stay that way. He leads us beside the still waters. He restores our souls, our spiritual energy, our inner spirit.

I say again: This old world gives you a beating, a buffeting. And you get haggard, tired, and weary. The cares of this world can weigh you down, but God, the Shepherd, will restore your soul. The Shepherd does not let you get overtired. He provides the strength according to the responsibility. Do not ever get those things out of balance. God does not give you a bigger load than you can carry.

We need to use common sense here. He restores the soul, my soul. " . . . He leadeth me in the paths of righteousness . . . ." Now the first "leadeth" is concerning the still waters so you will be calm and composed. Then the next is He leads us in paths of righteousness. Here you have the work cut out for you: paths of righteousness.

Now why? " . . . For his name's sake." You are representing the Lord Jesus Christ in all that you do. So He leads us, not for the work that we are to do, but for His sake. I say again, when you sing a song, are you singing it for the professor? Are you singing it for the audience? Are you singing it for your own glory? Or are you singing it for His sake? When you preach a sermon, why are you preaching? When you are called on to pray, are you praying for the audience or to the audience, or are you talking to God out of your heart?

He leads us in paths of righteousness for His name's sake. If you do not walk in those paths of righteousness, you are bringing discredit to the Lord Jesus Christ. You know, if everyone of us, everything that we do in life, if we could do it for His sake—How wonderful! When you go on a date, you are going to behave righteously for His sake, His sake. You are not there to please your date. You are there, first of all, to please God.

When you take a job down the street—and listen, we have a good testimony in this town as a whole—you should not take a job and bring discredit to the Lord Jesus Christ. You are working primarily for His sake. You are to be a good worker because you are a Christian, you are known as a Christian, and you attend a Christian institution in this city. They know it. The fellow workers, they know when you goof off that that does not represent His name. If you should ever laugh at an off-color joke, they know that that does not represent His name. They take note of it.

So whether you date, whether you work, or whatever you do, you are doing it for His name if you are a Christian. In your studies, you may say, "It does not matter if I am willing to take low grades." All right, wait a minute. You have a testimony with your parents back home. Some of you have unsaved parents that may be paying your way through school. If you goof off and make poor grades when you could make better grades, you will not have a good testimony with your unsaved parents. You will not have a good testimony if your parents are saved. It will be known in the church back home.

Whatever you do, you are doing for His sake. Not what they will think of you, primarily, but what they will think of the Lord. How are they going to judge the Lord if I am His representative, and all they know of the Lord is what they see in me? He leads me in paths of righteousness—not because I ought to behave righteously—but for His sake. So "Whether therefore ye eat, or drink, or whatsoever ye do, do all to the glory of God." His glory is at stake. He will be discredited. His name will be hurt. You may get hurt in the process, too, but more than that His name is hurt.

Oh, how we have brought reproach upon the name of the Lord Jesus Christ by our carelessness, not realizing that what we do, we do for His sake. Listen, there are some people that you could never witness to. You have already missed the opportunity because of your behavior. Some of you could never win an unsaved boyfriend to the Lord. You cannot testify to that boyfriend because he knows you. He knows how you behave. You need not go to him and try to win him to the Lord, or to a girlfriend. You have already ruined it. They do not have any confidence in you.

More than that, though, they do not have any confidence in the Lord Jesus Christ. You have brought dishonor upon His name, and they may never be saved because of the way you behaved. You have got to remember who you are, and whom you represent. So He leads in paths of righteousness for His name's sake.

"Yea, though I walk through the valley of the shadow of death, I will fear no evil . . . ." We are walking through this valley of the shadow of death right now. You are living in the valley of the shadow of death, but are you afraid? He said we can walk through this world where there is death on every side and fear no evil because He is with us.

" . . . For thou art with me; thy rod and thy staff they comfort me." They keep me from being afraid. Just like a mother comforts a child that is afraid, our Lord comforts us as we walk through this valley of the shadow of death.

"Thou preparest a table before me in the presence of mine enemies . . ." that is, our needs are being supplied. That is the reason we have no fear. That is the reason we are calm and collected. He is supplying our needs.

" . . . Thou anointest my head with oil . . ." that is, He gives me the Holy Spirit to encourage me and to empower me.

" . . . My cup runneth over." Here you have the joy of the Christian life.

"Surely goodness and mercy shall follow me all the days of my life: and I will dwell in the house of the LORD for ever."

May we stand, please.

PRAYER

We thank Thee, our Father, again for Thy precious Word and for this time of fellowship in it together. Bless it to each of our lives. In Jesus' Name, Amen.

17

December 5, 1974
Scripture: Luke 8:1-3
Subject: The Ministry of Women

WOMEN WHO MINISTERED

I am always glad to see Brother Ronald Creech. He is the only student in the thirty year history of the school that I ever talked into delaying getting married. He is the only fellow. I think really that it was Mary Belle who did that. I am not sure.

I was just in the Tidewater area of Virginia, and just before that I was down in South Carolina. In both instances I had opportunities with several pastors, most of whom had been students in school here. Some of them I had more or less lost sight of. Some of them, of course most of them, I know of their ministry. God is blessing their ministry. Some of the ones that you sort of overlook and forget about, you wonder where they are. When you get out there where they are, you find out that they are rendering a real good ministry. And this is refreshing.

We thank God for the ones that are in places where you have reason to know about them, to hear of them. You hear their work talked about, and that is wonderful; but there are many fellows that for some reason they do not get in the limelight, so to speak. Not that anyone is trying to get in, but you just do not hear about them. But when you get out there, they are doing a good solid work for the Lord. It was very refreshing to me, in these two instances recently, to visit with these men.

We have a very unique situation in our denomination. I think it is reflected right here on this campus. You do not realize it, of course, like I would, but we have a harvest of men pastoring who are still young and yet they have had years of experience, and they are mature. That is a wonderful combination. They have maturity and still the vigor of manhood, young manhood. They are at their very best. We have an army of men that are now reaching their best years.

I dare say that, in our denomination, in our work for the Lord, we are going to see in the next 20 years the fruit of these men's ministry. There was a long time when we did not have this. We did not have it when I came along. I was one of a very few young men, very few, entering the ministry. I had to associate with men 20 years my senior. I had very little fellowship with men in my age bracket because they did not exist. We did not have them in the ministry. That is not true anymore. You can go to most any area where we have work, and you will find several young men many of whom came to this school. Some did not, of course, but they are men of God.

I want to say this: We thank God just as much for the men who did not come through this school as we do for those who came through if they are doing a work for God. You do not have to have this tag on you in order for God to ordain you. If you are a man of God, God will use you. We thank God for all these men. It is refreshing to me to go out and to meet with them and see what they are doing. It is good to hear them and to see through their eyes.

I do not believe that I have lost contact with the ministry. I may be a little obsolete. I may not use some of the methods that are current today, but there is a great deal of flexibility in the use of methods. Every man is going to have to decide under God what methods he uses. It will be according to his personality and according to his situation where God puts him and what God puts in him. There is no blueprint that we can turn to and follow one, two, three down the line and say this is the way God's work is to be done. You do not find it in the Bible. That is the reason God gave us the Holy Spirit.

Now where the Bible speaks, that is wonderful, and you do not argue, but the Bible does not speak on many of these things. He leads us to use our personalities and our calling to do the work of God. I think I have stayed fairly well up-to-date with what is happening in the church, but it is good to hear these men talk and to see them in action. And we do thank God for them.

136

I want to read from chapter 8 of Luke's Gospel. Several days ago I spoke to you from chapter 7 concerning a woman who interrupted a social occasion. A Pharisee had invited Jesus into his house for a meal. He did not wash His feet and he offered Him no kiss. He was not very hospitable, but this woman from the street came in uninvited. She kissed Jesus' feet, and she bathed His feet with her tears. She offered Him with a heart of love all the hospitality that the Pharisee had failed to offer Him.

The only description of the woman that we have is that she was a sinner. That is not very complimentary, is it? She was a sinner. That suggests that she was a certain type of sinner, of course, but it could be said of any of us, that we were a sinner. Whether in the sense of this woman or not, we have "all . . . sinned, and come short of the glory of God." Jesus forgave this woman of her sins and said, " . . . Thy faith hath saved thee . . . ." Not her tears. The fact that she anointed Him with ointment was not it. The fact that she wept; that was not it. It was her faith. Her tears were tears of repentance. Every tear represented a sin.

Then Jesus said, "Thy faith hath saved thee." You know, some people think that coming to an altar is what saves you. It is not. You can get saved sitting there in your seat. You can get saved out in the field plowing. I think sometimes we run the risk of making the altar a necessary gateway into the kingdom. It is not.

If I were pastoring, sometimes I would use the altar; sometimes I would not. When I thought that people were beginning to think that you had to get saved a certain way, at a certain place, I would quit using the altar for a while. We are peculiar people. You know, you may have a place of prayer at home; and if you are not careful, if you pray in the same place every day for a period of time, after awhile you will get to feeling that God will not hear you unless you get in that particular place. You have got to kneel in a certain way, and when you get to feeling that way, you had better change places. We get to worshiping the place or kneel a certain way. Now when you get to thinking that the altar is the only place to get saved, you better quit using the altar. You are worshiping the altar. It is all right to use it as long as we keep it straight. It was her faith that saved her.

Now I want to read about some other ladies, some women of Scripture. These are beautiful thoughts to me in the first part of this, and I am reading through perhaps verse 4.

> And it came to pass afterward, that he went throughout every city and village, preaching and shewing the glad tidings of the kingdom of God: and the twelve were with him, And certain women, which had been healed of evil spirits and infirmities, Mary called Magdalene, out of whom went seven devils, And Joanna the wife of Chuza Herod's steward, and Susanna, and many others, which ministered unto him of their substance.

That is through verse 3. When you read the Bible, it is very interesting to read of the ministry of women. It was usually a ministry that men overlooked, and there is a ministry of women that men are inclined to overlook. In fact, there is a ministry in the home that the husband, no matter how much he loves the children, cannot minister to the needs of his children like the mother. She has a mother's touch that is unique. Nobody has ever been able to describe it. The man or the father can do the same thing, in the same way, but it will not have the same meaning. God has built into women a quality that is indescribable. There is something that they that have men do not have.

Men can love as much. It is a rather pathetic thing for a man's heart to be filled with love and for him to be clumsy and not know how to express it. You know, he feels it. He wishes that he could express it, but when he tries to, he is awkward. His hands are made for the plow handle, not for the delicate, tender things of life. When a woman tries to switch places with a man and a man tries to switch places with a woman, things get out of order. That is where we are today. We are trying to switch roles and it is not working.

God saw that man needed a helpmeet. There was something about man that was not complete. I do not know why God did it just like He did it. I think God, being omniscient, knew this before He created Adam. Why He did not go ahead and create Eve at the same time, I do not know. But the way it works is that God made man, and then He saw that man needed something that he did not have: qualities that God did not build into man, into his nature. He did not have it. So God put him to sleep and He made a woman. Man and woman, when they become one flesh, are perfect oneness. Really, a man is not complete within himself, and he needs that helpmeet, that something that he does not have.

You know, in the work of God, there is a place that women can fill that men cannot fill. As you follow the ministry of the Lord Jesus, you find in some instances these women. Usually they were out on the outer fringe of the crowd, or either they were up near the cross. You never hear them speaking out. I do not know the significance of that. Even they were not counted when the ushers gave the pastor the report in those days. The women and children were not counted.

Now we count every shadow. I think sometimes we count birds that fly by the window. We say, "There goes one. Put him down." We are number conscious, are we not? But in those days, the women and children sat and they were overlooked. They said, "Count the men." They counted the men, and they said, "This many besides women and children." How would you like to be slighted like that? But that is the way it was. But here they were; they were not hurt. They were willing and glad to play this role. They were helpmeets, they had a ministry, and Jesus recognized it.

And what a ministry. I wish I could perform such a ministry. I wish that I had such tenderness and thoughtfulness and gentleness. I stand and admire and almost envy these beautiful, delicate, yet so essential qualities of womanhood. Refinement. You have it. You are equipped for it. You are made for it.

Here these women are. I wish we had time; we would read about some at the crucifixion. So many of them were named Mary. These are six Marys, I am told, in the New Testament. It is hard to keep them separate.

But anyway, here they are and what are they doing? Well, Jesus is preaching, in " . . . every city and village, preaching and shewing the glad tidings of the kingdom of God . . . . " How wonderful it is going to be, He was saying to those cities and villages, when the kingdom of God has come. There will be peace. There will be no more sorrow; there will be no more war, when the King has come. There will be a rule of righteousness and peace. He was showing them the glad tidings of the kingdom of God. " . . . And the twelve were with him." They were listening. "And certain women . . . . "

At first they are not even mentioned. "And certain women, which had been healed of evil spirits . . . . " All these women had had the touch of God. They were women who at one time knew the torture, the torment, and the hell of evil spirits. But now they knew the difference; and you know, that makes a good servant. A fellow who has been poor, hungry, and without a piece of clothes and then gets rich and forgets that he was ever poor, he cannot appreciate his wealth when he forgets his poverty. Some of you do not appreciate these buildings.

Brother Jack Williams preached to us yesterday, and what a good message he brought. He was admiring our new buildings. He said it is a long way from the back porch of Davidson Hall, these new dormitories. I said to myself, "I wish that we could put every student on the back porch of Davidson Hall for one week. Let him live there and then run him back to our nice dormitories, and he would not gripe anymore." You see, he said he almost envied you. He said, "I wish I could come back and live in these nice buildings." He could appreciate it. He slept on the back porch of Davidson Hall. You have never even been up there, some of you. Cold, old, open-face heaters were used. It was not much, but he could appreciate it. You cannot appreciate these buildings. You have never lived on the back porch of Davidson Hall.

Well, anyway, the fellow who gets saved and gets sophisticated in his theology and his advanced maturity in the Christian life, if he forgets that he was a sinner, he will cease being grateful. These women had not ceased being grateful. They had known the evil spirits and all the torture and the hell of such living. You have known, I am talking to you this morning, listen; if you got saved before you knew you were a sinner, you do not appreciate your salvation. That is one question I have about some of our youth work. We get them saved before we get them lost. I will tell you: You ought to get a man good and lost if you want him to appreciate his salvation.

These women had been lost. You were lost. Some of you have known the torture and the torment of a mixed-up life. Some of you even as young as you are, you have known deep sin. You have broken all your dreams, and all that your dreams are becoming is shattered. You have known it; some of you have. You can appreciate being delivered from it. These women appreciated it. They had had the devils cast out of them. Now what were they doing? Well, they were serving Jesus. Now they were expressing their love. They were not on salary. They were not getting; they were giving. They were serving out of love.

You know, I read in the Bible in Malachi that the time is coming when they will not close the door unless they are paid for it. He said, "They will not build a fire on my altar unless they are paid for it." They will not close the door, we are told, for nought. That is, if there is no money, no reward, they will not be closing the door. I think we will have to go on a campaign like that around here to get lights switched off. We will give you a nickel for every time you switch off your light when you leave the room. I believe we would get more lights switched off. But this professional attitude, they did not have it. What were they doing? They were serving.

" . . . And many others, which ministered unto him of their

substance." I say again, they were giving, not getting. Women ministering. They were saying, "What can we do? Jesus is preaching, and He is tired. All right let us have some good cool water after He gets through preaching in this city. Let us have some refreshment. Let us buy some *Kool-Aid.*" I do not know whether they had *Kool-Aid* in those days or not, but you cannot prove that they did not have. So they had something. In other words, how can we lighten the load? How can we help him? He is tired. What can we do? And I will tell you, women can think up things that men could never think of.

I remember my mother. My mother was a country lady. She did not have too much education, but, oh, she could think up so many things to refresh. About ten o'clock, while I was plowing in the fields, I might see my mother coming with a jar of water, and she would have baked a little cake of some kind. It surprised me. She thought of it. She knew that we were tired. We were thirsty. And a little cake hot out of the oven; how it would refresh you. On rainy days when things were gloomy, I remember so many things that my mother did. She was a creative woman. She could think of so many things to spice up life or make it better and richer. Only a woman can do that.

Listen, ladies, there is a ministry for you. It does not have to be from the pulpit. You have got a quality of life. You think of so many things. You do not have to play a man's role. Do not try to be a man. You have something unique to offer. Fill your place for God. You say, "What can I do? Nobody has hired me." All right, just go out and do something to refresh the hearts of a weary pilgrim. Think up something to lighten the load of those who are tired. There is a ministry. It is all around you. These women, they ministered to Him of their substance. I wonder what it was? I wonder what substance? Well, it was just a little cake or bread of some kind, and good cool water from the spring. Some of them did not have money, but they had hearts of love, and they could minister and Jesus wrote it down. He listed their names and we read about them.

May we stand.

PRAYER

Our Father, we thank You for these women who ministered to the needs of our Lord. He was so grateful that He caused it to be written in the Book, and we read about their ministry. Everyone here can have a ministry. We can lighten the load of somebody who has a burden. We can refresh their day, and in doing that, we will bless them, and we will be twice blessed ourselves. In Jesus' Name. Amen.

18

October 7, 1975
Scripture: 1 and 2 Timothy – 1 Peter 5
Subject: Emerging Role of the Pastor

THE EMERGING ROLE OF THE PASTOR
IN OUR DENOMINATION

I want to point out a few words from 1 and 2 Timothy. If you want to turn in your Bibles, you may. Then I will read some verses from 1 Peter, chapter 5.

There are varying opinions about the role and the work of the minister or the pastor in a local church. We have changed-- and I think that I could speak to this point about as much so as anybody in our denomination.

When I entered the Free Will Baptist ministry as a pastor more than forty years ago, we had primarily rural churches with half-time at most; and in most instances, they had preaching only once each month. I started my ministry under those conditions. In fact, in my early ministry, I had—I do not know how many churches I did pastor. I think I almost equaled Brother M. L. Hollis whom some of you may know; most of you would not. He pastored all of Mississippi and part of north Alabama. That was the type of pastoring we had in those days.

I pastored a great portion of southeast Georgia and a portion of northeast Florida. That was my pastorate. That was typical. Well, all that you did in those days was preach. You held conferences on conference days when they transacted the business of the church, but you were not expected to be active in the administration of the church's affairs. In fact, there was not too much administration. You did not have that phase of the ministry to concern yourself with. There was something to be said for that because you were known not as an administrator but as a preacher.

Things have changed. We could not go back to that. We

should not attempt to go back to that over-simplified way of doing things.

But now we have moved into another period when some pastors feel that they are to run the church. And I underscore the word *run*; that is, they are to tell the church what to do and the church is to do it. If the church will not do what the pastor says, he resigns or he takes a group out and forms another church with people who will do what he tells them to do. He feels that God has ordained him to have a special insight into what ought to be done. All he has to do is to tell the people and it becomes law—or should become law. He is the "big wheel"in the church, and nobody is supposed to oppose him because he is divinely ordained to have this authority.

Now, let me say first of all that our authority is unquestioned when it comes to preaching the Word. We are to preach the Word, to be instant in season, out of season, reprove, rebuke, exhort, etc. Our authority rests at that point, but the Bible has little to say about authority when it comes to the administrative affairs of the church. It does not say that you are to have this right or that right or the other right in the affairs of the local church.

But a great many preachers are taking that authority unto themselves, and there is quite a bit of confusion in churches over this point. Since we are emerging, and we are still in the emerging state—emerging from that once-a-month type ministry where the pastor did not have anything or very little to do with the administrative affairs of the church, to a full-time ministry—we are trying to find ourselves. We are trying to "hew out" a place for the pastor. Let me say this, too; I know many churches that did not know how to use a pastor when they got one. That is, they went from quarter-time to full-time, and they did not know what in the world a preacher was supposed to do, hanging around all the week. They were not used to it.

It was sort of like when you get married, you are not used to a husband that hangs around: he gets in your way, and you have to get used to him. You have to find a place for him. So churches have been going through that experience of finding a place, or a role, for the pastor; and the pastor has not known exactly what his role was supposed to be. So, if he found a vacuum, he just moved into it and filled it. We do not know whether it is Scriptural or whether it is practical. The fact of the matter is, much of the administration of the local church has to be settled on the practical side of things. What is wise? What is good?

I want to point out some words that Paul used in writing to Timothy. Notice what Paul said to young Timothy and the role he was to have in the church. We will say that this was the church at Ephesus, perhaps. In chapter 1, verse 16, there is an interesting word: "Howbeit for this cause I obtained mercy, that in me first Jesus Christ might shew forth all longsuffering, for a pattern to them which should hereafter believe on him to life everlasting." This may be a little out of context, but I thought that word "pattern" was very important. In other words, the apostle was to be a pattern.

There is not a great deal of authority that goes with just being a pattern. And yet there is a tremendous responsibility that goes with it. Do you see the difference? No special authority, but a tremendous responsibility to be a pattern. So he is not setting himself up here as an authoritarian, but he is setting himself up as a pattern. The Lord wanted him to be a pattern.

Now coming to another word in chapter 2, "I *exhort* therefore, that, first of all . . . ." This word *exhort* does not carry with it the idea of a great deal of authority. It is a persuasive term, a term used to excite or to encourage to action. And yet, there is no thought of authority. It is a leadership role, persuading, convincing you of what ought to be. So, I think this is also an interesting word that is used in writing to Timothy.

"I exhort therefore, that, first of all, supplications, prayers, intercessions, and giving of thanks, be made for all men." He did not say, "I command it. You must do it," but, "I exhort you to do it; you ought to do it. I hope you will do it. I encourage you to do it." I think this is very significant.

Chapter 2, verse 7: "Whereunto I am ordained a preacher." Notice, this is where his authority is. He did not say, "I was ordained an administrator." This is divinely-given authority. This is your main role, your main job: "I am ordained a *preacher*; a preacher, a proclaimer of the Truth." No one should question you, and you should never question your authority when you stand to proclaim the Word of God. Now you get on shaky ground when you claim to have authority as an administrator; when you tell people that "you have got to do this, you have got to do that, and you have got to do the other." Sometimes you have to stretch the Word of God to give you such a base for such authority as this—but not here. You have full authority, divinely-given authority, because he says, "I am ordained a preacher." Who did it? The Lord did it. He tells you back in chapter 1 that *the Lord* put him into the ministry. Herein is his authority.

". . . Ordained a preacher, and an apostle. . . a teacher of the Gentiles in faith and verity [or truth]." There are three things here: He was ordained a preacher, an apostle, and a teacher. He has this sort of authority.

In chapter 3 (1Timothy), he says that if a man desires the office of a bishop (the equivalent of an elder, a bishop, or a pastor), there are qualifications. He says that he must be *blameless*. He is not talking about authority here. He is talking about the quality of character. "You must be blameless, the husband of one wife." Some interpret this to say that a divorced man should not be in the ministry. I agree that that principle is good, but I do not think that is necessarily what he is talking about here. I think that he is talking about having three or four wives at the same time. But nonetheless, he must be the husband of one wife.

"Vigilant"; that is, circumspect, alert, not falling into traps, but knowing what is going on. There is no place for a sleepyhead in the ministry. Let us nail that down. Now, there are a lot of fellows who are not sleepyheads; they move around a lot, but they are asleep mentally. They are alive physically. I think that this carries with it the idea that you ought to let your mind work a little. There is not any place in the ministry for mentally lazy people. I will tell you one thing I have noticed: There are a lot of preachers who are physically active, but mentally lazy. They would rather get out and spin their wheels than to dust the cobwebs out of their brain. They are just lazy mentally. They do not want to think. Some of you may lay your books aside and value your ministry because you put 40,000 miles a year on your automobile, and you do not add one new word to your vocabulary in an entire year!

Vigilant! Alert! Certainly, I think it carries with it the idea of activity, but it carries with it activity from the head to the sole of the feet. I want to emphasize that these are some of the requirements, to be sober and serious minded.

Let me tell you, preachers. *Do not build your church on bubblegum, roller skates, and parties.* Now you can weave a few of them in, perhaps, but I tell you, you cannot use these things to build your church. (This is sort of a pet theme of mine.) I cannot help being a little glad—and this is a little depravity that is still left in me—when I see a preacher come in with a sprained ankle, bruised up from a fall on roller skates on Saturday night. I like to see him hobble in. He had no business being out there in the first place.

You cannot build a real work for God on that; you can get the crowd—but listen, crowds do not build churches! Barnum and Bailey could beat us all to pieces on this. But that does not build a church; you have to have people. What I am saying is this: Do not use these methods to build your church.

If you think your people are over-worked or under a strain, remember Jesus took His disciples on a vacation one time. I guess you could take yours somewhere for a social; but He did not use it to get crowds, and He did not use it to build a church. In fact, one of His sermons drove them all away. I am not advocating trying to drive people away, but I am saying that there has got to be more to it than frivolous games.

Sober, serious-minded, of good behavior, given to hospitality, apt to teach; that is, qualified to teach. These are some qualifications. They do not carry with them any idea of unusual authority over a group of people, but are qualified by character and ability to perform the work of the ministry.

In chapter 5, he tells you how to treat elders; that is, people who are older than you. "Elder" means older. I like this part today because I qualify. "Rebuke not an elder." What does it mean not to rebuke an elder? Very simple: Do not use your authority to get your deacons told. God forbid. We have had so many churches torn up because some arrogant, upstart felt that he was an authoritarian and would speak in a rude way to good, gray-haired men, who had been the pillars of the church for years and years, simply because he wanted to get them "moving" and spinning their wheels.

Even if their wheels are stuck in the dirt and the mud, you are still not to rebuke an elder. You just do not rebuke an elder according to the Word of God. You do not have that right unless sin is involved. (Compare 1 Timothy 5:19, 20.)

Now, what *do* you do if he needs to be talked to? Well, entreat him as a father. You might say, "I tell my father off." If you do, you do wrong. Entreat him; that is, plead with him, reason with him in a kind way, recognizing his eldership and recognizing who you are. But you do not go vested with the authority of a pastor to tell off an elder. Oh, no. You do not have that authority; I do not care how many ecclesiastical robes you have wrapped around you. You do not have it. You are to entreat him as a father.

And in regard to the younger men—you are not to tell them off, either, but treat them as brothers. You say, "Well, I tell my brother off." Yes, and he bloodies your nose, too. And a lot of times these young men in the church are bloodying your nose. How do you talk to them? You are to talk to them kindly, as brothers.

Now, how do you treat the old women? (That is not a good

term, perhaps, but some of them are old; and they are women.) The elder women are to be treated as mothers, as gentle as you would talk to your mother. You do not go to your mother in an arrogant fashion and tell her off, not if you are a Christian. You respect her; and if she does not agree with you, you say, "Well, we will drop it. You do not have to do it, Mother; I think it would be wise, but you do not have to." If she says, "Son, run along and let me alone." You run along. You do not use some ministerial authority to go tell your mother off, or the elder women of the church either.

Now this has always been interesting to me. "The younger as sisters, with all purity." There is a danger. And he puts that word of caution in there. When you are dealing with the younger women, you do it with all purity. *All purity*. Oh, how that needs to be emphasized.

I wanted to point out these words of emphasis that you find in Paul's writing to this young man who was put in charge of the church in Ephesus. It was a thriving church in a commercial center where there were so many needs and so many wonderful opportunities. But he was a young man who needed to know how to carry on in the work of the ministry.

Notice the words that he is using here—all through his instructions to this young man—in 2 Timothy.

Let me read from 1 Peter 5 to support this thought:

> The elders which are among you I exhort, who am also
> an elder, and a witness of the sufferings of Christ, and
> also a partaker of the glory that shall be revealed.
> [Notice the word he uses.]

> Feed the flock of God which is among you, taking the
> oversight thereof, not by constraint, but willingly; not
> for filthy lucre, but of a ready mind;

> Neither as being lords over God's heritage, but being
> ensamples [there again, "pattern"] to the flock.

You do not beat them, but when you come to preach, there is the element of rebuke in the preaching; not in a sense of walking up to an elder and rebuking him, but letting the Word of God speak. Therein is your authority. And I will tell you what: If you will follow these principles, you will create so much respect for yourself that you can be an administrator without being an administrator. They will just want you to tell them what to do.

Your authority comes out of the respect that people have for you. I do not care whether it is written in a constitution or not. I would not give you ten cents for all the constitutions of all the churches in the denomination as far as my operation is concerned.

We used to have teachers sign a contract. There is not a teacher on this platform who is under any kind of written contract. I would not give you fifty cents for contracts. Now all other schools say they ought to have them, and that it is the thing to do. I do not care for contracts. When you have to force Christians to do right because of legal technicalities, you are in trouble! And if out of a good spirit of *heart* you cannot get cooperation, you are in trouble.

And so it is with the church, when you have to go in there with a big club, vested with all kinds of legal authority, you are in trouble! But when, because of your life and your ministry, people have respect for you, they will follow you—and you can throw the constitution out the window. Now if you want a constitution, have one; but I do not care for them. I do not care if they have a dozen constitutions, it would not bother me a bit because if I cannot win their hearts and their confidence, I fail.

And if sometimes they say, "We do not follow you; we do not believe what you are doing is right," I bow to them and say, "You may have more sense than I have." I will tell you, that makes them feel good, too. And many times they *do* have better sense than you have.

You respect them and their judgment, and when you

respect them and their judgment, they will respect you in return.
What a beautiful relationship it is.

May we stand.

PRAYER

Our Father, help us to learn from Thy Word, and the Spirit
of Thy Word, in doing the work of the ministry to which Thou
hast called us. In Jesus' Name. Amen.

19

October 8, 1975
Scripture: Psalm 119:50
Subject: Pastors and Pastoring

PASTORS AND PASTORING

What I had to say yesterday and what I will have to say today pertain primarily to pastors and preachers, but I think all of us can benefit from it.

I enjoyed many years in the pastorate. Many people forget that. They think that I have always been here (at the college), but I have not. I look back upon some very good years in the pastorate with a great deal of fondness and happy memories. And I am also delighted, as I look back, at some progress that was made in churches that I pastored.

I think I can honestly say that I never had a major church problem as a pastor. Now, I do not think I did exactly like a brother of mine. I asked him how his church was doing and he said, "Oh, all right. I preach like *I* please, and they live like *they* please." So they got along beautifully. But that was not my attitude, and really it was not his attitude either. But you know, there is some truth to that. People *are* going to live like they please. Now, it is our responsibility as preachers to try to get them to please live right. There is one thing about it; you cannot force them to live right. You are going to have to create a motivation or some way to get them motivated to live right.

There is only one way in the world to do that, and that is through the preaching of this Word. This Word, when it gets into a person's heart, will cause him to want to live right. The Spirit of Christ will make a person want to live right. Until that happens, all the beating and all the threatening, and everything else that you may bring to bear will not get the job done.

I say again, as I have said often, I think that much of the church activity that we see today may indicate that we have lost faith in the power of the preached Word. We are having to support it with so many other things.

Now I know that there are methods, and I take that into account. I recognize it, and I accept it; but after all is said and done, God has left us only one instrument to use in correcting men's lives—that is the Word of God. That is all.

And He has chosen to ordain men to preach this Word. There is something special and something peculiar about it. I do not know what it is; I do not know how to describe it. But there is something peculiar about the preaching of this Word by a man who has been ordained of God to preach it. I *do* believe in a God-called ministry. And I do not believe that there is any substitute for it.

I know that people can do many other things, and we ought to involve lay folk in many ministries that the preacher cannot do, but when it comes to proclaiming this Word, there is something peculiar about the power that a man has when he preaches it under the anointing of God. You may not recognize it immediately, but follow his ministry over a period of time and if he is a God-called man, anointed of the Lord, then you are going to see some fruit from his ministry. You will recognize that he is a man that is called of God.

I believe in Sunday School work, but a Sunday School teacher cannot take the place of an anointed man of God preaching the Word. They can supplement it; they can teach it; they can get people to understand the Word of God. They can even cause people to accept the Lord—and that is wonderful— laymen can go out and witness, and they ought to. But there is nobody who can take the place of an anointed man of God as he stands and proclaims the Word of God.

If that is not true, there is no such thing as a special call to the ministry. There is no such thing as a special anointing to preach it. But I do believe that there is. I do not want to bother you with any personal testimony because I do not hold myself up as an ideal minister or preacher of the gospel, but I would not be

in this business at all unless I was sure that God put me in it. I had
no *personal* desire to be a preacher. In fact, it was the farthest
thing from my mind until I recognized that God wanted me in it.

And wanting to do the will of God, I could not get out. I had
to do it because God wanted me to do it; or at least I *felt* that He
did, and I have been sure over these years. Please do not ask me
to tell you how you know that you are called to the ministry. I
cannot tell you. I cannot tell you because if I told you about my
call, you would recommend to the Cumberland Association,
which meets in a few days, that they take my license. You would
come to the conclusion that God did not call *me*. My call was
different. Yours may be different. But nonetheless, you can be
sure that God put you in the ministry.

Now the ministry has changed, of course, since I was called
into it. I told you yesterday about the church condition or the
situation in our denomination at that time. I am talking now
about our own denomination. Our denomination is peculiar. Do
not measure our denomination by other denominations. We
have a peculiar history, and you have to understand it in order to
appreciate it.

When this school was started in 1942, every student could
have sat on these front ten rows of seats here, and we would have
had some seats left over. Nobody thought that we would ever see
the day when there would be as many young people attending
this school as we have today. We have had no plan to have a big
school. We have never said that in five years we would have so
many students, and in ten years we would have so many more,
and so on. We still do not say that. We do not know. Next year we
may have 300. I do not know. I would be surprised if it took that
big a drop, but we do not know. We have no numbers set—up or
down.

Now some people can set goals. They say the Lord leads
them to have so many in attendance in so many months. Well,
that is all right. I never have been able to get a WATS line to
Heaven, though, to get that sort of information. God may give

that to some people, but it smacks to me of Madison Avenue type of goal setting, and the General Motors type of quota system that we impose upon ourselves to try to motivate people into service.

I want to say this, it may be all right—I will leave this to individuals if they want to set goals; that is all right—but I will tell you what: Goal setting will not endure as a motivator over a long period of time. It may work for a little while for some sort of special campaign, but eventually you are going to have to fall back on what motivated Paul: "The love of Christ constraineth me." That will keep you going through the ups and downs. Goal setting is a "roller coaster" type church program. You set the goal for six weeks from now, and you shoot up and up and up. When you reach the goal, everybody is so exhausted and over-extended at the end of it that they take a nose dive for a while. You have got to stay in this race day in and day out.

Listen, preachers, you have got to set a pace for yourself physically and emotionally that you can sustain day in and day out. Remember it. Some people delight in saying that they are burning out for Jesus. I will tell you what is burning them out; many times it is ambition and nervous energy. I am not encouraging laziness now. I know that people jump to that conclusion. But there are a lot of preachers who are fidgety and nervous and cannot sit still to counsel people because they are exhausted.

I want to look good at seventy—I am doing all right at sixty. But that is not the point. If God wants me to work at seventy, and God gives me good health, I do not want to be foolish and get the nervous jitters because I do not get enough sleep and over-extend myself at fifty. "Oh," you say, "you are lazy." No. Sensible. And you ought to recognize when you have driven the horse too hard.

If you are going to set goals—and I am not saying that you ought not to—watch the psychology of it. Goal-setting churches usually are roller-coaster churches. I had rather see that steady development.

You say, "Well, you pastored a long time ago." Yes, I know. I realize that. But I think I pastored in some of the most difficult days. I pastored in days when churches had no vision whatsoever; they had done nothing. There may have been one or two exceptions in my very earliest ministry, but I think I can say —and I hope that I am not boasting—I never left a church but what I felt that it was much better off than when I went to it. And one of the happy delights of my ministry has been to be able to observe the ministry of pastors who followed me and to see a particular church develop under their ministry. There is a delight in feeling that I had something to do with laying a foundation and helping that church get into a position to move on.

Now, pastoring is a wonderful ministry, a wonderful thing. We have different philosophies that are afloat today, and I would not say for you to go out and try to pastor the same way I would. But you have to become yourself at some point.

When you first go out, you are not going to be yourself. You are going to be a little bit of this one, a little bit of that one; a "Heinz 57 Variety." You will not have found yourself when you begin your ministry. The depth and the strength of your own character will determine how soon you become yourself. Some people never become themselves. They are copycats all their lives.

I do not read other men's sermons today very much. I read them occasionally just for my own blessing to hear what they say, but I do not read sermons to preach them any more. I do not say that I would not pick up an idea if I read a man's sermon and some idea struck me; yes, surely. I am not so independent that I say all that I preach is original because it is not. No man is. But I do not read other men's sermons to preach their sermons any more.

Now there was a time when I had to preach anything I could get hold of, regardless of whose it was. I just changed it a little bit, enough to put my name on it. You will go through that period. Do not be too critical of yourself while you are going through it, but always be working toward becoming your own person. Let God use your *own* personality. Then, be satisfied with being yourself.

There are just a lot of people who are mad with themselves. You know, if you have a grudge against somebody else, you are subject to get ulcers, but if you have a grudge against yourself, you will get two ulcers. The worst hatred in the world is self-hatred and not being pleased with yourself. You should become your own person, your own style.

We are going to have a Pastor's Conference here in a few weeks, and I hope it will be helpful. But even though we have pastors' conferences—and I think that we ought to attend some things occasionally to refresh us and to stimulate us—we are not to depend on such conferences for our total knowledge of the ministry. In other words, let it be a little stimulant to you and a refresher, yes. But as far as these "how-to-do-it" packages are concerned, I would advise you to read them cautiously. That is some other man's style. Some other man with a different personality wrote that, and when you try to harnass that on your personality, it may not work. Preaching is a wonderful thing, and I think we need to understand what it is.

What is a pastor? I am talking about pastors this morning. Webster says, "a spiritual overseer." Well, what is an overseer? It is somebody who watches over the members of his flock, keeps an eye out on them. Not as a foreman. It does not say that he is a foreman.

Now, a foreman is a type of overseer, but not in the sense a pastor is an overseer. He is watching out, not to make the sheep work necessarily, but for the welfare of the sheep. If he sees the sheep that does not get up in the morning to go out to eat, he knows that there is something wrong with that sheep.

I will tell you what a lot of pastors do when a sheep fails to get up in the morning to go out to eat with the other sheep. The pastor gets a club and goes and beats the sheep. He says, "Get up!" He kicks him and says, "You are lazy; you are backslidden; you did not tithe yesterday," or something like this.

When a sheep does not get up to go to work, there is

something wrong with him. But you do not go and kick him; you go to try to find out what is wrong with him. He may need doctoring. He may need some sympathy. All the other sheep may have been rough on him yesterday. He may be discouraged, and you want to be an overseer in the sense of "What is wrong with that sheep? I am going to see if I can help him."

See, an overseer is watching out for the welfare of the flock. On Sunday morning, do not get up in church and talk about that sheep that did not go out to eat, exposing him before the crowd. That is not the way to do it, either. There may be an occasion for that, but the overseer is interested in the flock, and he is pleased when the flock is in good order. But he is distressed when some member of the flock is not behaving as he ought. When something is wrong with him, the pastor is going to try to correct it.

This involves several things. One thing is knowing your sheep. It is hard to get acquainted with people if they are afraid of you. If you are the type person who is harsh and rude and always critical, they are not going to let you get acquainted with them. The first thing that I think a preacher ought to do—a pastor especially—is to get to know his people.

Here on campus my heart breaks sometimes when I learn that a person has had troubles and has been bearing problems and heartaches that I did not know about. And I have wished so much that I could have known about it so that I might have offered some help. We have some students right here in school today who have had problems this year, and it amazes me that you have been able to bear them.

Now, many times if you know your people, and you knew their problems, you could be sympathetic instead of critical. If you knew the kind of husband that that dear wife has to live with, you would be very sympathetic, and you would wonder how in the world that dear soul gets the children ready to come out to Sunday School. They do not do just all you would like, but you would marvel that they come at all. Sometimes if you knew what kind of wife a man had to live with, you would marvel that he could still keep his testimony. And many other problems, of course, that people have that we do not know about. Get to know your people.

I wish that there were some way we could get to know all of you and understand your problems. I wish you could know us. It is possible that right here on campus we could go through an entire year and never get to know one another. A teacher can teach a class and not know his students; he knows whether they made A's or B's; he knows some things about them, but really he may not know them. You may not know the teacher. You may have an attitude toward teachers in general that hinders you from getting to know them. Teachers may all be bad in your sight. They may be "stuck-up," or conceited; they may "know everything"or you think they think they know everything. "They are just not quite human," you think, but they are. It would be a wonderful thing if right here on campus we could know one another. We would be more understanding.

A pastor by all means ought to get to know his people. And then he ought to let them get to know him; that is important.

Then, there is another thing a pastor ought to do: love his people. You have no business being in the ministry unless you love people. Absolutely, you are disqualified, no matter how much ability you have, unless you have an interest in people. Now I am talking about their spiritual welfare in particular; but it goes beyond that. It includes the whole of life—being interested in people.

We talk a lot about loving souls. I wish we would change that. I wish we would start talking about loving people. I think that brings it a little closer and makes it a little more personal. Just loving people, and loving Christian people; loving those who serve God faithfully, loving those who are erratic in their service and devotion to God. Loving people will draw something out of them.

Then I want to close with this thought: I have talked about

knowing people, loving people. Now I want to talk about prescribing a remedy. This is the procedure a doctor follows. When you go for an examination, he asks you all kinds of questions. Some of them seem so silly. You are given a big sheet to fill out while you are sitting in the waiting room, and they want to know all about you. When the doctor takes that, studies it, what is he doing? He is trying to get to know you. Then when he comes into the office to see you, he ought to be concerned about you.

Have you been to doctors whom you felt were so professional they did not care about you? You did not go back to them. But when he gets interested in your case and your problem, he is going to prescribe a remedy. First of all, he has got to know you; then he has to develop an interest in you.

This is what a pastor is; this is what we do. We prescribe a remedy. Listen, a pastor is not a dictator. He is a shepherd. His authority rests in the respect that people have for him. And it does not rest in his administrative rights or skill. I will tell you, you would be wise to leave most of that to the laity of the church. They have got some sense. The laymen know how to run a church. They have been running it before you got there. They are going to be running it after you leave, perhaps. And it will surprise you that some laymen have some sense. But they do have. And I would leave much of the administrative load to the laymen; they ought to have it. That is an area where they can function.

But your chief thing would be to be a shepherd pastor who has the oversight of the people—and I would not check up on everybody's tithing record on Monday morning. (If I did, I would preach about it the next Sunday. I do not want to know.) A lot of things you are better off not knowing concerning the details of people's lives. It will hinder you in your preaching. You will get hung up. You see, you say you ought to preach to people's needs. Yes, that is right. You can know people. They have a lot of needs, but you do not need to know about their tithing record.

Now, for prescribing the remedy. How do you do it? This

Word. Right here. Are any of you having any emotional problems? Are you thinking about going down to see a psychiatrist? I am not saying that there is not a place for that, but I believe that a major portion of people's emotional problems would be solved if they would just read this Word faithfully every day, and bathe their souls in it and come to believe it—and appropriate its teachings to their lives.

The Bible says, "Thy Words counsel me" (Psalm 119:50). "This is my comfort in my afflictions, for Thy Word hath quickened me."

October 23, 1975
Scripture: Psalm 23
Subject: The Lord, our Shepherd

THE LORD IS MY SHEPHERD

It is wonderful how you can look at such familiar passages of Scripture in the Bible and have your soul refreshed. Not that you necessarily see something new in it, but you see a new blessing. "The LORD is my shepherd"—a fact that is stated—and "I shall not want."

Now David wrote these words. He had enough confidence in the Shepherd to know that all of his needs would be taken care of. Do I have that confidence in my Shepherd, in my Lord? "No good thing will He withhold from him that walketh uprightly." Do I believe that? —no good thing. "All things work together for good"—to whom? To those who love God, and who are in His will, called according to His purpose.

I think all of these statements mean the same thing. David, being a shepherd lad, used the shepherd as an example when he said, "My Shepherd will take care of me just like I took care of my sheep when I had them out in the pasture; I would not let any animal molest them."

David was tested. When he went over to visit his brothers and the giant was out there threatening them, he wanted to fight the giant. Saul wanted to know what his credentials were. "Well," he said, "I do not have many, but I killed a bear one time, and a lion, and a few simple things like that when they came to harm my sheep. These are the only qualifications I have." In other words, he protected his sheep and saw that they were taken care of. So, he said, "Now, if I would do that for my sheep, my Lord is a better Shepherd than I could ever be and I know that He will take care of me and I shall not want."

Suppose somebody came to you today and said, "I am going

to take care of all your needs and all your wants, and you can have confidence." There is no human being who can do that. Your parents cannot do it. Your banker cannot do it. There are some needs that you might have that nobody can take care of but the Lord. The Lord can take care of ALL our needs. "I shall not want."

This means that David put his life in the hands of the Shepherd and that he gave control to the Shepherd. All the responsibility for his life and his needs rested in the hands of the Shepherd. Oh, that we could come to that point where we could just relax in the Lord and have such confidence that He is guiding and taking care of everything, then we would not have these worried expressions on our faces. We would not go to the dormitory and wonder, "Am I going to make it? What about my finances? What about this and that?" Instead of worrying, we could just rest in the Lord and let Him take care of it. That is a wonderful statement to me. I hope I can learn to trust Him and believe it. That will take the tension off; it will take the worry away.

Verse 2, "He maketh me to lie down in green pastures."This suggests to me a rest, a relaxation, a confident rest. Now the Christian life is not finding a good cool place somewhere and stretching out under a shade tree. That is not the thought, but all the tension is gone. You have relaxed in the Lord. You are fully trusting the Lord, and you are not worried. You are not anxious.

"He leadeth me beside the still waters." Here is leadership. The still waters, the calm waters; not the worried life, not the tempestuous sea most of us live in, with the spray in our faces and the worry of what is going to happen—but the still, calm waters. Here you have a beautiful picture of the Lord in control and a full trust and confidence in Him.

Not only that, but if something should happen to me, "He restoreth my soul." He restores that which is wounded. If the cares and problems of life get to me, if something hurts me, then the Lord restores. "He restoreth my soul."

Sometimes we get tired of trying to be good. (Now, I know that some of you did not study during the nine weeks, and you are behind, and this is chapel time. And this is not the time to catch up on that which you did not do during the nine weeks. So put your books aside, take your eyes off your books and notebooks, and look up this way.) Sometimes we get frayed, we lose our courage, we get tired of bucking the depravity of our hearts and our lives and the disappointments of life.

You know, pastors get that way. I find a lot of pastors who are tired or discouraged. They are doing the best they know how to do, and they are not getting the results they would like to get. They are discouraged.

But notice here, "He restoreth my soul." He is the Shepherd; we are not going to want. And He restores our souls, the inner being. You know, we can keep up a front, we can put on a smile, even fool people, but inside we can be tied in knots. We can be defeated inwardly and still keep going and nobody knows anything is wrong.

Every now and then a student will drop out and everybody says, "I thought he or she was happy. He had such a good smile." But they did not know. If all could be known, inside there was discouragement.

Now that may be true of somebody now. School work is hard work. The routine—any routine—is hard. This is an age that is not accustomed to routine. If you do not get what you want on one channel, you switch to another channel. If you cannot find it there, you switch to another. Who would be stuck with a television that had just one channel! Variety! We are accustomed to variety. If we get tired of this place, we jump in our automobiles and race down the street, get an ice-cream cone, get a hamburger. Just variety!

That is the reason there are so many divorces. We are just not accustomed to sameness. Marriage is like that. You better think of it because there is a lot of sameness in marriage.

I tell you, there are some things that we ought to get

accustomed to. We ought to get accustomed to doing our duty. It is not always thrilling to do your duty. That is the reason some housewives stack the dishes away and have about two days of dishes in the sink; they do not like to wash dishes. It is awfully monotonous to wash dishes three times a day; and when any woman tells me that she likes to wash dishes, I have a little difficulty believing it. Making beds every morning—every morning the same routine. But you know, life is like that.

But now, wait a minute. Who restoreth? The Lord restores your soul. The Lord can keep life fresh, a sparkle in your eye, and a smile on your face. You have to wait on Him. You have to give Him an opportunity to work.

You take your automobile down to the mechanic for him to restore it, but you have to wait on it. A man (sitting on this platform) told me that he is very sorry that it happened, but he let his brakes go out, and he had to buy a new set of drums because he did not have time, would not take his car down for drums. Do not look up here, he might be blushing. He would not get it restored. He should have had it restored for $25 or $30, but instead—because he would not take the time, it cost him around $160. It took time. It takes time to keep up an automobile.

I rode with somebody just recently. I got into this nice new car, at least it looked new. But about the time we started I noticed a bump, bump, bump, and I wondered what in the world. It was a lady's car. She said, "You know, something is wrong." I said, "Yes, there is." She said, "I wonder if I should have my wheels balanced." I said, "I think it might be a good idea, except it is too late. Your tires are already ruined." And they were. She knew that she should take care of the problem, and had been planning to, but just did not take the time. She had worn out a good set of tires, and it cost her a lot of money. She would not have it "restored."

This is a simple illustration; but wait a minute, what about you? What about that inner man? What about that soul of yours? Are you getting tired of being a Christian? Getting tired of living a

168

Christian life? Are you afraid? The Lord can restore your soul. When you read this Book with all the wonderful promises that God is taking care of you and meeting your needs, you can get thrilled. You can get mighty excited when you read this Book, just to know that the *Lord* is your Shepherd and you shall not want. Your soul can be restored. There are some people here this morning who need to have their souls restored.

"He leadeth me in the paths of righteousness for his name's sake." Here you have leadership, work, activity. Do not go out on practical work in your own strength; do not walk up to a man and buttonhole him because you have got to witness to somebody. You will do more harm than you will do good. I have seen some people in services do a lot of harm by going to people in the congregation, speaking to them, embarrassing them, and that person never coming back again. Now there are times when that can be done. But do not do it just because you are revived, and you want to see somebody else get saved.

All of our Christian service ought to be done under the leadership of the Shepherd. "HE leadeth me. He leadeth me in the paths of righteousness."

There is somebody down the street to whom the Lord will likely lead you; and if He leads you to that person, He has prepared that person for the seed of the Word. Now you may not get a decision out of him, but the soil is prepared if the Lord leads you. So you can drop the seed of the Word, but only as He leads.

How much praying do you do when you go out on practical work? Do you pray for the leadership of the Lord? We ought to.

What about our preaching? I come to this platform several times a week usually, but I do not come here without whispering a prayer, "Lord, there is somebody out there who might have a need for the portion of the Word that I am going to speak on this morning. Lord, lead me, that the Word may fall into some needy heart; that somebody may be blessed and helped." We ought to do that.

"He leadeth me in the paths of righteousness for his name's

sake." Notice it does not say He leads us to keep us out of trouble, although He will keep you out of trouble, but notice that it says, "... for his name's sake." You are not living a Christian life just to protect your testimony, and not for your sake. You are living a Christian life for the glory of the Lord. You wear His Name, and whatever you do, and whatever I do ought to be done for His Name's sake.

He has a mighty good name. He has a name against which there is not one mark or one blemish. There has never been anybody who has been able to pin one thing on Jesus Christ that was wrong.

He has got a perfect name, a holy name. He wants to keep it that way, and He does not want us to tarnish His name. And whatever I do today, I want to do it for His name's sake. He leads me in paths of righteousness, not to keep me out of trouble; not simply to give me a good testimony for *my* sake, but He leads me in paths of righteousness for *His* name's sake. He wants His name protected.

Have you done anything in the dormitory lately that tarnished His name? Or anywhere else?

I spoke yesterday about a few business people who have called us recently, "I do not know why or what happened; you fellows used to be the best workers in town, but something has happened." We are having a few bad reports. I hope that is just an exception.

But wait, when you go down to take a job, it is not just that you are doing it for pay, but remember that God's name is at stake if you are a Christian. If you come from this school, they expect something out of you, not only because of the name of this school, but the name of Jesus Christ is at stake.

Why do we insist that our boys have their hair cut and combed? Listen, some get their hair cut, but they have not learned how to *comb* their hair yet. If you will come by my office, I will give you a little lesson on how to comb your hair. It is a simple thing. You take a comb and you run it through your hair and comb it back. Girls wear bangs. I like to see girls wear bangs; but you know, I have not got used to boys wearing bangs yet. It looks just a little odd to see a fellow with his hair down in his eyes.

The way you dress, your behavior in every way, is for His sake.

"Yea, though I walk through the valley of the shadow of death." We usually apply that to the time of death when the Lord goes with you through the valley. But wait a minute, we are walking through the valley of the shadow of death now. There are enough germs loose in this building now to kill every one of us in twenty-four hours. You are breathing them. Do not stop breathing now. You are breathing enough germs right now to kill you if there was not a defense mechanism that God built within you. If that defense should break down and you should lose your resistance to disease, we could all be dead in a short time. We are in the valley of the shadow of death with dangers everywhere. There are the lions of passion and greed; the venomous, hissing reptiles of lust and immorality to destroy us.

As you travel through this valley, you see the carcasses of young and old, rich and poor, bums and kings who have been destroyed. Beautiful young women, who in a moment of weakness let the roaring lion of lust overcome them, and the carcass of their purity is bleached in this valley of the shadow.

But you know, He is with us. "Even though I walk through the valley of the shadow of death, I will fear no evil." I will not fear the evil One who would like to destroy every one of us. If you are amounting to anything for God, the devil would like to destroy you. God is with us, "I will fear no evil: for thou art with me; thy rod and thy staff they comfort me. Thou preparest a table before me in the presence of mine enemies." In other words, He is supplying all our needs.

"Thou anointest my head with oil; my cup runneth over. Surely goodness and mercy shall follow me all the days of my life: and I will dwell in the house of the LORD for ever."

May we stand.

PRAYER

We do praise Thee, our Father, for Thy great promises to us, and for Thy presence with us. How good Thou art. How secure we feel when we are in Thy care. Help us to live such lives that we can remain in Thy care and under Thy protection and Thy guidance. Thou art supplying all of our needs. Take the fret and the worry and the care from our hearts this day and give us a sense of faith and peace as we trust Thee. In Jesus' Name. Amen.

MAN'S EXTREMITY: GOD'S OPPORTUNITY

If you have your Bibles and would like to turn to the reading, it is in First Kings, beginning with chapter 17. We are going to take a brief excursion through the main portion of the life of Elijah, pointing out a few practical things I trust will be helpful.

Elijah comes on the scene very suddenly, and he is introduced here in chapter 17 of 1 Kings. The first announcement that he was to make was that there would not be rain for a number of years; three and a half years there would not be rain in Israel. This was a judgment, an announcement of judgment. Immediately after he had made this announcement, the Lord told him to go to the brook Cherith, and he went there and the Lord fed him for a certain length of time. In all of this I think that we should note that God is preparing him progressively for the work that He had for him to do.

God does not thrust one of His servants out without adequate preparation. God was going to school him; He was going to put him through certain experiences, and these experiences were necessary. Had Elijah flunked out on these experiences, then of course, I do not think that God could have used him. These were not all exciting, pleasant experiences. Now I suppose that one at Cherith might have been, but that was not too easy for a man like Elijah. Elijah was a robust man. He was an "activist" we might say. It was not easy for him to be down there letting ravens feed him. Elijah was the kind of man who had never depended on anybody. Perhaps he had been very self-sufficient, but God was teaching him some things here at the brook Cherith that he needed to know.

I want you to notice some words. I think you should underscore these words as you study this passage of Scripture.

Verse 2: "The word of the LORD came unto him, saying . . . ."
Then verse 8: "The word of the LORD came unto him, saying."

First, the Word of the Lord told him to go to Cherith. Now the brook had dried up in Cherith, or the Lord had ceased feeding him there. I suppose the Lord will not feed us when we are out of His will. A lot of people are hungry today spiritually because they are out of God's will. As long as you are in God's will, there is a spring; there is always water, there is always food, that inner-water, that inner-food. There is a well of water springing up within your soul if you are in the will of God. God will always feed you when you are in His will. The inner-springs never run dry when you are in God's will. They only dry up when you are out of His will. I think a lot of us get out of God's will. Our souls get dusty, dry, and parched and we are thirsty.

When you are thirsty and hungry you are restless; and you get easily discouraged. So, God let the brook dry up. Elijah, however, listened to the Word of the Lord after the brook dried up. If God lets your brook dry up, He has another message for you; just wait. God has not forsaken you just because the brook dries up. If God lets it dry up, it is for a purpose. So Elijah listened for the Word of the Lord, and the Lord came to him again and told him to go to Zarephath and there he would find a certain widow. (They laugh at Southerners for saying "widow woman," but this is what the Bible says in verse 9, so we are more Scriptural than any sophisticated Northerner.)

Anyway, he went to Zarephath and found this widow. She was out at the woodpile. Now you do not know what a woodpile is. But that is where wood is piled. Those of us who were reared in the country before the days of gas and electricity know what a woodpile is. She was out at the woodpile gathering stovewood. She was going to bake the last bread that she had. She was a very discouraged woman. She was totally defeated.

Let me say this to you. You may think that you are the only person who has ever been defeated. You may feel you are at the end of the road with no where to turn. But any man who has lived for God has been right up against the wall more than once with no where to turn. Helpless. Empty. No resource.

We know what it is. And this woman was there. She had saved perhaps as best she could, hoping that something would happen to alleviate her problem and to meet her needs. Nothing had, and now this was the last meal in the barrel. These are not pleasant experiences at all, but after you pass them and see how God has worked, you thank God for the bottom of the barrel because it is then that you turn to God. When all human resource is gone, God moves in at your moment of desperation. God does the impossible. It is then that God becomes bigger than your problem. He is glorified.

Now some of you here in school have faced these situations. It will not be the last time you will face them. God is getting you ready for something. I do not know what it is. You may not know what it is, but God is preparing you if you can trust Him. You say, blind faith? It is not blind faith. It is faith in a God that you cannot understand at the moment, but He is doing something. He is working something out.

If you are His child, in His will, God is working something out for you no matter how painful the experience you are going through. God is working something out that is going to strengthen you, and it is going to turn out for His glory and for your good.

Well, this woman responded to the request that Elijah made. The first request she responded to it favorably—some water. You see, Elijah had not gotten real clear what he should ask for. God was leading him. He asked for water when he should have asked for bread. But he was not clear on that, and the woman was going to get water, and he said, "Well, I'd better ask her for some bread." So he asked for some bread. She turned around to explain the situation as politely as she could.

This should have been enough for any man to have accepted. She said, "I only have a handful of meal and I am preparing it for my son"—I do not know whether she said for herself or not. But she said, " . . . that we may eat it and die." I do not think she was going to eat any of that bread. If I know a mother and a mother's heart, I do not think she was going to eat any of that bread. I think she was going to maybe feign eating it, pretend that she was eating it; but I think she was going to give all that bread to that boy because this was the last bread in the house. She wanted him to have it. Perhaps she did not mind dying too much, but it is awfully hard to watch your child die of hunger. She explained this to Elijah.

I have often said that I used to get angry with Elijah; I did not think that he was a gentleman at all. After explaining this, he should have said: "I am sorry, lady, very sorry to have embarrassed you. You just wait here and I will go down the road to see if I can find somebody who has some bread, and I will bring it back." But you know, he was hard-hearted. He said, "Go bring me some first." How selfish can a man be! How cruel can God be to take all that you have! The last meal in the barrel. See, he was acting under the direction of the Word of the Lord. This was not necessarily Elijah speaking. It was God speaking through him, and God is going to take away something. He is going to take away the last human resource so that He can become God. That is the only way that He can become your God. As long as you have human resources to lean upon, you are your own God. You supply your own meal; God cannot get the glory. As long as any human resource is left in you and you are leaning upon your own staff, in your own strength, ingenuity, and know-how, you are your own god. You glorify yourself.

You know, one thing that bothers me in religious circles today is all the promotion and publicity. I get a little concerned sometimes that the servants of God in the Name of God are using God's name to promote themselves. Oh, how sickening. You know, you cannot judge men's motives. I do not think it is proper for me to jump up and tell you every time that I pray. I do not think it is proper for me to tell you every time I speak to somebody about his soul. Human nature is such that if I do much of that, I am going to be casting the light upon myself. I have to be very cautious, and you have to judge your own heart when you say anything about what you do that reflects favorably upon you. You have to be very, very cautious. How subtle Satan is, even in the work of God. We want people to know that God is using us, and sometimes the "us" is underscored more heavily than the Lord.

But anyway, this woman was destitute. Have you ever been destitute? She said, "We are going to die." Here was God's opportunity. Now she was empty of all human resources. She had to fall back upon God! The only time we fall back upon God is when all human resources are gone. That is the only way I got saved. I tried to save myself every possible way. I did the best I knew how. I quit this; I quit that. I did this; I did that. I was just doing *everything* and *not* doing anything. I was not getting anywhere. It was only when I became destitute and quit trying and said, "Lord, I cannot make it. If I ever get saved You have got to do it"—God stepped in. My barrel was empty and this gave God an opportunity. I cannot take any credit for it because I had tried long and hard and could not make it. But God did it so simply when I came to the end of the road.

Now, if you are at the end of the road, cheer up. Thank God that you are at the end of the road. Say, "Thank You, Lord, that I cannot do these things and cannot work my problem out. I know that You are about to do something. You want to do something. You want to take over." Instead of letting it discourage you, just have a prayer meeting of thanksgiving. You say, "That is foolish. I cannot have thanksgiving until God does it. I do not know for sure that He is going to do it." That is our attitude.

Well, moving on rapidly from this: God did not let the barrel go empty. One other thing we need to mention, though, is what happened after this miracle—now, wait a minute—God may do something for you that will thrill you and put you on what we ordinarily call "cloud nine" and then you may be let down again. You know, that is what happened to this widow.

When Elijah prayed and day after day the barrel was not

empty and the cruse of oil did not fail, I think this woman was singing in the kitchen as happy as could be. But you know, something else happened. Her son died, her only child. The child that Elijah had saved by coming on the scene. The cruse of oil had not failed, and the barrel had not been empty, but now the child got sick and died. Oh, what grief! How let down she was! God lifted her up just to let her down. The Christian life is a mixture of sorrow and song.

"Must I be carried to the skies on flowery beds of ease, while others fought to win the prize, and sailed thro' bloody seas? Sure I must fight, if I would reign; increase my courage, Lord." I will tell you, you will have some ups and downs. This was the worst jolt to her, and so she complained to Elijah and said, " . . . Art thou come unto me to call my sin to remembrance . . . ?" I do not know what sin she was talking about.

There are some of you who are blaming yourself for some sin that you have committed that you have asked God to forgive, and you will not believe that God has forgiven you. You are insulting God. The reason God came in the Person of His Son was to forgive sin. This woman had been blaming everything bad that had been happening to her on her sin. You know, some people go through life like that. Everytime they get sick, they say, Well, I remember that I did something back down the road of life that was not right, and God is judging me. Every time a reverse comes in life, they say, "God is judging me," and they feel so guilty and unworthy. She had a guilt complex that would not quit. Here she said, "My sin has been brought to remembrance again."

Wait a minute! If your sin has been put under the Blood, it will never be remembered again. We ought to accept that. Elijah brought the son back to life. This was another schooling. This was not only a benefit to the woman and to the son, but to Elijah. You know, while you are helping somebody, you are being helped. It is a two-way street. God may have been performing more in Elijah's heart than He was for this widow. We witness to somebody, and they get saved; we look upon the benefit as being for that person, but what does it do to you? What a thrill to present this son back to the mother.

In chapter 18, " . . . The word of the LORD came to Elijah in the third year, saying, Go, shew thyself unto Ahab . . . ." You remember this experience. He met Obadiah and Obadiah hesitated, but finally, he met Elijah. I like the dignity of the man of God saying, "Go tell the king to come to see me." You know, that is not the way it usually works. Listen, there is not anybody who holds a higher position in God's estimation than a servant of God. Finally, they met but we will not go into that aspect of it.

Then they had the contest on Carmel. Elijah won. Can you see old Elijah after this experience, there on the mount, herding the 450 false prophets up, taking them down to the brook, and having them slain? That was not a gory sight to Elijah. Elijah liked that kind of business. Elijah was thrilled. Four hundred and fifty prophets slain at the brook! I think he took them to the brook so that they could wash off their swords, clean up after the slaughter. That is the only reason I know.

But anyway, here is Elijah. A moment of triumph! A moment of victory! First we find him at the brook, having to rest and wait on God. Then we find him at Zarephath, praying and the meal being supplied, the child being raised from the dead. Sensational things. Oh, any man can be religious like this. I will tell you when you are winning such victories, you feel very religious. I am sure the word spread throughout the whole country that Elijah had been victorious and everybody was talking about 450 slain prophets. Elijah was soaring now. He was still acting, though, under the Word of the Lord.

Ahab went home that day and told Jezebel what had happened. The scene is going to change now. Elijah is not any longer acting under the command of the Lord. He is not any longer listening to the voice of God. He did not wait long enough for God to tell him what to do when he heard about Jezebel. He took off running. It is always dangerous when we do not act under the leadership of God.

Here was a man of God who had had tremendous victories. Sensational experiences! His name was flashed on the headlines of all the papers. (They did not have printing presses, but you explain that.) His name was on everybody's lips. Elijah, the man of God. Four hundred and fifty slain prophets! The widow's son raised from the dead! Miracles! Elijah! Elijah! The man of miracles!

But now, here is Elijah the coward. You know what he did. He ran.

(I want you to wake up. Do not come to chapel and insult me by sleeping. If you came to visit me in my home and went to sleep, I would ask you to leave. If I went to your home and you started to entertain me and I caught you sleeping over there, I would get up and leave.)

Here is Elijah, running from Jezebel. He had lost something. He had lost his courage. He got under this juniper tree, and he said, "I am not worthy to live. I want to die." See, he was a coward. He did not have courage to commit suicide. He wanted God to do the dirty work. Some people want God to do it, but since God will not, they go on and do it themselves. Defeated! He had just experienced a tremendous victory, but now he was begging to die.

Notice what he said in verse 4: " . . . For I am not better than my fathers . . . . " In other words, "I am a no-good. I am a nobody. I have never amounted to anything. I cannot do anything." I am telling you he was really defeated. Is there anybody here who feels that he is a no-good? Just absolutely no good? Elijah felt that way. You just move over beside Elijah, and say, "Elijah, make room for me. I feel that way, too." So he said, " . . . I am not better than my fathers."

Now, what did God do? God said, "Take a nap!" Take a nap! Nobody in this age will tell you to take a nap. I have just told you to wake up. But God said, "Take a nap, Elijah. You need to take a nap."

And as he lay and slept under a juniper tree, behold, then an angel touched him, and said unto him, " Arise. It is time for breakfast, Elijah." Thank the Lord for a good nice gentle wife who wakes you gently in the morning when she has breakfast ready. She has tiptoed around and let you sleep, and now she comes and says, "Time for breakfast."

I think God told that angel, "Do not be rough on him. Do not wake him up too suddenly. Just touch him and tell him to get up; it is time for breakfast." He was letting him rest and He was feeding him; taking care of him. There was a cake baked and he ate. God said, "Elijah, the journey has been too great for you. Just a little more than you could take. You got too excited there at that brook watching those false prophets being killed. You got beside yourself. You got too worked up, Elijah. And then, Elijah, you got too frightened when Jezebel got after you and you ran too hard, too long, too fast. The journey has been too hard for you." See, God knows when you need some rest. God was very gentle with His servant.

Well, he got up and ate. "And he said, Go forth, and stand upon the mount before the LORD. And, behold, the LORD passed by, and a great and strong wind rent the mountains, and brake in pieces the rocks before the LORD; but the LORD was not in the wind: and after the wind an earthquake; but the LORD was not in the earthquake; And after the earthquake a fire; but the LORD was not in the fire: and after the fire a still small voice."

Elijah had known the God of the tornado. He had known the God of the earthquake and the God of the fire, but He had not become acquainted with the God of the still small voice. And you know, there is the God of the still small voice. Some people who know the God of the tornado, the fire, and the earthquake do not know the God of calmness, quietness, gentleness, and rest.

So now, the Lord was presenting Himself to Elijah as the God of the calmness of spirit, the serenity of mind and soul, and the peace that only God can give. What do you know about God? How do you know God? Do you know God only when He is shaking things by the tornadic winds, the jarring earthquakes, or the leaping flames of fire? Is that the only way you can recognize God? Or can you recognize God as a God of the still small voice, that inner-peace. You do not have to see something external; it is something internal that assures you that God is God and that He is in control. You do not have to see signs and wonders. You know that God is with you because of the still small voice. Now there is the God of the tornado perhaps, and the God of the fire; but there is also the God of the still small voice.

May we stand, please.

PRAYER

Our Father, we thank Thee for these truths we find in Thy Word. May some portion of it meet some need in our lives this day. We pray in Jesus' Name. Amen.

22

February 13, 1976
Scripture: Ruth 1:14-17
Subject: Courtship; Engagement; Marriage

COURTSHIP; ENGAGEMENT; MARRIAGE

I am reading some verses from chapter 1 of Ruth, beginning with verse 14, a very familiar passage: "And they lifted up their voice, and wept again: and Orpah kissed her mother-in-law; but Ruth clave unto her. And she said, Behold, thy sister-in-law is gone back unto her people, and unto her gods: return thou after thy sister-in-law. And Ruth said, Intreat me not to leave thee, or to return from following after thee: for whither thou goest, I will go; and where thou lodgest, I will lodge: thy people shall be my people, and thy God my God: Where thou diest, will I die, and there will I be buried: the LORD do so to me, and more also, if ought but death part thee and me."

This portion is sung at many weddings, and it is supposed to represent a great love story. And it does, but this particular part illustrates the love of a daughter-in-law for her mother-in-law; but that might suggest also the deep love Ruth had for her husband who had died.

I do not want to become known as an Ann Landers, but there are some practical things that I think ought to be said to young people today that are not being said. Right here on our campus, I think it ought to be said because every year we have some deep emotional problems caused by love affairs, break-ups, and so on. What I say, I want to say very seriously. We joke about things that are serious sometimes that we should not. Because of our own feeling of uneasiness, we laugh at things that are serious. I do not know why it is that we feel so uncomfortable talking about these things that touch everyone's life, something that all of us face, and something that is absolutely normal.

That is this matter of courtship, engagement, and marriage. Now, it is not God's will for everyone to get married. I know in our day, we think it is terrible if a person does not get married, and perhaps there is nothing more terrible than to get married to the wrong person, or to get married if you should not get married. Everyone should not get married; I am sure of that. Most people are going to get married at some time in their lives, and they are going to have to make a home. They are going to have courtship; they are going to be engaged; they are going to get married; and they are going to make a home. I think it is very important that we take this very seriously.

As I said, here on our campus every year we have people who get engaged and before the year is out, you hear that so-and-so has broken up and rings have been given back, or some problem has occurred that greatly disturbs the people involved. I think much of this could be avoided. I hope you will listen to what I have to say. I hope it will be helpful.

Now, first of all, it is normal. Now you who are married just endure this. You can say something about these things to your young people if you are a pastor or a pastor's wife. You are at a time in life when you are to consider these issues, and you will be considering them very seriously. In fact, you have already considered them. Maybe not seriously, maybe not in relation to some particular individual, but you have already thought, and you will be thinking very seriously about marriage and home in years and months to come. This is a time when you are dating, most of you; or you will be.

Now, it is absolutely normal for young men to be attracted to young ladies and for young ladies to be attracted to young men. God made us this way. There is nothing to laugh about; there is nothing abnormal about it at all. Usually the attraction begins at the physical level. I am not talking about sensual things either. Usually, you are first attracted to a person by some physical characteristic: the way the person laughs, the way the person smiles, the way the person dresses (he is neat, nice, or he has good manners), just some physical, outward thing that is obvious.

Some people say that this is love, that they fell in love at first sight. I do not believe in falling in love at first sight. You have to know a person to love a person, and you cannot possibly know a person at first sight. Now, you may have been attracted to that person at first sight—some physical characteristic or personality—and as you get to know the person, you get to love the person and you relate the love to that first experience, but it is not love—it was not love because you did not know the person. But as you get to *know* the person, you may get to *love* the person. So, to me, there is no such thing as love at first sight.

This matter of falling in love is an unfortunate expression. It indicates that something happened to you that you could not help. In other words, it was sort of an accident. You fell. You know, when you fall, that is an accident. The terminology itself I think is unfortunate because getting in love is a process. Dating is normal. Dating is a very wonderful experience because it is always a wonderful experience to get to know any other individual, whether it is a young lady, a man, a roommate; it is a wonderful experience to get to know people. Dating is a time of getting to know people or a person. That is the whole purpose of dating or courtship.

Now in every date, there is a possibility that it will lead to marriage. I know that there is such a thing as casual dating, just friendship dating, and all of this; but even *that* could lead to marriage. We have been disturbed in these days about some of the aspects of dating, beginning so *early* in life. Children ten-, twelve-, and fourteen-years old do not know enough about life to know how to evaluate the person. The only thing that can happen to them is physical excitement and the arousement of the physical nature. They are not mature enough to evaluate character and personality; and so many times dating starts at such an early age until it can be nothing but physical. But, at your age level, it is a time when you can evaluate personality and character. You can look for those qualities within the person you are dating to see whether or not he or she is the kind of person that you would like to know better. Such relationships help you to see if you could like and love, and eventually, if it develops far enough, you would marry and that person would become a part of your life.

This is the whole purpose of courtship; it is not just to have a good time. This business of dating and courtship is serious. Now, it can be fun and excitement and all of this; but beyond all of that, there is something very serious because you are evaluating one another, and this evaluation should go on long enough until either you decide that this *is not* the person for me, or this *is* the person for me.

Now, it is more than just an emotional thing. It is a time and a period when good, solid, sound judgment should be used. Emotion should be laid aside in great measure. You should look as objectively as you can at the quality of character of this person. Of course, emotion will be there. It must be there and should be there, but there also should be good, sound, sensible judgment.

Many times I think we fail at that point. We take an emotional ride; we go on an emotional binge; and the person, because of physical characteristics, appeals to us emotionally. But we do not apply good, sound, solid judgment and we make a mistake. This is why every young person should talk to his parents, very seriously. It would be ideal if the relationship between parents and child could be such that the child would be willing to listen to his parents, to help evaluate character. If you do not have that relationship with your parents, you should find somebody in whom you have confidence and to whom you can talk about this matter of helping you evaluate character. This is a thing that is going to be important thirty years from now.

Your opinion of the quality of character of the person to whom you marry is a thing that respect has to be built upon, a foundation upon which respect rests. His hair will turn gray and even fall out. He may lose that slim, trim waistline, and all the other good physical qualities—but I will tell you there is one quality that will never fade, and that is good, solid character. It will

186

grow to be the most *important* thing in any good marriage.

Now listen, believe me on this, I have lived long enough to know. I hope you can believe me. These are things to look for. This is the purpose of dating and courtship. Let that process go on until you have had time to evaluate. Now, I am not talking about putting things in a computer because emotions are going to be there, and those (I do not like to use the word) "psychic" things that you cannot define: what makes one person love another, and all those things that are involved. But still, these other things are the over-riding things that I am talking about.

In dating, you look for personal habits. Are there too many little annoying things that that person does? Does the person not know how to dress, and you wish he did? Does he embarrass you when he goes out? Does he know what colors go together? I would not kick a good fellow out because he did not know how to match up colors because you can do that for him, but I tell you, it always bothers me when a wife lays out the clothes, and says, "Now, honey, put this on today." I do not go for that. I would put on overalls if she told me to do that. Those are minor things. But I am talking about little annoying habits that, you know, you just cannot get over. All of those things are important.

Of course, you ask the question: Is he a Christian? Do not fool yourself there. Do not try to pretend that he is a Christian if he is not. Do not try to make one out of him if he is not. Just because he went to Sunday School with you one day, or to a Sunday School picnic one time, do not assume that he is a Christian. Now, this limits Christians, and this is one reason I want to talk to you here. Christian young ladies and young men have a problem. I do not like to inject personal experiences, but I had a problem as a young man. I had to go to a Christian school. I did not go there for that purpose, but it worked out that I found my wife there. I just could not find Christians that shared my standards and with whom I could have that normal rapport and that freedom of communication; I could not find them. I had a problem of communication; I could not find them. I might have ended up an old bachelor, I do not know. But it is a problem; do not forget it is a problem. But it is something that binds you—you are limited.

Now who limits you? God limits you. God's Word limits you. There is no choice; there is no argument. ". . . What fellowship hath . . . light with darkness?" "Can two walk together, except they be agreed?" "Be ye not unequally yoked with unbelievers . . . ." And if you do not start at the level of this point of dating only Christians, you may end up marrying a non-Christian. So you have that point of consideration.

Look at the family background. You are marrying a family when you get married. Do not forget it. More than a mother-in-law, too. You are marrying a family background, a family history. And —listen, if you want to know the kind of wife that you will be living with thirty years from now, look at her mother now. Just take a look at her mother. If you can fall in love with your mother-in-law, then go ahead and marry her. No, seriously, take a look at the background; get acquainted with the family. Do not fool yourself to believe that "Oh, I know that there is nothing to them, but *He is* all right, or she is all right." Now, that can happen sometimes, but you want to weigh it with other things.

Be honest in your courtship. Do not go around here telling every boy that you love him because it is just a fad. Be honest. It is just as big a sin to lie about this as anything else. A lot of people sputter out all kinds of sweet things, and they do not mean a word of it. Be honest. Be serious. Take plenty of time. If there was somebody trying to push me or rush me, I would get suspicious. I am suspicious by nature anyway. I do not know whether there is anybody honest or not, but me. You know, when a car salesman starts to push me too hard, I walk out. You do not sell me things under pressure. I like to buy suits where the fellow shows me the racks and goes on and lets me alone. He tells me where my sizes are and goes on; then if I need him, I call him. I do not like one standing there saying this one fits, etc. I just do not like that. In courtship do not be rushed. Do not be pressured. *You must decide.*

Now, we have passed on from courtship. What is the next stage? Well, you could drop him, or her. No harm has been done. No commitments have been made. After evaluation you decide this person is not the person for you. You have not promised anything; you are not obligated. But now, you have come to engagement and most people do not take this seriously enough. They still have a basketful of doubts when they get engaged. They still say, "Well, I am engaged; I am going to take a ring," or "I am going to give a ring, but still, if I decide between now and marriage, I can still back out."

Do not go into engagement with that attitude. First of all, it is downright dishonest. Dating or courtship is a time of evaluation. Do not make any commitments until the evaluation period is over. Then when you are satisfied with the character and with the person that God wants you to marry, then and only then, enter into an engagement. Enter into it with the idea that it is binding. There is no backing out unless some new evidence comes to light that you did not know before and that had been withheld from you. There is no backing out.

The time of evaluation is over; courtship at the casual level is done with. Now you are entering into an agreement. You are entering into a commitment, a contract, and it is just as binding as getting married, unless some new evidence comes to light that changes things. That is, a basis for changing things because, in spirit, you have already gotten married when you got engaged. In spirit you have already said, "I will."

Now, I want to put a word of caution in here. Many times dating couples, when they have come to that point where in spirit they give themselves to one another, they think they can give themselves to one another totally; that is not true. There are still some limitations, even in engagement. But in spirit, and underscore what I am saying, *in spirit* you have already given yourselves to one another. You have already set yourself apart for this purpose in your heart and in your spirit. I am saying this to you because some of you are not taking engagement seriously enough. You are not looking upon that engagement, "I will marry you," as a commitment and as a word of honor on *your* part. Some of you are still having doubts in the backs of your minds, "Well, if I decide later on that I do not like him, I can give his ring back," or "I can ask her for it back, and it will all be over." That is dishonest.

You read in Matthew chapter 1 when Joseph found out that Mary was with child. You see, they did not call it engagement in those days, but that is what it was. There were engaged. They were going to get married, and Joseph found out that Mary was with child. Of course, he did not understand. Naturally, he assumed that something sinful had happened. God had not let Joseph in on it yet. You know what it says in verse 19, "Being a just man, and not willing to make her a publick example, [he] was minded to put her away privily." That is, he was minded to divorce her. That is what most of the versions say. The King James says "put her away," but it meant divorce her. You know, he looked upon the engagement so seriously that in order to get free of it, he had to go through a divorcement procedure.

That is how serious engagement was. And it *is* serious. Do not enter into it lightly or frivolously, and do not break one frivolously because you happen to fall in love with somebody else. You have no right to fall in love with anybody else unless there are just grounds for breaking an engagement. You have no right to be looking around at somebody else and considering somebody else because you have already given your word of honor, and you are bound by it unless, as I said, some *new* evidence comes to light that you could not have known before.

Now this makes dating serious, too. You have got to evaluate. You have got to investigate. Do not hesitate to ask questions during dating periods if you are getting serious. Find out what you want to know. Find out the background of this person, and if you find some things in the person's background that you have doubts about and you do not know how to evaluate, find somebody who has lived longer than you and in whom you have confidence, and ask them some questions: What would they do? I never count it a greater honor than for some young person here to come and discuss with me some problem about their courtship. Something they cannot know. I ought to know a few things that you do not know. I just stumble into a few things. If you live sixty-two years, you pick up a few things. I count it an honor when a young person values my judgment enough to seek my advice. But, you know, we ask questions about employment, about this, that, and others, and we go right on and use our immature judgment and never ask anybody questions about these serious things. Maybe we do not make you feel free to ask. I hope this is not true, but it could be.

No backing out, just because you happen to fall in love with somebody else or because you say I have decided I do not love him. What if this happened after you got married, and you decided you did not love him or her? What are you going to do? See? You have got the same problem. I will tell you what; I would not run off to the divorce court the first morning I got up and looked at him over there snoring with his mouth open, and I decided I did not love him. You will see that. Do not go to the divorce court right then. Wait. Wait until he shaves and gets dressed; you might fall in love with him again.

But it is wicked to get engaged and then fall in love with somebody else and come and say, "I have decided I do not love you anymore." *That should have been settled in the courtship stage.* After you have given your word of honor, and you have made your commitment, you have no *right* to back out. That makes courtship serious. It is serious business. We ought to take it out of the silly, giggling stage and make it serious because it *is* serious. You are making one of the most important decisions you will ever make in life: marriage.

Now, the commitment is total. You are already married in spirit when you get engaged. You are already off limits to anybody else. But now there are certain things that there cannot be total commitment in until marriage. There cannot be the physical commitment until marriage. A lot of young people because they get married in spirit, want to go on and be married physically, and they lose respect for one another. They fall out of love with one another before they ever stand before an altar because they want the total commitment before they are ready for it. This total commitment which involves the physical is reserved for marriage. In engagement, you are married in spirit; but when you are actually married, you are totally married in spirit and physically. Not until then. Do not take liberties that will jeopardize your respect for one another during the engagement period. May we stand.

PRAYER

Our Father, bless us in all the decisions that we make in life. May we do it for Thy glory. In Jesus' Name. Amen.

May 3, 1977
Scripture: Proverbs 22:1
Subject: A Good Name

23

BUILDING A GOOD NAME

(Dr. Johnson)

We are delighted to have Dr. Reeds with us today, and he will introduce the guests that are here. He is going to have a presentation at this time so we turn this part of the service over to Dr. Reeds.

(Dr. Reeds)

Thank you, Dr. Johnson. Some time ago Free Will Baptist Sunday School Department began publishing books. I do not know exactly how many titles we have published now. It is something like a hundred. I lose count and lose track of the various titles we do have.

Today we present to you a first. It is the first time we have published a biography of any individual in our denomination. We trust it will not be the last. We do want to recognize those who have been responsible persons in our denomination, who have helped to make our denomination what it is today.

I think some of us became concerned about our ancestry especially as a result of a recent television broadcast. Maybe you are concerned about who your granddaddy is and your great-granddaddy and so on. I am also concerned about my spiritual heritage. I know who won me to the Lord, but I do not really know who won that man to the Lord and so on.

I think we ought to recognize these who have pioneered the way and who are responsible for us being here today. We have come to recognize one of these men today. The first biography that we have published is titled *Founded Upon A Rock*. It is the life story of William Henry Oliver.

Let me share with you some of the highlights of Brother Oliver's ministry. I will not share with you his birthdate. He may want to do that himself. He is past my age, leastwise. He is, of course, a very well-educated man. He spent some time studying at Southwestern University in Clarksville, Tennessee. He transferred to Vanderbilt University in Nashville and graduated from there in 1926. His first position after college was at the Jere Baxter High School here in Nashville, Tennessee. Then he moved to Ayden, North Carolina, in 1927 where he taught math and English at Eureka College at that school and stayed there until that school closed.

He came back to Nashville to sell insurance for a period of time and then got involved in public education again. In the meantime, he also served several of our churches as pastor. He helped to establish and pastored for several years the East Nashville Free Will Baptist Church. He pastored while he was in Ayden, North Carolina, at the Ayden Free Will Baptist Church. Also, in the Nashville area, he pastored Bethel, Bethlehem, and Dunbar's Chapel Free Will Baptist churches here in Middle Tennessee.

He also has taught at Kingston Springs school in Cheatham County, Hume Fogg in Nashville, and then has served as activities manager at East Nashville High School for a number of years. He served as assistant principal for two years and held the principalship of that school for eighteen years. So he has had a very active life.

Then, in 1964 he retired for just one day, for the very next day he became a college professor at Belmont College. He served there until 1970, and then came to work here at Free Will Baptist Bible College where he has been teaching English and education courses. He remains in that position, of course, at the present time.

The book is authored by Miss Dale Edwards. Miss Edwards is a former student of this institution. She graduated from

Belmont College in 1970 and received her MA degree at Austin Peay State University in 1975. She has taught at Faith Christian Academy, Mount Calvary Christian Academy (all of these in North Carolina), and is presently at Maranatha Christian School in Florence, South Carolina. Miss Edwards is present with us. Would you stand, please? She also has her mother with her. We would like to recognize you, too. By the way, her father is in the hospital and has just undergone open-heart surgery. We might remember him in prayer. I understand he is doing very well.

Mr. Oliver, we would like to present you with this first copy. This is the first one off the press, and we would like to present it to you if you would come forward at this time. We congratulate you on a life well lived.

(Mr. Oliver)

Thank you. Thank everybody. I thank Brother Reeds; I thank Miss Edwards; I thank all of you. This is a great surprise to me. I knew the book was being published, but I did not know that it had actually been published yet and certainly did not expect this this morning.

It has been a long, beautiful road. I do not believe my guests have been introduced, so I would like to ask my brother and his wife, Hazel, to stand at this time, please. Thank you.

John has been with me most of the way. He is two and a half years younger than I am. As most of you know already, I am 73 years old and my sister-in-law, Mrs. Oliver (Hazel), was my student when she was in high school. So she is one of my former students. I officiated at the wedding of Miss Dale's parents some little while ago. Thank you very, very much. Thank you. Thank you, Brother Reeds.

(Dr. Reeds)

Brother Oliver will be in the bookstore immediately after

chapel this morning. There are copies of the book available, and he will be glad to autograph copies for you. Thank you.

(Dr. Johnson)

I think we have been very short in our denomination in preserving history. Back in the early days I think they were better at it than we have been in recent years. I do think we have been neglectful in expressing appreciation to those who have meant much to our work and to the cause of Christ and to our own individual lives. I think it is very proper that we be thoughtful in these areas, and I am delighted that this book has been written and this expression of appreciation has been shown to Mr. Oliver.

That brings me to some thoughts. I usually preach at least once a year, every two years at least, from a verse of Scripture that in one way is very simple but another way it is one of the tremendous verses in the Bible. I want to emphasize those thoughts this morning even though during this year I have emphasized them before. I want to emphasize them again.

Let me say, first of all, I make no apology for emphasizing certain truths. There is no happenstance. There are certain things that need to be emphasized, they need to be indelibly impressed upon us, and usually only those things that are repeated over and over again stay with us in life.

So this verse of Scripture found in Proverbs 22, verse 1, is a very familiar verse and you can quote it. "A good name is rather to be chosen than great riches, and loving favour rather than silver and gold." Now, when you read that you might get the impression that all you have to do is to decide or choose a good name as if you would go into a store and choose an article to purchase. There is more to it than that. "A good name is rather to be chosen than great riches, and loving favour rather than silver and gold."

The point that I always try to make in this is that you are

196

responsible for the name that you wear. I usually try to point out that in our early years we had to borrow names. Some of you will be looking for jobs when school is out. Maybe you have already written to some person seeking a job, and you used somebody's name as a reference. You picked out someone who had a good name. You did not pick out just anybody. When you go to list someone's name as a reference, you think of someone who has lived such a life that he is respected. His name will mean something, and you use his name.

People often ask you, or they ask me and others, of course, if they might use my name as a reference, and I am glad for them to if it will mean anything to them. I hope that for those who know me it would mean something to them. It depends on how I have lived and what kind of name I have earned for myself as to whether my name will mean anything to anyone or not.

Then, someone will ask you sometime to give a recommendation. That recommendation is worth only as much as the name that is signed to it. If your name is not worth anything, then the recommendation is not worth anything. So you have to earn a good name. As I said, early in life you borrowed names, but all the while you are building your own name.

Now, there is a lot that goes into building a good name. It is not easy. It means that you have made wise choices in life. Your decisions have been wise decisions. You have been honest. You are dependable. You are truthful. You are a person of integrity. How do people know this? They know it because you have lived such a life. You have demonstrated these qualities of life.

Now, it is not easy to be honest. There is a lot of pressure to be dishonest. All of us know this. Just to say that I am honest as if it is no trouble to be honest, that is too simple. There are times when pressure is brought to bear that it is not easy to be honest. That is the reason that some people are not honest. If it were always easy to be honest, then everybody would be honest. Everybody would like to be honest. They would like to have a reputation of being an honest person. But some people are not honest because when the pressure comes, it is not easy to be honest. The person who has built a good name has withstood the pressure, the temptation, to be dishonest. In spite of the pressure, he has been honest, and he has built that kind of name, but it is not easy.

It is not easy to be truthful. Now, if you say it is always easy for me to tell the truth, you have already told an untruth. It is not easy to always be truthful. To be truthful causes you to lose friends. It makes you unpopular at the moment with certain people. To be truthful embarrasses you at times. It hurts your ego to say that I just "goofed," I just played the fool, I was unwise in what I did. It is not easy to be truthful.

But a man who is known as a truthful man is a fellow who has withstood the temptation to tell lies. In spite of the pressure to lie and protect his ego or to get some advantage or advancement, he has told the truth. He has been tested over a period of time, and people have come to know him as a truthful man. It is not easy though. You know it is not easy to be truthful. I know it is not easy to be truthful. But a good name . . . you are building a good name, and you do it through discipline. You do it through making the right choices. You are developing character. You are developing conviction. You have integrity, and you live by the integrity of your own heart.

"The integrity of the upright shall guide them . . ." the Bible says. That is, what you are inside determines your behavior. You read about the good tree in Matthew chapter 7. It says, "Beware of false prophets, which come to you in sheep's clothing, but inwardly they are ravening wolves. Ye shall know them by their fruits. Do men gather grapes of thorns, or figs of thistles? Even so every good tree bringeth forth good fruit; but a corrupt tree bringeth forth evil fruit."

In other words, what you are determines your behavior. Now you can live a hypocrite for a while, but what you are catches up with you, and eventually you cannot live under the pressure of hypocrisy. You have to settle down to what you are.

You become what you are eventually. You get tired of pretending, and you cannot carry that kind of life always. So here you are the fruit.

A good tree produces good fruit. A good person will produce a good life, but it takes discipline, hard work. I covet for everyone of you a good name. Now, you have been a student here, some of you four years, some three, and some of you this is your first year, some your first semester. Well, it does not matter, I am lost in the crowd around here. Yes, it matters. Your roommate will remember you for something as long as he lives.

I have forgotten some of the names of the people that I roomed with in college, but I have not forgotten the people. I remember the kind of people they were. I could not tell you their names, some of them, but I remember them. I remember whether they had a good influence on me or otherwise.

They are going to remember you right here on this campus. You have been building a name, and when somebody mentions your name thirty years from now, something will flash in the minds of those who have known you here. They will think of you and remember the kind of person you were. It is very important right here on this campus to build a good name.

Some of you are going out to pastor. Your church will not know you. They are going to be looking you over for a year, two years, to find out what kind of person you are. You may not be the greatest preacher in the world, but if you are a good person, they can say, "You know, he is a good man. He is honest. He is truthful. He works. He prays. He practices what he preaches." They can put up with mediocre preaching, but they cannot put up with shoddy living and a shoddy character. They will not put up with that. They will not tolerate it. It is very important to build a good name. You have to be careful. One little slip up can put a mark against your name that will be hard to erase in the minds of those who know you.

In an unguarded moment, in a thoughtless act, you reveal the kind of heart you have and the kind of person you are. You have to watch it every day. It is a life of discipline. But you know, it is not so hard if you have the right kind of heart. You have to start there. You cannot build a good name with the wrong kind of heart.

The life of Saul is very interesting when he was made king. He was not looking for the job. You know, you had better watch these people who are looking for the job. They might not be the ones that ought to have it. Usually God taps people who are not looking for the job. They were doing what they were supposed to be doing at that time, and God used them, chose them, for a certain work.

Anyway, Saul was made king of Israel. It was not God's will for him to be made king of Israel; but He went along with the demands of the people, and God told Samuel to anoint Saul as king. But an interesting thing happened. God gave him another heart. That is, God was saying, "If you are going to be king over My people, and if you do a good job, you have got to have the right kind of heart."

So He knew that Saul's heart was not the kind of heart that would make a good king. He knew Saul's heart. He knows our hearts. So He said, "Now, I am going to fix you up so you can be a good king. I am going to give you another heart." And as he turned to go from Samuel, God gave him another heart.

Now, you start there. You have to get your heart right. When your heart is right, then you can begin to build a good name because you are a good person. Only God can make the heart good. You cannot. I cannot. You cannot do it through self-discipline. Now, after you have got the right kind of heart, then you start practicing or putting into life's experiences the character of your own heart through good deeds and good acts. A life of discipline, yes, for a Christian.

Oh, you say, "God does it all. He comes into your life and takes it over . . . . " Wait a minute. Yes, God gives you the possibility of being what you ought to be, but God does not make you that unless you practice discipline. Paul said, "By grace

[God's grace] I am what I am . . . . "

God's grace does not guarantee success, but God's grace does make success possible. God's grace does not guarantee that you will have a good name, but God's grace makes it possible for you to have a good name. But you will have to practice discipline.

"A good name is rather to be chosen . . . . " You start off with getting a good heart, getting right with God, and giving yourself to God. Then He has given us the Word of God to instruct us, to encourage us. He has given the Holy Spirit to indwell us, to empower us, and to give us the spirit of a good life. Then in the Word He has taught us discipline which is a part of building a good name.

When you see a man who has earned the respect of his fellowmen, it is a wonderful thing. It is a wonderful thing to mention Mr. Oliver's name in this city and among people who know him across this city, I have never heard anybody question his character or his name. Otherwise, I have heard many good comments made. He has lived here among people in this city for many, many years. They have watched him. He has had students, he has had teachers to teach in his schools, he served as principal of the school system here in this city for many years, and all the teachers of the city knew him. He has been watched. They know him.

It is wonderful to have a good name. But it is not accidental. It did not happen in a day. A consistent day-by-day, week-after-week, month-after-month, year-after-year, as they came and as they went, living among people builds a good name.

You can build a good name. You will have to work at it. Get right with God. Start there, then start practicing by saying "no" to those temptations when they come and saying "yes" to that which is right. It is just as hard to say "yes" to right as it is to say "no" to evil. It goes together. Making wise choices by the grace of God, you can build a good name. I covet it for everyone of you. May we stand, please.

PRAYER

Our Father, should there be one here today who does not have a good heart, we know he can never build a good name in Your sight. We pray that we will all examine our hearts to see whether our hearts are right or not. Then we pray, Lord, that You would give us the grace, character, and integrity to discipline ourselves according to the teachings of Thy Word so that we will have a testimony. The kind of name we have determines the kind of testimony we have. We cannot be used unless we have a good testimony, a good name. Bless us to the end that all of us will be known as godly men and women, for Your sake. Amen.

24

May 4, 1977
Scripture: James 1:13-15
Subject: Temptation

DESIRE—THE ROAD TO THE GRAVEYARD

We would like to thank the pastors, the Christian education directors, and others who have been instrumental in bringing so many fine groups to our campus this spring. I know that somebody has to be back there to suggest and to plan these visits, and we certainly do appreciate those who have done that.

James, chapter 1, verses 13-15: "Let no man say when he is tempted, I am tempted of God: for God cannot be tempted with evil, neither tempteth he any man: But every man is tempted, when he is drawn away of his own lust, and enticed. Then when lust hath conceived, it bringeth forth sin: and sin, when it is finished, bringeth forth death."

I was reading those verses again the other day, and I began to think of people that I have known and experiences that I have seen in the lives of other people. These verses took on a new meaning to me.

Now, first of all, let us notice in verse 13: God does not tempt people. Sometimes we say God is trying people, and we leave the impression that God is tempting people or testing people. God cannot be tempted with evil. I think there you have the answer for the impeccability for our Lord Jesus Christ. Our Lord could not be tempted. That is, there was no response in His soul to the temptations that the devil offered Him. With you and with me, there is a response, at least a possible response. There was not a possible response for our Lord to have a desire for evil. That is not true of you and me. We can have a desire for evil. Our Lord could not. He had no sin in His nature. We have sin in our nature. There was no depravity in Him. There was no appetite for evil. There was nothing within Him that sin could appeal to but that is not true of us. We can be attracted to evil. Desire can be kindled within us for evil, not our Lord. So, I believe definitely in the impeccability of the Lord, and I guess you have studied that and maybe argued over it. Here I think you have the answer.

"... God cannot be tempted with evil, neither tempteth he any man." Anytime that you are tempted, do not blame God. God does not tempt you. But it tells us now where temptation comes from. "But every man is tempted, when he is drawn away of his own lust, and enticed." In other words, the depravity of your heart is the source of temptation. There is something within you that responds to evil.

So lust, the depravity of our hearts, makes it possible for us to be tempted. There is where we have our trouble. I am talking to an auditorium filled with people every one of whom has the problem of temptation. You grapple with it daily. It is a lifetime struggle. I know that some of you think, "Well, when I get older, I will have no problems with temptation." No, that is not true at all. The devil is going to have a set of temptations for you when you are young, middle-aged, and when you are old. You never get past temptation.

Abraham pulled some big boners when he was rather old. Other characters of the Bible did the same thing. David, for instance, was no young man when he fell into temptation and into sin and on it goes.

So, " . . . every man is tempted, when he is drawn away of his own lust . . . ." It would be wonderful to believe, I suppose it would be, but it would be awfully frustrating in another way, to believe in the doctrine that when you get sanctified, there is no more temptation. Those people live in a dream world. The only way in the world that you can harmonize that is to stop calling sin "sin." You pretend that it is not sin any longer.

I suppose any of us could rationalize and call sin something else and say that we are not living in sin. I was shocked several years ago when one of our brethren, I think he was a good man, but I think he was ill informed, said, "I have not sinned in twenty years."

Well, I do not know how he feels, but if that could be true, it would be wonderful, would it not? But the temptations come as a result of our depravity. You have depravity. You are going to face temptations today. You are going to face it in examination periods. Some of you will have the answers so convenient. I would suggest that you not take any material with you that would make it convenient because the pressure can get great when you know that you know the answer if you could just get the first two words and get started. You would be all right, but you cannot think of those first two words. So you will be tempted during examination period.

You will be tempted this summer. There will be many temptations this summer. All of us will have temptations as long as we live here in the flesh. So when you talk about temptation, you talk about something that everybody knows something about, and you do not get past it.

So he tells us where the origin of sin is. Let us read on: "Then when lust hath conceived . . ." that is, out of the depravity of your heart you have lust. There is desire born. Now, perhaps it is not sin as yet, I do not know. I do not know where it turns into sin, but you have first of all in verse 14 desire, or lust. You are enticed. Then in verse 14 this lust conceives.

We do not know what is going on in our bodies. You may have some disease that you are unaware of that is taking hold, or will take hold, of your body today that will eventually kill you. It may be a long time before you are aware of it; but that disease fastens itself on some organ of your body, and it goes to work silently, unknowing to you, but it goes to work. Five years, ten years later, you say, "There is something wrong with me." There has been something wrong with you for years, but you did not know it. This is the way sin works.

"When lust hath conceived . . ." first of all it is desire, that inordinate desire, lust. You had better control your desire. Take a look at your desires. Every man of God who stays true to God finds himself at times, I am sure of this, getting in love with some things that are wrong. He checks himself. He says, "This is not right." I know preachers who have said, "I got interested in making money, and it was getting hold of me, and I had to quit it." I have known men who quit their business, a good income, because they could not control it.

Desire. Every man who goes off into immorality, every person who goes into immorality, before he commits the sin of immorality could have stopped. If he had said, "This desire is not right," and he realized where it was taking him, he could have stopped. But he lets that desire take hold of him. He lets that desire conceive. It is born in his heart. Here is where sin is born. Here you have the birth of sin, and you have the graveyard of sin mentioned in this passage of Scripture. Here is where it is born—when desire has conceived the birth of sin.

You had better check those desires. You read the wrong kind of literature, and that literature stirs up unholy desires. You had better check it. You had better throw the literature away. If you are in association with somebody that is a temptation to you, you had better change your associates. If your job brings in so much money that you are strongly attracted to material things, and you do not want to live on a preacher's salary any more, you had better quit that job. This old world has a lot of wonderful things to offer to the flesh. If you are much of a preacher, you could make a lot more money than you will ever make preaching.

Now, people ought to take care of the servants of God. Those who minister the Word should be ministered to. You had better quit a job if it is getting you involved in money making, and you are getting accustomed to a living standard that the ministry will not support. You had better get out of that job if you are going to stay in the ministry. A lot of people are frustrated at that point today. They have been accustomed to making so much money until they do not see how they could go into the ministry.

Sin is born in your heart when you let lust conceive. It takes hold. Life is there, and that life of sin goes to work. It draws you gradually away from God toward some act of sin out there. It has not gotten to the act yet. It has not been delivered. It has been conceived, but the time of delivery has not come yet. There has to be a process, but sin is at work. It is conceived in the heart. It is there; it is growing. One of these days sin will be delivered. The hour of birth will come, and the act will be committed. The lust that started back there when you started thinking about the thing, conditioning yourself for it, you were just simply waiting until the convenient time to commit the act, but it was growing all the while.

Am I talking to anybody today where sin has already conceived or maybe it is still in the lustful stage? You are thinking about it. Mulling it over. Conditioning yourself for something that you really know is not right. Getting ready for the act of sin. There comes a moment somewhere when that sin is conceived and you say, "yes" to it. Under the right circumstances, you will do it. You had better weed it out of your mind and out of your heart. Say "no" to it.

" . . . When lust hath conceived, it bringeth forth sin . . . ." Now, you may be enjoying it up to this point. It may be pleasurable. Nothing has gone wrong yet. You have thought about it. You are enticed by it. Your desire for it is whetted. Your appetite was built and you looked forward to it, maybe with a little nervousness and a little fear to be sure because you did not know just what the results would be, but you had thought about it. Now it has been conceived. Lust conceived, it has turned into sin, and it has all been a thrill. It has been pleasurable, no bad results.

Wait a minute. There is another step. There is a graveyard. It always ends in the graveyard. You know, everything that is conceived and born ends in the graveyard. You will; I will. That sin that is born in your heart, it has been pleasurable. You have enjoyed it, but there is a graveyard out there. I have thought of some people, as I thought of this verse of Scripture, that are in the graveyard. Some of my friends are in the graveyard. I am not talking literally. They are still walking around, but as far as their usefulness to God is concerned, they are in the graveyard.

I am thinking of one fellow who as far as I know (God is the judge, I realize that) is now in the graveyard. He used to be a good preacher. I never hear of him anymore as far as his preaching is concerned.

He was used of God, but he could make money. I got a little envious of him at one time. He was just making it so fast, and looked like he was getting along so well. I did not think he had any more sense than I. I may have been conceited, but he did not seem to be any smarter than I. He could just turn things into money right and left. He still preached. It seemed like he was going along all right. It was not hurting his ministry, it did not seem.

But wait a minute. Something happened somewhere down the road. No church that I know of could support that man with the standard of living that he was able to enjoy. He could not go into the ministry without going way back down the ladder as far as the standard of living was concerned. No church in our denomination, and I do not know of any church hardly, that would support him like he could support himself with the money that he could make. But somewhere, he stepped into a grave, and I do not ever hear of him anymore as far as the ministry is concerned. It got him; it took hold of him. That lust for material things got hold of him.

Let me tell you a little something. Most of us come from pretty poor backgrounds. We have not had too much in life. I want to just throw out a thought. The less you had, perhaps when you grew up, the more problems you may have with material things when you get older. The fellow who has never had anything gets a taste of it. It is like a country boy going to town when I was growing up and getting a cone of ice cream. He just liked it and went wild.

A fellow who has not had anything when he was growing up, and he gets a taste of it, I will tell you, he can go wild over it. I have noticed people who have grown up with it, had a little something all along, they are not nearly as likely to go off the deep end. The fellow I am thinking about, he came from way back deeper in the woods than I. I do not know whether he had any less than we had or not, but if it could be possible, I think he did. His wife had not had anything. I will tell you they went wild over it. They have got it now but I do not hear anything about his ministry. Death. The lust for material things got hold of him.

I am thinking of another friend of mine. We were about the same age. He owns a big farm now. There is nothing wrong with owning a big farm. There are a lot of white-face cattle on that farm. He has other securities and just retired a year or two ago from another position where he had quite a financial interest and he has that pension. Oh, he is fixed, but he used to be a flaming evangelist for God. Now you never hear of him. Lust, desire, conceived and grew. One day there was delivery, birth, sin, then his ministry was gone.

I am thinking about a young man, well, he is not young anymore, but we were young together. One of the best personal soul winners I ever knew. If I called his name, some of you on the platform likely would know him. I used to be embarrassed and felt guilty around that fellow. He had a way of winning souls, a good personality, and was a good preacher. I remember living with him in a meeting one time. We shared a room together and I was impressed with the fellow. He prayed, won souls, and preached the gospel. Then a dirty, ugly, sin got hold of him. It ruined him. His wife left him, and his children had no respect for him. The last time I saw him he was in shabby clothes and looked like a bum. I said, "Could this be that man that I knew?" It was.

Lust conceived and turned into sin; death and the graveyard followed. He is not used of God, is out of the ministry, going from town to town as I have been told. How sad for that man that I knew as a soul winner. You say, "It could not happen." It did happen.

One day years ago somebody came into my office in this school and said, "I have heard so-and-so about this student. He is involved in a terrible sin, if it is true."

I said, "That cannot be. That is the best soul winner on this campus."

He would lead groups out, win souls, and talk to people about the Lord.

I said, "That cannot be."

But I checked it out.

I said, "I will check it out."

I knew in my mind it was not true. I called him into my office. (My office was over here in this building at the time.)

I said, "This has been reported on you, and I know you should know it and should get it straightened up," because I expected him to say, "No, it is not true."

I could not believe it. I said, "This is being reported about you."

He said, "That is right. I am guilty."

Then he started telling me about his sin, and he was not embarrassed about it at all. In fact, he was telling me how wonderful that sin was.

I said, "You get out of my office! Shut up that mess! I do not want to hear it!"

I said, "You pack your things and get away from here."

A fellow that was known to be the best soul winner on this campus. One of the best that has ever been on this campus as far as I know. He was caught up in this terrible sin. We "shipped" him.

Lust conceiving, turning into sin put one in the graveyard.

A young lady came to this school . . . I will not tell that story though. She lost her purity. Somewhere out there, somewhere, nobody knows but God. I do not know whether she knew or not, but somewhere out there in her life, lust took hold. She planted it. It grew. It conceived and one day sin was born and her purity was gone: death.

Young people, you are living in trying times. The world is against you. The world says, "It is all right. Do any old way you want to." No shame anymore. "Have your illegitimate children."

210

No shame. "Get divorces." No shame. "Go on and live like you want to." No shame. The world says, "It is all right." God says it is not. God says, "Death."

Whom are you going to believe? Are you going after the fashions of this old world, and let this old world set your standards? Then you are going to end up in the graveyard. You will not be worth that much to God.

The progression—you had better deal with it early. If it ever conceives, it is awfully hard to have an abortion. It is hard to get it out of your system, your mind. You had better deal with it early. You had better not let it happen. If you feel yourself drifting and if you are in association with somebody here that has agreed with you on a sin, *separate!* It is not worth it. A moment of sin is not worth a lifetime of tears and regret. It is too big a price to pay. You have sinned against a holy God, too, and you have ruined your prospects of being what God would want you to be.

I could give several illustrations if we had time. David let lust conceive. It was born. Everything was going all right so far. Ah, but you follow the life of David from there on out. There is one heartbreak after another. The "sweet singer of Israel" let lust conceive. It was not worth it. Read Psalm 51. It was not worth it. Death to self-respect is death to conscience. Your conscience can get hard and seared. It is death to the power that God can put in your life to be used. It is death to fellowship with God. It is death to usefulness. It is death to the soul. Do not play with sin. May we stand.

PRAYER

Our Father, put a fear in our hearts to sin. Put a love in our hearts for God. Give us character to withstand temptation. In Jesus' Name. Amen.

25

November 8, 1977
Scripture: John 21:1-3
Subject: I Go A Fishing

I GO A FISHING

Reading from John 21:1-3.

"After these things Jesus shewed himself again to the disciples at the sea of Tiberias; and on this wise shewed he himself.
There were together Simon Peter, and Thomas called Didymus, and Nathanael of Cana in Galilee, and the sons of Zebedee, and two other of his disciples.
Simon Peter saith unto them, I go a fishing. They say unto him, We also go with thee. They went forth, and entered into a ship immediately: and that night they caught nothing."

An interesting story of some people who had some wonderful experiences, but now they were discouraged. It is very interesting about Simon Peter. If you go back to Matthew 4, after the temptation of the Lord in the early parts of that chapter, you find that Jesus walked by the sea of Galilee and He found two brothers who were fishing, casting their nets. And He said, "Follow me." That was all that was said at the time. "And they straightway left their nets, and followed him." And He journeyed on down the seacoast and soon came to two brothers who were with their father, and He called them—James and John. And they also followed the Lord. So, first of all, you find the call that God gave to this man Simon Peter, and now you find him very, very discouraged.

In another place in one of the gospels—Luke's Gospel—we not only have the call of Simon Peter, but we have his commissioning. It also surrounds another fishing experience.

And when you first read it, you think, "Well, perhaps this is the same incident." But it is not. There were *two* nights that Simon Peter fished and did not catch anything. In this chapter 5 of Luke's Gospel, the disciples had toiled all night, and they had taken nothing. And the Lord came to them and encouraged them in a manner. Then He said to them: "From henceforth thou shalt catch men." In other words, the futility of fishing for material things as compared to fishing for men. I do not know why they had toiled all night, or that the Lord had allowed them to toil all night and catch nothing. It was unusual, I am sure, for skilled fishermen to toil all night and catch nothing.

I think He was telling them at least this much: When compared to fishing for men, fishing for the fish of the sea is nothing. They had caught nothing, and He said from henceforth you will fish for men. So they were commissioned. And after that, of course, through the life of the disciples and especially Simon Peter, he had some wonderful experiences with the Lord. He had seen many, many miracles; he had heard many lessons taught; he had seen the dead raised to life. He had had the transfiguration experience and many, many other experiences. Experiences of walking on the water and various other experiences that he had with the Lord.

But now after the crucifixion, after the burial of the Lord Jesus Christ, and even after His resurrection, we find Peter very, very discouraged. That so often happens to those who have had wonderful experiences with the Lord. It is possible to get discouraged. Those who have heard His call, those who have heard His commission, and those who have seen many other things happen in service for the Lord are not exempt. I think this is one of the things that we are encouraged over as we read this, to be encouraged by others' discouragement. But the way it turned out should be a very encouraging experience. God's people can become discouraged.

Now, they had been through trying times. Elijah became discouraged after he had been through some trying times. After he had seen the wonderful miracles of God, you would think he would never doubt God, that he would never be discouraged, but he did. He had stood up to Ahab; he had stood there before the false prophets on Mount Carmel, and God had answered by fire. God had done everything that Elijah had asked Him to do, but now you find him, after this wonderful experience, very, very discouraged—running—asking God to let him die. Some think that Elijah had a nervous breakdown; I do not know whether he did or not. But I know that after some wonderful experiences you can certainly hit some low points.

Now, right here on this campus, that can be true too. We have our campus revivals. We have our missionary conferences. We go out on soul-winning teams, winning people to the Lord. We have our prayer meetings and sometimes feel very close to the Lord. And yet in the midst of all of that, we can hit some very low points, and can feel like quitting just like Simon Peter did.

So, after all these wonderful experiences, at this low point, he made a decision. Now, I would like to warn you about making a decision on Monday morning if you are a preacher. Making decisions when the grade cards come out, and you do not make the kind of grades that you thought you ought or were going to make is not a good time. The grind of school work, the monotony of it, it can get to you. Do not make important decisions when you are low. You wait until you are at your best to make important decisions.

And I would say this, do not make decisions regarding getting married—that is an important decision, too—I would wait until I went to my room and thought it over. I would not make a decision while I was gazing into my girlfriend's eyes. Or I would not make the decision while I was looking at his wavy hair and broad shoulders, you know, whatever is attractive about a man (I have never figured that out). But whatever it is, I would not make the decision. I would at least get alone and think it over, and think it over seriously. And that, of course, would go for any other important decision that you might be called on to make.

Simon Peter said, "I go a fishing." In other words, "I am quitting. I am going back to my old life." I believe that every Christian at some point has been tempted to go back to the old life; he remembers it. Every Christian has his low points, his discouraging days, and he thinks about the old life and how it was. It seems rather glamorous sometimes to think about it, the nostalgia, the good old days as we would call them, the carefree days; out from under the discipline and the routine of things, the grind. We would like to think of those days as being better than what we are now experiencing.

I do not know how Simon Peter thought about it, but I think he had the same kind of attitude that the Children of Israel had when they were in the wilderness on the journey. They were there in the hot blistering sun as they traveled, tired, weary, no home, unsettled, on the move, and never knowing when the cloud or the pillar of fire was going to move. I can just imagine some of them going out the tent door and saying, "Well, the cloud is still there; it has not moved. The pillar of fire has not moved either, and we have been here now for so many days. What are we doing here?" Restless! Anxious to go, but having to wait on God. Not accustomed to waiting on God.

Now, they had been down in Egypt where they were told what to do. The task masters told them when to go to work and when to quit. They regulated their lives. Now they were out here under the guidance and control of some mysterious cloud and fire, and some God that they did not know too much about. Moses tried to tell them about Him, but it seemed rather weird to them. They could not quite grasp it. They wanted something tangible to go by. They got restless and grumbled. They wanted to go back to Egypt and settle down where they would know what tomorrow would bring, and what they could expect. Their lives could be more regulated than this. You know, the Christian journey is like that. You cannot always put your hand on things and you cannot always figure out what you are going to be doing tomorrow.

216

So, Simon Peter had gotten a little weary of this, discouraged. And he said, "I go a fishing." Now, I do not know whether any of you have had any thoughts like that or not, but if you have not, you will. There are a few already this year—not too many, comparatively speaking—but some for one reason or another have said, "I am going fishing. I do not like this grind." And let me say this, It is a grind. And life is going to be a grind. Life is not going to be filled with thrills and excitement every day.

Now I know there are some who talk like that. You can read your Norman Vincent Peale's and a few like that, and always smile, but it will be a hypocritical smile about three-fourths of the time. Life is not always a big excitement, a circus affair. It is a grueling, monotonous sort of thing, doing the thing that has to be done, whether you like it or not. But someway we have painted the Christian life as a sort of utopia where all of our problems are solved. Some envision that we are just floating around above our problems, and when we happen to have a problem—stub our toe on a problem—we say something is wrong with us. We have sinned, I suppose. But you can be in the will of God and have problems. Jesus said that. He said, in essence, "Do not think that you are going to have it easy. If you follow Me, there is a cross, there is sacrifice, and there are hardships and persecutions. Beware when all men speak well of you."

Even in the will of God, right here if this is God's will for you, it can be grueling; it can become monotonous. And to tell you a little secret that I have heard about: Marriage can be that way, too. Oh, you say you go around holding hands all the time. Well, you can always be suspicious of these people who have been married very long who hold hands very much. Something is wrong—they are trying to put on a front. Any area of life that you take is going to be filled with hardships and hard work. You will be tired at the end of the day. Sometimes you cannot see light out of the tunnel in the darkness, groping along, feeling that you are not making any progress. Then, once in a while God will let the sunlight come through and the breezes blow in your face for a while, and you get new courage and go on. But then you go right back to the grind.

"Oh," you say, "you are painting an unrealistic picture." No, I am not. I am painting a realistic picture. You say that these professors have it easy; they have already got their degrees. All right, you sit down to a stack of papers so high and start trying to grade them. You cannot read the handwriting, and none of them have the right answer. Yes, it is thrilling! There at twelve or one o'clock in the morning trying to find some way to pass people who really did not pass, but you are trying to find some excuse to pass them. You say, "No, they do not; they try to flunk you." You succeed when people succeed under your teaching.

All the hard work has not gone because teachers sit here on this platform; it is still there and it will continue to be there. You hear the good reports of these churches, people walking the aisles joining the church, everything going fine—well, that is just one side of the story. You go behind the scene, back of the curtain, and you see that pastor and the people who work with him. You see the disappointments, that person who started out and now he is backslidden. Somebody is cantankerous in the church, and the preacher's heart is broken during the week. He is facing Sunday, and he does not know what to do. So life is not easy. It can be very discouraging.

So Peter got discouraged. He said he was going fishing. Now, he influenced some other people. And you always do that. It is easy to influence other people to quit. Did you know that if you quit, there may be another fellow down the hall who will quit because you quit? If you quit, there is another girl on another floor of the dormitory who knows you, and she will quit? And if you stay with it, somebody will say, "Well, if he can do it, I can. I am ashamed to be the only quitter on my floor in my dormitory. I am not going to be a quitter; I am staying with it." If you stay with it, listen, you will influence somebody else to stay. If you quit, you will likely influence somebody else to quit. So Peter went fishing, and others went with him also.

Now, why did Simon Peter go fishing? Well, of course, you know he got discouraged, but I think there are reasons why he got discouraged. He must have forgotten the call that God gave him that day as he and his brother were fishing close to the shoreline of Galilee, and Jesus said, "Follow me." Now, I do not know what happened that caused Peter and Andrew to follow Jesus. There must have been some kind of change that took place in their lives. It must have been more than just a verbal call. There must have been some spiritual experience that we are not told about that took place. Two grown men out there fishing would not normally lay their nets down and take off and follow Jesus.

I cannot but believe that something happened inside them. There was some power; there was some change; there was some force in that call. We are not told about it here; it just simply says that Jesus said, "Follow me." You would think that that would be all there would be to it, but I think more happened. I believe that Peter must have forgotten it, and I believe that he must have forgotten the miracles that he saw, the dead that were raised, the blinded eyes that now could see, those who were blessed by the ministry of the Lord Jesus Christ. Surely, he must have forgotten that transfiguration experience. Surely, he must have forgotten walking on the water and beginning to sink and Jesus lifting him up. He must have forgotten all that. Something caused him to forget.

Let me tell you a danger: If you forget what God has done in your life, if you do not reflect and recall from time to time what God has done for you and what you have seen Him do for others, if you let that slip from you and grow dim in your memory, you too can get discouraged. One of the best ways in the world to keep from getting discouraged and wanting to quit is to recall quite often what God has done for you. I think that is very important; Paul was always reciting what God did for him on the Damascus Road. He was telling about it. And if you will just tell it over to yourself whether you tell it to anybody else or not, relive that experience.

Now, it does not hurt, I suppose, in marriage to relive some of your courtship experiences. Why did you propose to that girl? Why did you want to marry her in the first place? She is the same person now that she was then, and some people forget. They think, "Well, she has changed." She may not have changed much at all, but you have just forgotten. And so it goes in life. If God has spoken to you and changed your life, it is going to be hard to forget. You should not forget.

I think Peter must have forgotten that. He must have forgotten the miracles and the other things that he had seen Jesus do, and the lessons he had heard Him teach. Surely, he could not have forgotten the feeding of the multitudes out in the desert. But all of that seemed to have slipped away from him now, and he said, "I want to go back to the old nets."

Now, I do not know where those nets were. It would be interesting to know. I do not know whether Peter had to go down to the store and buy some more, or make some more, or what. But I wonder if he did not keep them around. He put them up on the shelf somewhere. I do not know about that, but I do know this, that some people keep the old nets around and some people keep the excitement of the old life fresh in their memory.

I cannot help believing that Simon Peter must have been thinking more than on just this occasion about the excitement of the sea. I suppose he could feel the tug of the nets, the fish in the nets, and pulling those nets in and counting the fish. I think that he relived too often going down to the market place and finding a buyer for those fish and getting the money in his hands and counting it. The excitement of success in material things— surely, he must have been thinking of that. Had that been erased from his memory, could he have gone back?

You know, there is a danger for you to spend too much time thinking about the old life—thinking about what you could have been and what you left behind that was exciting. You had better forget it; you had better tear up the nets, burn them. Get rid of them. Then there will be nothing to go back to.

I have said quite often that I am glad that about the only thing that I can do is preach. You take me away from that and I would not have anything else to do. It has been so long since I was involved in anything else, my nets have pretty well rotted. I do not have much to go back to, and you know that is a blessing.

Some people get prepared to teach school in the event that preaching does not work out. They can fall back on teaching. God pity you if you teach school for that reason. It is all right to teach school if God has called you to do it, but do not have a crutch back there, something you can lean on if it fails. If God has called you, He is not going to let you fail if you will be true and faithful. Other people have other things as crutches. I think of people now who had good ability to preach, good preachers, but they also had some ability to make money. And they could not get away from it. They got started in the ministry, and yet the old nets are back there. They can pick up their "nets" and make money, and I have known some of them who have done it. They have divided their lives between making money and preaching, and some of them have gone back entirely. What a pity! What a pity! At some point they said, "I go fishing, I go fishing."

Now, some of them do not make a complete break; they say, "I am just going fishing today, and then I will get back into the ministry tomorrow," or "I am just going fishing out there and make some money so I can get my security all prepared for old age and then I am going to preach." You know, there were people in Jesus' day who said, "Let me go bury my father; let me go bid farewell to them at my father's house." Jesus said, "No, let the dead bury the dead." You leave all and follow Me.

The happiest people in the world are the people who are totally involved. The most miserable people in the world, the most confused people in the world, are people who are living in two worlds. Two worlds. They have a divided heart, a divided interest.

Now, young people, some of you as I said awhile ago, may have become a bit discouraged and disenchanted. Some of you, and this could be especially true of freshmen, it could be true of others too, but primarily freshmen, may have had a wrong concept of what school was going to be like here. The thrill may have worn off by now, whatever thrill there was. You have found that this is hard, grinding, grueling work. You never quite catch up; the papers are never quite all in. The assignments are never quite completed, and you are running behind. The excitement of getting out here and doing service for the Lord is gone, the glitter is gone, and you are getting tired. "Going fishing." God forbid.

If God put you here, stay true. Stay with it until the task is finished. You will have more self-respect. If for no other reason, suppose you do not need to learn anything else—you know all that you need to know, which is not true, of course—but just take for granted that you did know all that you need to know, you ought to stay and complete the job for the self-respect, to know that you were not a quitter. You could say, "I was not a quitter." You will always be proud of that fact.

Let me tell you this. If you are a quitter in one area of life, you may be a quitter in other areas. It does not confine itself to just one area of life if you are a quitter. And I will tell you that is one reason why we are having so many divorces in this country today. We do not have a generation of people who learned to stick with it. When the excitement of marriage wears off, they run to the divorce courts, and we are having as many divorces as marriages, just about equally divided. And that can be true of all of life. Just the self-respect of knowing that you did not quit a job will mean much to you down the road of life, and I will tell you what, it will mean something to that wife or that husband that you marry, too.

Do not let somebody talk you into getting married before you ought to. A fellow who tries to talk you into getting married before you are ready is not worthy of you. And the girl that tries to talk you into it, if there should be those, I would not have her.

You ought to be mature enough to look at life realistically and realize that it is important that you get prepared. Anything that runs a risk of causing you to quit before time is not worth it. Now, it does not mean that getting married always causes you to quit, but it could. So I would consider it very seriously. Peter said, "I go a fishing. I go a fishing." And he went, and took others with him. And they caught nothing.

Now, I am going to close with this thought: Every person that I have ever known that God called or who said they were called, and they quit, they have never amounted to anything. They have never caught anything. Their nets have always been empty. Their lives are empty, and I guess it was a disgrace for professional fishermen to have to come in dragging empty nets. Now I would not be embarrassed. In fact, I am used to it, when I go fishing I really do not expect to catch anything. I guess that is the reason I do not catch anything. I have been defeated so much. But now if I were a professional fisherman, supposed to know how to fish, I am sure I would be embarrassed to come in and have to admit that my nets were empty. I have seen men who started out with God, who decided to go fishing. I have never known of one single one of them to amount to anything for God. Barren lives, frustrated, critics, sneering at the work of God, making light of it. What a pity! What a pity. Do not be a quitter.

May we stand.

PRAYER

Our Father, Thou hast called us. Not all of us to be preachers, but You have called us to be followers. Help us to be faithful followers and never even consider quitting. If there are those luring things of life back there that we left, we pray that we will refocus our vision, and get a new vision of Him who saved us from our sins and called us, commissioned us. We pray in Jesus' Name. Amen.

26

November 10, 1978
Scripture: Ecclesiastes 5:1-12
Subject: Riches Do Not Bring Happiness

RICHES DO NOT BRING HAPPINESS

I am reading from Chapter 5 of Ecclesiastes:
"Keep thy foot when thou goest to the house of God, and be more ready to hear, than to give the sacrifice of fools: for they consider not that they do evil" (verse 1).

In other words, some people talk too much; some people do not listen because they are always talking. I guess most of us are afflicted with that bad habit. It is a good one to break if you have it.

"Be not rash with thy mouth, and let not thine heart be hasty to utter any thing before God: for God is in heaven, and thou upon earth: therefore let thy words be few" (verse 2).

In my early ministry, I tried to wring out of people all the commitments I could get. I thought that was the way to do it, and maybe it is. But I have changed my mind. I do not now exert as much pressure to get commitments as I used to because I have seen so many people make commitments they could not keep. You have to have certain maturity in order to support certain commitments. We can make commitments that are over our head. I remember that story in the Bible about Simon Peter. He told the Lord that he would die for Him. Let all the others forsake Him if they would, but he would die for Him. He tried to prove that by cutting a man's ear off. Simon Peter meant it when he made that commitment. He was as sincere as any of us have ever been when we made commitments, but he could not keep that commitment. Now Jesus knew that he would not keep it, that he was not prepared to keep it, that he had overstated the commitment. Jesus looked at him and said, "Well, now, Simon, before this night is over you will have denied Me three times. Before the cock crows in the morning, before break of day, you will have denied Me three times." That was a shock to Simon Peter. I am rather sure that he doubted what the Lord said because he had his fervor up. He was in good spirits, and he meant every word of it, or he thought he did. Have you made commitments that you could not keep?

There are several applications that you can make of that thought. You can borrow money that you cannot pay back; you can get too deeply in debt. Your ability to borrow is more than you are able to pay back. Be careful. When you give your word about doing something, be careful because you have got to analyze yourself. Are you the kind of person who stays with a job until it is completed? Or are you the kind who intends to stay with it but you never do? Think about yourself. How is this going to be when the going gets rough? Look at yourself, your abilities.

You can apply it to spiritual things also. You may say that you are going to go to the mission field. In a missionary conference you may hear someone speak and you are moved and you make a commitment. Well, there is nothing wrong with that if you are able to keep it. How are you going to feel a week from now, or a year from now? How are you going to feel when you fall in love with that girl and she does not want to go to the mission field? Or you fall in love with that fellow and he does not want to go to the mission field?

So, think about your commitment. Let us read that second verse again: "Be not rash with thy mouth, and let not thine heart be hasty to utter any thing before God: for God is in heaven, and thou upon earth: therefore let thy words be few." That would be good in your love affairs around here. You should not get engaged until you are a senior. Some of you have been engaged to three or four fellows. I do not see how you meet them on the street. Maybe they too have already been engaged three or four times. There is no need for that. There is no need for telling a fellow that you love him, or a girl that you love her, until you have tested it. Sleep over it for a long period of time; see how you are going to feel when you catch her with her hair in rollers. That will cure you if anything will. No. Be careful about your commitments. Be not hasty with your words. You know, some people have to do as much backing up as they do going forward. A reverse gear is put on a car for a purpose, but it is to be used in a limited way. You do not use a reverse gear as much as you do the others. Some people are always having to back out of trouble. They are too hasty with their words. They over-commit. When they feel good, they can do anything. When they feel bad, they can do nothing and want to commit suicide. Up and down. Good advice: "Be not rash with thy mouth."

"For a dream cometh through the multitude of business; and a fool's voice is known by multitude of words" (verse 3).

How do you fulfill a dream? By hard work. Hard work begets more dreams. This institution is here because somebody had a dream. I take my hat off to those men who labored in those years when it was only a dream, and they labored faithfully because they saw it in a dream. They were willing to sacrifice for it.

Every man who establishes a successful business, first of all, sees it in a dream. Then he goes to work. He says, "I believe it can be done." And he sets out to do it. Hardships will not stop him; discouragements will not stop him—because that dream keeps him going. The dream stays alive. If you are going to be a preacher, you should have a dream of being the best preacher you can be. Whatever you are going to do, have a dream. "A dream cometh through the multitude of business; and a fool's voice is known by multitude of words." Now if some of us could make a success out of our words, we would be very successful.

We are always talking about what we are going to do, but we never seem to get around to doing it.

> "When thou vowest a vow unto God, defer not to pay it; for he hath no pleasure in fools: pay that which thou hast vowed" (verse 4).

If you have given your heart and life to Jesus Christ, stay with it. Keep your life on the altar; you will not always feel like it, but keep it there. You have told God you would. If you get married, stay married because you are married—not because you feel like staying married. But stay married to the person whom you made a vow to. And that is true in courtship, too. And that will also apply to what I said a bit ago about being too hasty to commit yourself to getting married, and then having to break it up. That shows that you may be that kind of person throughout your life. If you will take time, you will not have to do that.

> "Better is it that thou shouldest not vow, than that thou shouldst vow and not pay. Suffer not thy mouth to cause thy flesh to sin; neither say thou before the angel, that it was an error: wherefore should God be angry at thy voice, and destroy the work of thine hands? For in the multitude of dreams and many words there are also divers vanities: but fear thou God.

> "If thou seest the oppression of the poor, and violent perverting of judgment and justice in a province, marvel not at the matter: for he that is higher than the highest regardeth; and there be higher than they" (verses 5-8).

You will see a lot of injustice in this world, and you are going to be inclined to jump in and correct it; and sometimes maybe you should, but remember that God is the one who sets things in order. Some things God has to do. That applies in the church as well as anywhere else. I have known many pastors who tore up churches because they were trying to correct things that only God could correct. God can take vengeance. Now you are going to be inclined to take things into your own hands. I have just a few experiences in my life when I think I know that God took vengeance, and I am glad I let Him do it. If I had done it, I would have made an awful mess of it. But I have seen God work things out and straighten things out that I never could have done. So when some cantankerous person in your church (if you are a pastor) gets after you and somebody has done you wrong, you will have to turn some of that over to God; you cannot retaliate. Get rid of this spirit of retaliation. That will ruin you. It will ruin you. Some fellow bumps into you and trips you up on the basketball court; what are you going to do when you run down the court again? Are you going to sneak around and stick your toe out and trip him up? See? Get even with him. That is the way friendships are broken up, too. "Well," you say, "he did it to me." Yes, he did. But he is the one who is going to be hurt more than you are in the long run.

> "Moreover the profit of the earth is for all: the king
> himself . . . . He that loveth silver shall not be satisfied
> with silver; nor he that loveth abundance with increase:
> this is also vanity" (verses 9, 10).

Have you ever known a rich man to have all he wanted? I do not think I have. The more he gets, the more he wants. I was standing in a hospital hallway one night here in this city several years ago. One of the outstanding businessmen of the city was in the room, and his loved ones and friends were standing out in the hall. I overheard part of a conversation. They told about the man who was seriously ill in the room, and I think he died shortly thereafter. They told that he set his goal to be a millionaire at a certain age, about 27 or 28 years old, and he was more than a millionaire at that age. He thought when he started out that that was all that he would want—to make a million dollars, and then he would have it made.

After he got the first million, he set another goal. He wanted in a much shorter period of time another million, and I heard that it went on up to several million. I do not know how much he was worth, but he was worth several millions of dollars. But I thought that was an interesting conversation. The first million he would be satisfied; but when he got there, he wanted the second million worse than the first, and the third more than the second, and on it went.

And so it is, I think that is true and is truly stated right here. "He that loveth silver shall not be satisfied with silver; nor he that loveth abundance with increase." You cannot satisfy the flesh's desire. The most restless, miserable people I know are the people who are traveling to and fro across this country. They have plenty of money, but they are restless, not satisfied. They go to New York, they go to London, they go around the world, and they are trying to find satisfaction.

You know the most satisfied person—if I went to look for one—I wouldn't look for the socialite, and I would not look for the millionaire. I would go back somewhere in the mountains and find a hollow somewhere where some poor person had lived and had hardly ever gone out of that hollow. Maybe he had never traveled out of that county, but perhaps had reared a large family, sacrificed; all he had ever known was sacrifice and hard work. Went to bed at night tired, and could sleep because he had worked hard all day. That is where I would go to look for the happiest, most contented person. I would not look for the fellow who has a bank full of money, and can go and come as he pleases. He goes to his wardrobe and looks and gets confused because he has so many suits, and he cannot decide which one to wear. That is no problem for some of us, you know. We just pick up the same one, or the one we wore day before yesterday. But anyway, this verse right here tells us something.

I have never known of more men getting out of the ministry today because of their love for money. I spoke to you not long ago about this thing; some men's standard of living is so high that they cannot afford to go into the ministry. They cannot make it, and they cannot make themselves satisfied with a lower standard of living. How pitiful! How pitiful! Having food and raiment, let us be satisfied. That is the teaching of the Word of God. So, "he that loveth silver shall not be satisfied with silver."

Do you know where the second highest suicide rate in America is? I may have said this here. I read it not long ago and it shocked me. It is among college students. College students.

I got to thinking about that. I went to college during the Depression. There was no money; many many days you would go without money to buy postage stamps. You did not go to the snack shop because you did not have any money. You had it hard.

Now, it is different. I would be the same way, I am sure, as you are, and other college students. But every month or six weeks, you board an airplane and go home, spend a hundred or a hundred and fifty dollars. My, my, that would have taken you through a semester of college when I was going to college. But you know, you got there and you were satisfied—you knew that you could not go home.

Some of you would be much more satisfied if you could not go home from the time you came in August until Christmas. You say, "My, that would kill me." No, it would not. You would be much more satisfied. But you know you can go home every few weeks. You go home just enough to keep yourself homesick. You go home and see the old cat and the dog; you do not even have time to forget them. And you come back to school homesick. You stay frustrated. This traveling to and fro does not satisfy you. Having abundance does not satisfy.

A businessman's secretary came in one day. She was elated and just thrilled. She called all the other girls around her and they were thrilled. You know what she was thrilled about? She had been able to take a pair of shoes out of layaway. She had them on layaway for several weeks, and finally the day had come and she was able to get those shoes out of layaway. She had all of her friends rejoice with her. You know what that businessman told me? He said, "I wish I could think of something that I could buy that would thrill me." He had plenty of money. But if he wanted a pair of shoes, he just added a pair to the dozen he already had. No thrill. No thrill. If he wanted a new suit of clothes, he just added it to the wardrobe of plenty. There is no thrill in buying a new suit of clothes when you have all that you need and can think of.

Now I thought, "How pitiful." Here is a man with plenty of money, and he cannot think of anywhere to go that he has not been. He cannot think of anything to do that he has not already done. His money will not buy him anything because he is already full. And here is a little girl that works in his office, thrilled to death that she has been able to take her shoes out of layaway.

What a thrill. Who had the day that day? She had it. And he had his money. But nothing that he wanted to buy. I will tell you, this verse is right. I have seen it in life.

Ah, listen. I heard a couple talking the other day, I believe on this last trip or one of the recent trips, this couple was talking about how it was with them when they first got married. They did not have any money to pay the preacher. They had to get somebody to take them in an automobile to get married. They had no furniture to speak of and very little to buy groceries. This wife said, "Those were the happiest days of our lives." And now they have plenty. They can go anywhere they want to; they have money, not rich, but all that they need and all that they want. And she said as she looked back on it, "Those were the happiest days of our married life." Now what does that tell you? It tells you that money and things will not satisfy you. That is what he is saying here:

"When goods increase, they are increased that eat
    them: and what good is there to the owners thereof,

saving the beholding of them with their eyes?" (verse 11).

In other words, you just sit there and look at your stocks and your bonds. You figure it up every once in a while, and you are worth a hundred, two hundred, five hundred thousand dollars worth, whatever you are worth. And you look at it and say, "My that is wonderful. I remember when I was poor." But when you look at yourself you are not happy. You are not happy. I will tell you, we ought to learn in this country that things will not satisfy. If you are going to serve God, you had better learn it quickly. If you are really involved in the service of God you may not have many of the things of this world.

> "The sleep of the labouring man is sweet, whether he
> eat little or much: but the abundance of the rich will not
> suffer him to sleep" (verse 12).

He has indigestion because of that big steak he ate. He has indigestion because he stuffed himself. The poor man works hard. He is tired when the end of the day comes. He did not have much for supper, just enough to satisfy his hunger, but he said to his wife, "Do you not have a little more somewhere?" She said, "No. That is all we have." He said, "We will make out," and he divides it with the children. He gives most of it to them, so he goes to bed half-hungry. But he is tired, worked hard, been honest, and he goes to sleep and he sleeps soundly.

The rich man is tossing and tumbling. He cannot sleep. He takes a little nap, then wakes up thinking about his investment, thinking about that one that went wrong, wondering if this deal is going to pay off. Restless. See? But here is the poor man, sound asleep. That rich man would give a thousand dollars if he could sleep like that one night, but he cannot—and you cannot buy it. See?

Now what is real life after all? What is real life?

27

November 16, 1978
Scripture: 2 Timothy 4
Subject: Fought, Finished, Kept

FOUGHT, FINISHED, KEPT!

In chapter 4 of 2 Timothy, Paul talks about his departure from this world. Beginning with verse 1 (he starts out with a charge):

"I charge thee therefore before God, and the Lord Jesus Christ, who shall judge the quick and the dead at his appearing and his kingdom;

[A very serious charge; it is before God who knows all of our hearts, all of our deeds, all of our attitudes.]

[Now the exhortation:]

"Preach the word; be instant in season, out of season; reprove, rebuke, exhort with all longsuffering and doctrine."

I need, and you need, every one of these aspects of the ministry. We need to be reproved, and the Word of God does reprove us. We need to be rebuked, and the Word of God will rebuke us. We need to be exhorted (that is, encouraged—there should be encouragement, encouraging us to live for God in trying times). "Exhort with all longsuffering and doctrine."

Now, he gives us a forecast: "The time will come when they will not endure sound doctrine; but after their own lusts shall they heap to themselves teachers, having itching ears [that is, having itching ears, they are going to get people or teachers of this Word supposedly that will tell them what they want to hear]."

There has been a change in our pulpits of this country in recent years. Now much of it has been for the good. I believe that—there is better preaching going on than ever before—but there is one aspect of it that worries me. That is a softness or a dodging, unconsciously I think, some of the aspects of the preaching of the Word. As far as I know, the plan of salvation is accurately presented in our pulpits across our denomination. I am glad for that. The most outstanding evangelist in the world today—I am glad that he preaches the gospel; that is, he tells people how to be saved. I do not think he preaches all the Bible. But he does preach the gospel; that is, you are lost without Christ, here is the way to be saved. I thank God for that, and that is true in our pulpits across the denomination. But I do not know that we are getting in every instance the well-rounded preaching that we ought to be getting: That is, it is not popular to rebuke people and reprove them with the gospel.

It is popular to encourage them, and that is one aspect of it—and that should be done. No man's preaching should always be negative, rebuking, lashing out at people. That is true in your home—you should not always be correcting your children, and never approving what they do. That is the easiest thing in the world to do; be conscious when they are doing something wrong and fail to commend them when they are doing right. That is sort of human nature, I suppose.

When you give directions to somebody in this town, what do you say? Go to the first red-light. Have you ever noticed that? Whoever said, "Go to the first green-light"? I never have been given directions like that. "Go to the first red-light; turn to the right." Negative by nature. And if we are not careful, we will be that way in the home, in our preaching. It is easy to do. But it is also a danger to preach just encouraging sermons, and never reprove and never rebuke. That is when you get into trouble with people in your church who are not living right, and they may be the most influential people in your church.

But here you have the well-rounded gospel, the message of

God's Word, and you are not preaching the Bible unless you preach every aspect of it, every truth in it. So watch your preaching; do not let it get centered in this or that to the exclusion of something else. I need to be reproved. I need to go to church and hear a message that will bring me up short, make me conscious of how I am living; but I also need to be encouraged.

But "the time will come when they will not endure," they will not put up with it. I hear preachers even in our denomination saying that that is becoming more and more true; people do not want to hear anything that is negative, or when it gets down to where they live and rebukes them for the way they are living. I hope you will stay with the preaching of the Word, but watch your preaching. Be sure that it does not center in just one of these truths.

Now, in building churches, you are going to drive some people away. I do not believe in people going out the back door as fast as they come in. I do not believe in that philosophy, but you are going to lose some. They all are not going to stay with you. Now, test your own reaction here in chapel. What kind of message do you like? We have speakers coming here all along; what kind of message do you like? Do you find sometime that you resent the truth that is touching you and the way you are living? You know, we have to watch that. When I resent the truth, I may be needing the truth more than at any other time.

So, you have to be honest with yourself when you are listening, and there is as big a responsibility on the part of the listener as there is on the speaker. We are going to be held accountable for what we hear and the opportunities we have.

There is going to come a time when you may not be able to build big churches. I do not know whether we ought to be trying to build big churches, anyway. We ought to be trying to get people saved. Whether they are in big churches or little churches, it does not matter too much.

You know we have the comprehensive school system in this city and other cities across America, and you know we are having more problems than ever before. The more comprehensive they get, the more comprehensive the meanness gets and the problems, and they cannot deal with them. Right now in this city, we have a school that went comprehensive just recently, and they are having a riot out there. We do not know how bad it is; much worse than we have been told, I am sure.

But anyway, I do not know that I am for these big comprehensive churches. It sounds good, but I do not know that that is best. I am not opposed to big churches, necessarily, but I do think you fare better when you are in a church where you know the people and they know you, and the pastor knows you.

The pastor cannot know a congregation of two thousand people. It is pretty hard to keep up with knowing a church of five hundred, when you know the people. I do not know that one man can really know five hundred people, like a pastor ought to know his people and keep up with them. Can one shepherd take care of five hundred sheep? I do not know. I do not know how many sheep a shepherd can take care of, but I know one thing: I had rather take care of fifty than try to take care of five hundred. I feel I could know them, and I think that is true in a church situation. But anyway, I do not know that in the end time you are going to have people flocking to the Lord, wanting to live right, begging you to show them how to live right. I do not know how sincere people will be if they do ask that. But they will "not endure sound doctrine."

"And they shall turn away their ears from the truth,
and shall be turned unto fables" (verse 4).

Why do we have a proliferation of new religions in this country? Oriental religion is growing in this country. It is being imported from the Orient, and it is growing by leaps and bounds in some areas. Why is it? People are turning their ears away from the truth. They are turning their ears to fables. That is the reason; they seem religious.

Some of these off-brand religions you will find the adherents more dedicated than true worshipers. The Moonies; they do not mind being embarrassed. Latter Day Saints—two fellows nicely dressed and some of us could learn something from the way they dress. They walk up and down the streets, in mid-August knocking on your doors. They are dedicated. They will suffer embarrassment, rejection. They are dedicated to it. They have turned their ears away from the truth and are turned unto fables. Do not be taken in by the dedication of these false religions. They are very dedicated, very dedicated. Communists—the Communist is very dedicated. Sometimes we wish that Christians would be as dedicated.

"But watch thou." Now here is further admonition. We are told to preach the Word, we are told what will be the response to it, and now he admonishes us to watch in all things. Be careful. This is a day when we need to watch. So, we need to know what we are watching for. We need to be alert.

"But watch thou in all things, endure afflictions. . . ." This is not very encouraging, is it? "Endure afflictions." Afflictions are going to be a part of it for the Christian in the end times. Now listen, we have got to prepare a generation in this country in a hurry. We may be too late already. Affliction and persecution are going to come to the Christians. We have not known it in this country. Over and over again I feel compelled to say that Americans, Christians in the United States, this part of the world, have got to learn how to live in a pagan culture and still be Christians. We have got to learn how to deal with a pagan government and still be Christians. The government is moving in on every religious institution, gradually, gradually.

Now we have brought it on ourselves to some degree. When these big denominations get rich and have all kinds of foundations and tax-exemptions and nobody knows what goes on with the millions of dollars, the church has no business with this kind of business enterprise. Take the big denominations that own much of the down-town section, and it would be hard to identify their worth with the true ministry of the gospel. It is related in a loose sort of way; but now the business community, the governmental officials, etc., look at that and they wonder, and they have a right to wonder. As long as the church would stay with the business of preaching the gospel, we had a leg to stand on when it came to claiming tax exemption, but when we got into investment business (and many of these denominations have investment experts—they have to, to invest millions of dollars; they have portfolios on Wall Street, millions of dollars).

I would like to say this to you pastors. A fellow said to me just the other day, "My, we are doing real well; we have four or five I forget how many thousands of dollars in the church treasury." I said, "You ought to be ashamed of yourself." He looked at me; he was shocked. I said,"Are you going to have a building program?" "No, not necessarily. The Lord has really blessed us." Blessed us to take the tithes and offerings of God's people and run down to the bank and put it in savings?

I do not want my money down there in savings. I want it out there in service. No need to be down there in savings, and I would not give a dime to a church that is going to take my money and invest it somewhere, and put it in savings. I had just as well get it as the church unless there is a real purpose. And these churches that boast about having thousands of dollars in savings and think God is blessing, God is going to curse that church because that money should be out there blessing people. If we do not have anything to give it to that can be a blessing, then do not ask people to give it. So there is no need for all this.

But nonetheless, the government, as the church has deteriorated and lost its power and its influence, is moving in on us. That would never have happened in America if we had stayed with the preaching of the gospel. But when we get off on these subsidiary movements that are only loosely related to the church, we can hardly convince people that this is a part of the real ministry. I think we need to be careful.

"But watch thou in all things, endure afflictions, do the work of an evangelist, make full proof of thy ministry" (verse 5).

Full proof, *full* proof of thy ministry. Now he says, "I am now ready to be offered, and the time of my departure is at hand." In other words, "I am ready." It did not mean that Nero was ready; he was ready too, but Paul said, "I am now ready; I am ready."

Now when you get my age, you begin to ask yourself, "Am I ready?" Well, you can ask yourself, because young people die too. But have I come to terms with death and with the other world? Is it possible for a man in spirit to say "I am ready"? Now people say that on their death beds, and that is a comfort to loved ones, and I suppose you can come to that point, but do you have to wait until the death bed experience to say "I am ready"? Paul said he was ready: "I have fought a good fight." I would just like to think of that word, "fought."

Young people, the Christian life is no picnic, You do not expect to live here on the top rung every day. Now that is ideal, that would be ideal, but most of your life is going to be lived with tears in your eyes and in your soul. You wait until you get married and have a family. Now you tuck your little ones in at night and the mother sighs a sigh of relief and falls down into a chair for a few minutes rest at the end of the day, and you are glad they are all in. One of the happiest times you will ever have is when you tuck the little ones in at night and you are tired at the end of the day; but then after a while that old saying goes:

> When they are little, they are on your toes,
> When they are old, they are on your heart.

And you are going to be involved in the heartaches of your family and your children. You are going to carry their tears in your heart and in your soul. When they have reverses, you are going to suffer them with them.

If you are a pastor, you are going to weep with the ones who weep and rejoice with the ones who rejoice. And—there will be more weeping than rejoicing. You are going to suffer dying with the dying; when your people suffer, you suffer. And if you cannot suffer, do not get in the ministry; do not get in the ministry. Whether you get in the ministry or not, there is going to be a lot of heartache, and you are going to have to fight and toil and struggle.

You say, "Give me something encouraging." I am giving you something that is fact. And you just as well get used to it. Right here on this campus is a good place to start. First time some of you have broken away from home, and you do not know how to get the answer to your problems. Well you have got a lot of professors to help you, but most of the answers are going to come from you yourself. You are going to have to make the final decision after everybody else has contributed his counsel. You are going to have to learn to stand on your own and after a while you will have nobody to run to.

So, there is going to have to be the fight. "I . . . fought a good fight." Now this gave encouragement that he could say "a good fight." All of us fight but not all of us can put that word "good" in there. Some of us cannot put that word "good" in there; some of us have not been very good fighters; we have lost; we have quit. But Paul could say, "I have fought a good fight, I have finished my course." I like that thought, "I have finished my course."

I have told the illustration here many times of a farmer who farmed for my daddy long ago. I remember it so well. I do not know what the reason for it was, but I know they laughed about it. It worried and irritated my father. I know where he lived—but he never would finish a field. He would plow in this field today, the next day he would be over here in another field, but the other one would not be finished. My father would say, "Mr. _________, why do you not finish . . . ?" He would say, "Well, this over here needed doing." He just got tired of finishing the field; he would not stay with it.

Now, you know, that is an illustration to me of a lot of people and a lot of things; they do not finish the job. Some people do not finish college. They do not finish, and they will always go through life defeated in their minds. They do not finish. Some people do not finish a marriage; they jump from here to there. Some people jump from job to job; they just do not finish, and they lose self-respect. "I have finished—I have finished the work God gave me to do." No wonder, Paul said, "I am ready." I have finished the job. I hope you will finish the job. Do not stop. Do not stop. Learn to stay, stick with it.

Listen, what about those term papers that you have not gotten in yet? You have got one page written; you went to the library and spent 30 minutes. You saw a friend pass the window and you said, "I believe I will go with him." You heard somebody crank up a car in the parking lot and you said, "I believe I will get to this later." What about those assignments that you do not get in on time? Some of you pretend to be sick the day they are supposed to be turned in? Listen, do not start that silly kind of little insignificant pattern; after a while it will be something you cannot break; something you cannot deal with. Finish the job. If you cannot write but one page, that is all you know and all you can find, and the professor asks for ten, then write one page and say, "This is all I know, but I am finished." Now the professor may not be finished with you, but you finished! Do what you can do, but FINISH! Do not have things hanging over your head all the time. "I have finished my course. I have kept the faith." FOUGHT, FINISHED, KEPT—good words.

May we stand.

PRAYER

We thank You, our Father, for the warning of Thy Word. How we need it day by day. Help us to hide a portion of it in our hearts today that will help us in future life. In Jesus' Name. Amen.

28

February 22, 1979
Scripture: 1 John 1
Subject: Once Saved

ONCE SAVED

If you have your Bibles, turn with me to 1 John. John was permitted to live to be an old man; I think God had a very special purpose for this. There were some heresies that would come to the newfound religion, the new church, and God seemed to hold John over to answer some of the questions that would arise out of these heresies. At least, he did live to be an old man, and he is writing as an old man.

But in this first chapter I want us to notice a few practical things:

"That which was from the beginning, which we have heard, which we have seen with our eyes, which we have looked upon, and our hands have handled, of the Word of life." Now can there be any better evidence that a man could have than these evidences that he presents here? First of all, he says that "we heard it." That is, "I heard it." Talking about the apostles, the disciples, he says, We have seen him; we have looked upon Him; our hands have touched Him. There could not be any better evidence, any more intimate relationship with our Savior, than John had. Now he says,

"(For the life was manifested, and we have seen it, and bear witness, and shew unto you that eternal life, which was with the Father, and was manifested unto us;)

That which we have seen and heard declare we unto you, that ye also may have fellowship with us: and truly our fellowship is with the Father, and with his Son Jesus Christ."

In other words, John is saying, "I want you to come in now and share with me what I have shared." He is opening the door and we are walking in. He is making us a part of that fellowship, that intimacy that he has known himself having seen, heard, looked upon, and handled. He is saying "Now, I want you to have this fellowship that I have known."

"And these things write we unto you, that your joy may be full." In other words, we do not want you guessing. One of the most miserable states a person can live in is that of doubt about his salvation. Everyone needs to know whether or not he is really saved and whether it is trustworthy to put his faith in the Lord Jesus Christ and feel secure that he is saved. Now if you do not have this, you do not have joy; you do not have peace.

Over the years one of the things I have noted here in this school among students (and I experienced that one time in my early Christian experience—did not know the truth) is that sometimes people come here who think they have been saved but they are not sure. They are going on feeling, and they feel saved one day, and the next day they do not feel saved. They are in and out and they feel that if they happen to miss the mark or the ideal that they have established for themselves as a Christian that they are lost. If not, they feel saved. When they break their standard, their ideal is lost through the weakness of the flesh. Then they wonder if they are not lost, they worry about it, and they think that every time they do something that is not according to their standard of being a Christian, they are lost, and they have to go back and get saved over again.

We do not believe in repeated regeneration. It is not necessary to believe in repeated regeneration to be a Free Will Baptist in belief. We do not believe in salvation by works, or salvation by feeling. We believe as much as anybody, I hope, in salvation by grace through faith; and we do not want to overlook that. It is not according to our righteousness, our works, but according to our faith in the Lord Jesus Christ. By His grace we are saved. We receive the unmerited gift of God when we believe.

So, we need to nail this down if we are going to have any peace and any joy in our Christian life. We need to know that we are saved.

Now I know that those who call themselves eternal securitists cannot comprehend that we can believe in salvation by grace and also believe in the possibility of apostasy. Do you know that our statement of faith says, "There are strong grounds to hope that the truly regenerate will persevere unto the end and be saved " but some people want to interpret it, "We have strong grounds to believe that everybody may be lost." Our position is not that. We believe that there are strong grounds to believe that a person will persevere. But since it is by faith that we come into this experience, then we believe that a person's faith can be lost, that he can renounce his faith and face the possibility of apostasy. But we also believe that is an extreme situation and that if a person commits apostasy, that he can never be saved again. We do not believe in repeated regeneration. We believe in "once saved." We just do not put that other part on it. We believe in once saved.

"And these things write we unto you, that your joy may be full." Nobody should have more joy and peace in his salvation than a person who is a saved Free Will Baptist. We do not need to go around worrying and wondering. We can have all the assurance that anybody has. If you are trusting Jesus Christ, then you are saved. You say, "Well, I am not perfect." No, nobody else that I have ever met is perfect, not in the flesh. Now, that is no excuse for going out and sinning. We are just not perfect. We are perfect in the Lord. We ought to be striving for perfection, and we ought to be growing into perfection more and more every day. But we will still be growing when the Lord calls us home. No matter how much we grow, we will still be growing.

"These things write we unto you, that your joy—your joy . . . ." You know, we used to sing a little song, It was "Cheer up, ye saints of God, there is nothing to worry about." I think a lot of Christians ought to cheer up and get the assurance of salvation that they are really saved. ". . . That your joy may be full [complete]."

"This then is the message which we have heard of him, and declare unto you, that God is light, and in him is no darkness at all." Here you have light representing holiness, sinlessness; darkness representing sin and evil. "In him is no darkness at all," not any shadows—no darkness at all. "If we say that we have fellowship with him, and walk in darkness, we lie, and do not the truth." That, they tell me according to the original language is "the habit of your life"—if you are habitually walking in sin, then you cannot have any assurance of salvation.

Now these people who get saved and then say, "Well, I got saved thirty years ago and my name is written in the Lamb's Book of Life. I do not have to worry any more. I go out and do this and live like a sinner, and my habits of life are the habits of any other sinner." Why, they have no assurance. They have no grounds, according to my understanding of the Word of God, to believe that they are saved. Now they can belong to the biggest church in Nashville. They can give the biggest gifts. They can do a lot of good things, but according to my understanding of Scripture, if a person is habitually walking in sin, he is not saved. If he is walking in darkness, if that is the characteristic by which he lives, then he has no reason, no hope, no grounds for saying that he is a child of God. Now it does not mean that a person may not stumble; it does not mean that a person is perfect and sinless. The weakness of the flesh may overtake a person, but he will not live like that habitually.

So he says, "If we say that we have fellowship with him, and walk in darkness"—the habits of our lives are characterized by sin—then he says, "we lie, and do not the truth." If we say that we are saved or walk in the light and have fellowship with Him then our lives will reflect it. If the habits of our lives are Christian habits and we walk in the light, we are characterized by doing right, righteousness, and righteous living. Then he says that if we walk that way, "we have fellowship one with another, and the blood of

Jesus Christ his Son cleanseth us from all sin." And I understand that means "a continual action, continuous action." The blood of Jesus Christ, God's Son, is moment by moment cleansing us. Jesus Christ, the High Priest, is seated at the right hand of God the Father. There He pleads for us, intercedes for us, and His blood is a covering at all times for our sins. Therefore God looks at us as saints, as children of His. We are counted sons of God because of the COVERING of His blood. The high priestly ministry is absolutely essential—Jesus' continuing ministry.

Now I know that the atonement has been made; the blood will not have to be shed again. There will be no more atonement, but as a priestly ministry, Jesus Christ is not there just resting. Jesus Christ is there representing us before God the Father. We are not perfect in our walk, in our attitudes; so as the High Priest, He is there interceding for us. This is an absolute essential for us as we live here, and God the Father accepts His intercessory ministry. His blood covers our sins and He intercedes for us as children of God, pleading the blood as a covering for our sins. His continuing ministry—what a thought!

I know He said it was finished; redemption was finished there on the Cross in that sense, surely. But there now He is acting on your behalf and mine. I am glad we have an Attorney in Heaven, presenting our case before God the Father, because I believe the devil accuses us before God as he did Job. And if the devil could say to God the Father, "Look, I know that So-and-So was saved thirty years ago. I will acknowledge that he got saved, but I want you to look at his life since then. Do you think that he has lived a godly, holy life since then?" And God would have to acknowledge that we have not, and then He would say. "Well, now, he hasn't lived like a Christian; he has sinned some since then, hasn't he?" Yes. "Well, then, he is a sinner." But you know, Jesus Christ, our High Priest, says, "Yes, but My blood is a covering," and He is there to represent us as our Attorney before the Father, pleading the Blood.

And God has never looked at your sins since that day they

were covered by the blood. He does not turn back the pages and look at the soiled things in our lives that have been covered by the Blood. We have been covered, been cleansed! Jesus Christ, our High Priest, reminds the Father of that, and He intercedes for us in our weaknesses, too. I am glad for that. We do not have to worry; we have got a good Attorney in Heaven. We have a good representative before God the Father, and our case will never be lost. Thank God for that. As long as He represents us and we have faith in Him, He has never lost a case yet as our representative.

So, "We have fellowship one with another, and the blood of Jesus Christ his Son cleanseth us from all sin. If we say that we have no sin, we deceive ourselves, and the truth is not in us." The most obnoxious people I have ever met have been "sinless" people. I do not know whether I am just so bad until I feel uncomfortable around them, but I surely do feel uncomfortable around sinless people. You know, these people that do not commit sins? They are just so holy—oh, I tell you, that is not what John says.

Now remember, he is writing to children of God, sons of God. He says, "If we say that we have no sin, we deceive ourselves." You know, and I know, that we are not all that we would like to be, not all that we *ought* to be. We get so disgusted with ourselves; we fall so short, even in our best moments. We fall so far short of God's holiness. We long for it; we cry out to God and confess our sins. Oh, you say, "You are talking like a sinner." The closer you get to God, the more you are going to realize your unworthiness. The closer you get to the Light, the more you are going to see the specks of sin in your mind, in your heart, and in your soul. If you want to feel comfortable, get out there in the shadows. If you want to feel comfortable, get away from the Light. But when you move close to the Light, God's light shines into your heart, and you see things that disturb you. And you cry out to God for mercy, and God likes that. He says that He will honor a contrite heart, "a broken and contrite heart." We are realizing our unworthiness. Realizing that Jesus Christ shed His blood at Calvary and we are saved by God's grace makes us want to live right.

I will tell you if you have the proper attitude, that will make you not want to use it as a license for sin. It will humble your heart. "If we confess our sins, he is faithful and just to forgive us our sins, and to cleanse us from all unrighteousness." Now notice what that says, "He is faithful. . . ." God is faithful to His nature; God is faithful to His Word. Do not make God a liar by having repented and believed in Jesus and then getting up and insulting God by doubting Him. You take God at His Word.

If you want to be saved and you have asked Jesus to save you, then believe that He saved you. It is an insult to God to say, "Lord, I want to be saved. Oh, please save me, Lord. I confess my sins, Lord, I want you to save me," and then get up and say He has not saved you. He has to be true to His Word; God cannot lie. "Whosoever believeth in him." The Word of God is clear on that. And if you have believed, trusted—you say, "Well, I do not know whether I have trusted or not." Well, just trust. Just say, "Lord, I cannot save myself." And you cannot. Just say, "Lord, I surrender. I give up. I want you to save me, Lord." And then believe Him because the Lord says that He will. So, he says, "If we confess our sins, he is faithful." He is true to His nature; true to His Word.

". . . And just to forgive us our sins, and to cleanse us from all unrighteousness." Now He forgives and He cleanses, forgives and sanctifies at the same time. It is a wonderful experience. "If we say that we have not sinned, we make him a liar, and his word is not in us."

May we stand, please.

PRAYER

Father, we thank You for this day; thank You for Your Word. Be with us in all our activities and responsibilities; keep us from sin; keep us from evil; keep us in health; give us wisdom. We pray in Jesus' Name. Amen.

29

February 27, 1979
Scripture: 2 Timothy 4
Subject: Preach The Word

PREACH THE WORD

"I charge thee therefore before God, and the Lord Jesus Christ, who shall judge the quick and the dead at his appearing and his kingdom;

Preach the word; be instant in season, out of season; reprove, rebuke, exhort with all longsuffering and doctrine.

For the time will come when they will not endure sound doctrine; but after their own lusts shall they heap to themselves teachers, having itching ears;

And they shall turn away their ears from the truth, and shall be turned unto fables" (verses 1-4).

Of course, Paul is talking to Timothy here. He is talking about preaching the Word of God. The power of the Word of God is indisputable. If you are a Christian, you know that. Some of you became Christians when you were very young, and this may not have the same meaning to you that it would have to others. But to some whose lives were already scarred by sin, you thought that you never would be a Christian, that you could not be a Christian. You figured that Christianity was for somebody else, the good people, the people who could discipline themselves; but not you. You had already lost hope.

But God moved in your heart and there came about a change, and you cannot explain it to this day. Of all people, you are most surprised that you are a Christian. And you are more surprised that you have been able to live the Christian life with all your weaknesses; you would have thought it impossible.

There are a lot of people out there in the world who would like to be Christians, but they look at themselves and all their weaknesses and they say to themselves, I cannot be a Christian. I am too weak. They do not understand the power of the gospel. They do not understand the working of God's Holy Spirit through His Word, and how He can change your life and make you into a new person, a new creation in Christ Jesus. There is not any doubt, I say again, about the power of the Word of God.

Now, we have the Word of God to tell us something about that, but even if you did not have the Word of God to say this to you, you know it from experience. The Word of God is powerful. Anybody who will live for God in this day and age, in fact any age I suppose, with all the temptations that are about us, and all the weaknesses of your life, anybody who can live the Christian life must admit that there is a power outside of himself that enables him to do that.

In Hebrews, chapter 4, verse 12, we read, "For the word of God is quick [that is, it is alive], and powerful [it changes lives], and sharper than any twoedged sword, piercing even to the dividing asunder of soul and spirit, and of the joints and marrow, and is a discerner of the thoughts and intents of the heart."

So God tells us something about the power of this Word that we are to preach. The gospel is the power of God: it is alive, it is quick, it is powerful; it changes lives. We would not be here today if that were not true.

Now Paul charges us. He charged Timothy; he charges us. It does not mean that you have to be an ordained preacher to do this, but it would apply particularly I guess to ordained preachers, but for anybody who might teach a Sunday School class, or give a witness, this charge is given:

"I charge thee therefore before God . . . ."

The seriousness. This makes it very serious.

"And the Lord Jesus Christ, who shall judge the quick
and the dead at his appearing and his kingdom."

In other words, we are going to be judged in the light of what
we do with this Word. Now he says,

"Preach the Word . . . ."

"Preach the Word . . . ."

Just a word to you who are going to be preachers. There are
almost 200 of you here who are going to be preachers, or that is
your plan; you feel that you are called to preach the Word. First
of all, you are going to be tempted to lose faith in the power of the
Word. You are going to preach it Sunday, Wednesday night, and
Sunday again, and sometimes you are not going to see the results
that you would like to see. You are going to wonder if the Word of
God has lost its power. You are going to be tempted to switch to
something else, to some gimmicks of some sort, or some
psychological approach because the Word is not working—
or so you think. Now, the Word IS working; it tells us here that
the time is coming when people will not listen to the Word. And
we may be approaching that day.

I thank God when I hear of a church, or an area, and
sometimes it is rather strange how this works—you can take a
man and put him in a certain place and his ministry will be
mediocre, but you might move him into another place and he will
have a rich, fruitful ministry. Or you will hear of an area
sometimes where the ministry of the Word of God is very fruitful.
I am thinking of some places now in our denomination where that
seems to be true. But then I can point to you other places where
there are faithful men of God who are preaching the Word, doing
the best they know to do, good men, and it seems that the fruits
of their ministry are very, very meager. They get discouraged.
They do not see people saved. I cannot explain that, but that
seems to happen. Why, I do not know.

But it says here that we are to preach the Word. Now there
is a negative—this is put somewhat in the negative; it tells what
they are not going to do. It does not tell us that everybody is going

to get saved if you preach the Word; it does not tell us that the altars are going to be filled with people repenting and accepting Jesus Christ; it tells that the time will come when this will not be happening. But the Word of God is still powerful; it will change some hearts and some lives if you preach it. But you are going to be tempted to lose faith in it.

Then here is another danger as a preacher. I have found myself doing this, when I was pastor, and sometimes even here. I get to saying (or I did when I was pastoring)—What is the need of my church? And I think of somebody out there who might be having a problem, maybe he is backslidden, or he is not doing what I think he should do, and I pick him out, and I try to fashion my sermon to meet his needs—in other words, what am I doing? I am playing the role of psychologist when I do that. As I look back over my ministry, I helped more people when I did not know I was helping them than I ever helped knowing that I was helping them.

I believe that is true. The sermons that I preached and I did not know why I was preaching them, I just felt that I should preach this sermon, but I had nobody in mind. Maybe I felt, "Well, this does not apply to this congregation," but I had some strange feeling that I should preach it, a certain message. And I, through that message, was meeting some needs that I was totally unaware of.

I am not psychologist enough to know how to fashion my messages to the needs of the people. Now I think that surely you should have common sense and think about such things in a general way. But when you are preaching to people who have particular needs, and you are trying to play the role of a psychologist and apply your message to their needs, you may create resentment. Then you will be somewhat self-conscious and the person to whom you are preaching may be self-conscious. So avoid that tendency to play the role of a psychologist trying to determine the needs of the people and fashioning your messages accordingly.

If you do that, you will finally develop a very narrow type of ministry, and we should preach the whole Word of God. Remember this, whether you have anybody in your audience that you think a passage applies to or not. When you are preaching it faithfully and God has laid it upon your heart, then God is using it. You may not know it; you are unaware of the need because you cannot know the needs of people's hearts and lives. You may know some of the surface ones, but you cannot know them all.

People are not going to tell you all their needs, in the first place. Mostly they tell you what they want you to know, and they keep the other away from you; but God knows the deep needs, the secret needs, needs that are not known to anyone else. He can take the message and through the Holy Spirit, He can meet those deep needs. So do not get hung up on just preaching to obvious needs. If you do, you will be picking proof texts, and you will not preach the whole Word of God. So, preach the Word. Preach the Word.

Then another thing you will want to avoid is when you are angry with somebody—I do not want to know, if I were a pastor, who tithed and who did not tithe, and who gave big gifts and who did not. Now some of that information will get to you without you seeking it out. But I would be half angry with that fellow who made a thousand dollars a week and only gave five dollars in the offering. I would beat him over the head every Sunday morning if I knew it. I do not want to know it because I do not want to be mad with him when I am preaching.

You will get mad with enough people without looking for excuses to get mad with them. That fellow who says that he tithes and you know that he does not tithe, that he is lying and all of that—you look out there and you are half mad with half the congregation, and they are half mad with you. So just do not know too much.

That is good in rearing children too, by the way. It is good around here a little bit. Now we want to know some things, but we do not want to know all. And you do not let us know all anyway, so there is no danger.

But anyway, preach the Word, preach the Word. All of it! All of it! Preach the Word; it is powerful. And it surprises you what it does. Have confidence in it. Believe in it. Whether you know that it is applying to anybody or not, faithfully preach the Word. God is going to take it; it is His Word and all of it is there to meet the needs of our lives. We need to preach it all. So, preach the Word in season, out of season. When you feel like it, and when you do not. Sometimes you go to the pulpit just itching to preach. That is wonderful. But you go to the pulpit and you do not have a message, or you go out to witness and you do not want to—that may be some of the most fruitful witnessing you will ever do. Some of the most fruitful preaching you will ever do is when you do not want to preach. You wish you did not have to preach.

Now some people may say, "Well, I always want to preach." Well, I could say generally I do. I like to preach, but there are times when I do not have anything to preach and wish I did not have to preach. I may have something that I do not want to preach. I am just not in the mood, maybe, And you will be like that. But you are to faithfully preach the Word. You do not get up every morning, and jump up and down and say, "I am glad to go to work." There are some days when you may feel that way, but they will be the exception. But you go to work whether you feel like it or not. And you preach whether you feel like it or not. So, be faithful in season, out of season.

"Reprove"—now you can do that when you are mad, but you are not mad with anybody; you love the people. They just gave you a new suit, raised your salary, then they bought you a new car, or at least you are hoping that they will. And you do not want to get mad with them. See, you do not want to rebuke those people.

Not only that, but you can find an excuse for their behavior if you know them very well. That may be one of the curses of a small church; there are a lot of advantages of a small church, but there may be some problems. You know everybody. You know their ups and downs; you know their weaknesses; you know their grandma; you know if they had had the right kind of a daddy, they would be better; and you can find excuses for their behavior.

You know, you can just alibi for them. Have you ever seen a pastor who alibied for his people? I have. You get that grandfatherly feeling toward them, and you know they are just children; you knew them when they were born. That is, if you have been there long enough—you watched them grow up, and they are all your children ; all of them were saved under your ministry. And you can excuse ALL of their sins, all of their misbehaviors. You know the reason why they are not behaving and you take that grandfatherly attitude.

Listen, you had better watch that grandfatherly attitude. I am a grandfather. I know about that feeling. I can excuse my grandchildren for things I used to wear my children out for. See? I have got it! They cannot do much wrong—except after about the first hour—then after about the second hour if I am left alone with them, they begin to do some wrong. But you know, you have that grandfatherly attitude.

You are not fit to rear children when you are a grandfather. That is the reason grandfathers do not have children. See? That grandfatherly attitude. That can be true in a pastorate, and in your ministry. Why, I watch it around here, my attitude toward you. Why, I see some of you doing things that thirty years ago, I would have flown into you. I would have—I used to be mean. I have lost my meanness. That is the reason I am retiring. When you cannot be mean any longer, you are not worth anything. Listen, I can find excuses for people behaving the way they do better than I used to. I cannot reprove them; I can find excuses, "They are just children."

I hate to say this to you, most of you are just children to me. You know, I can find excuses. Listen, you had better watch that. The man of God is not to find excuses for people's sins because they lived on the wrong side of the track, or because they had a mean daddy. Their mama did not take care of them like she ought to have, and all of this and that and the other. We can excuse EVERYTHING!

God holds people responsible for their misbehavior. That is what the Bible says. You know our speaker talked about humanism the other day. The sociologists of this country—I wish we did not even have to teach sociology here. It is good if you just do not take it too far, and I think that we handle it all right. It is just the idea; it has been abused so much; they have found why everybody is doing what he is doing and they have excused him. There is no responsibility for people's misbehaviors, and we have passed that off and got a generation of people believing that.

But it says here, "Reprove. Reprove." This means to chide as blameworthy. That's what the dictionary says, "to chide as blameworthy." You are to blame. You are responsible, the man of God says, for your misbehavior even though you were born in a poor family, and even though you were put down and left out of everything, and even though it did affect your personality. The Word of God says that God can change that. And then He holds us responsible. It says that when the man of God preaches, he is to reprove, to chide as blameworthy, to censure. Then rebuke is very similar to it, "reprimand." Reprimand people for their misbehavior.

"Reprove, rebuke, and then exhort." "Exhort with all longsuffering." Encourage people. Some people need to be reproved and rebuked. Maybe you do today. Tomorrow maybe you need to be encouraged. You need both; you see the balance? But you know, the tendency of a preacher is that he is a rebuker or a reprover with fire in his eyes. He has a harsh voice. That is the image he has every time he gets in the pulpit, or either he is a grandfatherly type old fellow who is always just exhorting and never does reprove and rebuke. He ought to do both. You ought to do both.

"Reprove, rebuke, exhort with all longsuffering and doctrine." Then it tells you what will happen. "For the time will come when they will not endure sound doctrine." But you are to keep on in season, out of season, just the same. "But after their own lusts shall they heap to themselves teachers, having itching ears."

I can go places where I used to do a lot of reproving, and I can preach a message along that line today, and it does not go over like it used to. People used to accept reproving more than they do today. People resent it more than they ever did. I think it is slipping up on us, and the preachers may be backing off because it is slipping up on us and we find a resistance to it. We may be softening. We had better watch that. God will hold us accountable because one day we will have to give an account according to the first verse in this chapter.

May we stand, please.

PRAYER

Our Father, we thank You for the day. Thank You for Your Word and for this time together, to think together, to look into Your Word. We pray that it will be a blessing and a help to us. In Jesus' Name. Amen.

30

February 28, 1979
Scripture: 1 Corinthians 9:7
Subject: Muzzle Not The Ox

FINANCIAL RESPONSIBILITY OF CHURCHES

The Alma Mater of this school was written by a former music director here at the College, Mr. Ross Dowden. The words and the music were written by him; however, the music was changed somewhat by a later music director, Mr. Don Clark. We are indebted to these gentlemen for this. I think it is a very fine Alma Mater.

I would also like to say a word about Ray Lee. I do not suppose there are any of you who knew him, but Ray was a very fine person. Ray was a leader; he was a fine student, good musician (we have a song which was written by him that we sometimes sing here), and it is wonderful to leave a record and a name like that.

I would like to point up the fact that all of us are leaving a name. Now you are not aware of it, and it is a good thing, I think, that we are not.

Mr. Forlines spoke recently on "A good name is rather to be chosen," and so it is. Your name will be long remembered. You say, "Well, I do not do anything outstanding." Not many people do. Most of our lives are just ordinary, day-by-day living events. Very few persons have outstanding things that they can point to in their lives. It is an accumulation of day-by-day habits that determines what people think of you. It is so very important. So Ray Lee has left to those of us who knew him, a wonderful name, even though he was a young man.

We do not understand why the Lord would take a young man like that with such promise, but that is not for us to question. So, we still use the name of Ray Lee around here because he was a fine student, and a fine student leader.

We have had fine students over the years, and I would like to pause here to just point that out. We started with nine students in 1942, and if there is any one thing that I would say gave us a good start, it was the caliber of students that we had. If there is one outstanding thing that has contributed to the success of the school, it is the caliber, the kind of students that we have had over the years. We have had a loyal student body; we have had fine students; we have had Christian students. Now of course you can pick out certain individuals that would not classify as fine students, or even as Christian students; you could find a few, but not many. The thing that has characterized this school has been a good quality of students who believe in the same things that we believe in.

We have said often from this pulpit that you cannot force Christianity upon people. Now I know some people like to call us legalists around here; we know very well that you cannot force Christianity upon people. You cannot make them Christians by a code of ethics, rules, and regulations. We know that.

Most of our students would live as they live whether we had rules and regulations or not. However, when you live in a community of people, you always have to have rules and regulations. This city is a community of people. We have rules and regulations. When you get out on the highway, you are out there in a community of people. Some of them are not very good neighbors, the way they drive, etc., so the State has found out that we have to have rules, laws, by which to drive on the highways. Society is like that.

Anytime you find a society of people, you will find it necessary to have rules and regulations, or you have anarchy. The colleges and universities of this country have abandoned much of their responsibility by not having sufficient rules and regulations to govern people's lives. We still have some, as you know; but most of you would live the Christian life on your own. And you do—it is a thing that you have to live on your own—we cannot live it for you, and we cannot force it. We have had students who have believed in the same basic things that we

264

believe in, and that has given us a wonderful advantage.

Now there are people, and I run into this occasionally, who cannot believe that you can have a school of this kind without having total regimentation, and they have the feeling that students would have to be subdued. In other words, you have to take them and sit on them, or hold them down, to regulate their lives. Some think that this school is somewhat of a convent and an institution where there is no freedom or nobody ever laughs unless they are told to laugh. This is the concept some people have, and that is not true at all. I think you know that. Even though we have some regulations, that is not true.

I believe we have one of the freest student bodies in one sense that you could find—happy, where people want to live right whether we had the rules or not. So I just wanted to say that as a tribute to our students. Not only to this student body, but to the students who have made up this school over the years. We had a wonderful school spirit the very first year; we acted just like we had a big university. I do not think school spirit has ever been better than it was that first year with just a handful of students. That has characterized this institution over the years: a good school spirit. That has really contributed greatly to making the school what it is.

In chapter 9 of 1 Corinthians, Paul deals with a matter that is ever with us. He deals with a matter of gifts, material things, for the servant of God. Now I will not read all of this, but beginning in verse 7 of chapter 9, 1 Corinthians,

> "Who goeth a warfare any time at his own charges?
> who planteth a vineyard, and eateth not of the fruit
> thereof? or who feedeth a flock, and eateth not of the
> milk of the flock?
> "Say I these things as a man? or saith not the law the
> same also?
> "For it is written in the law of Moses, Thou shalt not
> muzzle the mouth of the ox that treadeth out the corn.
> Doth God take care for oxen?

"Or saith he it altogether for our sakes? For our sakes, no doubt, this is written: that he that ploweth should plow in hope; and that he that thresheth in hope should be partaker of his hope.

"If we have sown unto you spiritual things, is it a great thing if we shall reap your carnal things?

"If others be partakers of this power over you, are not we rather? Nevertheless we have not used this power; but suffer all things, lest we should hinder the gospel of Christ."

I am stopping at verse 12. I want to make just a few comments about this matter of the support of the servant of the Lord. It is very important, and very little is said in the average church about it.

There has been a tremendous change in the Free Will Baptist denomination since I entered the ministry. I entered the ministry as a young man. I have been in the ministry some 45-47 years. I have seen changes, unbelievable changes, and I want to tell you about some of them. When I entered the ministry, there were no, what we call, "full-time" pastors that I knew about in the Free Will Baptist denomination. The ministers that I came up under as a young man, boy, did not receive a living wage from their ministry.

Our church, I think, was very typical as a country church in those days. We had services one weekend out of the month. You have heard me refer to that. That characterized our denomination. We were a rural people—and are predominantly rural today; however, there is quite a change that has taken place in the past few years, a shift to the cities, the urban areas. But primarily in those early days we were rural, and had services one Sunday out of the month. One weekend out of the month, the pastor came in to preach. Perhaps he did not live in the community; most of the time he did *not* live in the community. He came from a distance and would come in and spend the weekend and preach. They would take up an offering. Sometimes it would be enough to pay his expenses; sometimes it would not be enough. That was the way of life; that was the rule.

In the fall of the year, harvest time, why, they tried to make up in a small way for what they had failed to do during the year. Most of the time, however, they did not make an effort to cover his expenses. One pastor I remember had to come by train, a hundred miles or so. It was quite a task to get enough money to cover his ticket, during what we might call the lean months of the year, when there was no income. In those days people farmed, and they did not have a job on the side; they had income about one time a year—harvest time. The other months there was very little income. It was quite a task to get up enough money to cover this pastor's train ticket, except in the fall of the year, as I say, they would try to make up for it somewhat. But if he received a hundred dollars a year, that was perhaps a good income. Naturally, he could not live on that.

Most of the pastors that I knew in those days were farmers; they had their own farm or at least they farmed or did something else on the side. When I entered the ministry, of course I expected to provide for my own living, and I expected to preach. If people gave me something, all right; if not, that was still all right. In fact, I was very embarrassed in those early days to accept a gift; I did not know how to react. Of course, I did not have to do much reacting because they did not give me much. But nonetheless, you were not expecting anything. People did not assume that responsibilty; the fact of the matter is, most of the pastors in those days depreciated the idea of giving, lest they be thought to be mercenary. One thing they did not want the people to think was that they were mercenary or that they wanted anything. They created the idea. It seemed to me that it would be sinful for a pastor to even desire or want anything. So they pretended that they did not want anything—at least they did not ask for anything—and the people responded accordingly.

Well, things changed. They have changed. We live in another day in our denomination. Now, our denomination may have been somewhat peculiar, and I suppose it was; but this was not only peculiar to our denomination in my part of the country, it was the general rule. Very few pastors of any denomination lived from the ministry. I am sure that was not true in the cities and the metropolitan areas.

But there has been this change, this turnaround, and I do not know that we have found ourselves entirely yet. Most pastors now have the stated amount, the stated income. Just recently I asked some people whom I knew very well about the way they financed a revival. I asked them also about how they took care of their pastor. I know this church and I know the people; they have come a long way, a long, long way from what they used to do and the way it used to be. I was somewhat shocked at their view and their responsibility, how they feel about their responsibility of taking care of the pastor, supporting revival meetings, etc. They thought they were doing quite well.

Since I knew the people so well, I figured I could talk to them. I pointed out some things, and they said, "We had not thought of this." Really, what it was—it pertained to revival meetings. Now I was not nosy because I knew the people well enough that I could do this. When it was all spread out and I pointed out a few things, they said, "We did not realize this; we are not giving the evangelist (they have been having the same evangelist several times) enough to cover his expenses. At least no more than his expenses. He has been holding our revivals really for nothing."

Yet the amount that they gave seemed rather good to them. They were rather pleased with themselves, until they added up the expense of the travel and the other things that the evanvgelist might be out. They really were doing no more than covering his expense, and they were embarrassed that they had been treating the evangelist this way. But nobody had thought it through.

Now this was the pastor's responsibility to point out these

things to this church, but he had not done it. The people were unaware of what they were doing. Now the reason I am talking about this is that (I am talking now primarily to you who will be pastors) you have a pastoral responsibility in this area. This is a part of Scripture, and you can talk about it. You do not have to talk about it as it relates to you; you can talk about it as a Scriptural principle, and the people will be glad that you have helped them understand.

This pastor had not done it; no other pastor had done it. They had gotten in a rut, and they had been doing the same thing over and over again. They had not taken into account changing economic conditions and travel that the evangelist might have, and other things. They had just been going over the same old pattern. Well, somebody needed to help them think and point out these things.

Now, the Bible principle that is stated here is that we are not to muzzle the ox that treadeth out the grain. What is that principle? It is easy to see. Taking an illustration from Old Testament days when the animal would tread out the grain. Now you could put a muzzle on the animal so that he could not feed as he would tread the grain. You could be stingy enough to starve the animal, getting the benefit of his service without giving him food. Now the principle is that this is wrong. The animal that treads out the grain is entitled to enough of the grain to meet his needs, and you are not to prohibit the animal. He is vital; he is necessary to the work. How would you tread the grain without the animal? You have benefited from his labor; therefore, let him have his needs met from his service to you.

Now this principle is a Scriptural principle. Here is a man of God, called of God to come and be your pastor. He preaches the Word of God; he specializes in studying the Word of God. You do not have the time; you are not anointed, we will say, as an ordinary layman (I know you can study the Bible for yourself, and we should all study the Bible for ourselves), but here is a man called of God.

In God's economy, His plan of things, He said that it is necessary for certain men to be anointed and called out and give themselves to the ministry of this Word. Now everybody cannot meet his own needs, or there would be no need for this man; but God says there is a need for such a person. Now this man is to give himself to the ministry. He preaches the Word to you. You learn what your needs are, your responsibilities toward God. He helps you, if you have children, to bring them up in the nurture and admonition of the Lord. After he has done all he can in the home as the father and the mother, as they work together, then the pastor is necessary—in child rearing. You say, "Well, I am not rearing people's children." Yes, you are if you are a pastor. You are helping people rear their children. You are helping them bring them up in the nurture and admonition of the Lord. You are pointing them toward God and getting them God-conscious, sin-conscious, getting them converted, helping the parents in this process.

So this man is a very important person in your life, in your home—not just in your church. In helping him, you personally stay aware of your responsibility and duties to God and understand God's will for you. Your children and the entire community benefit from his service and his life. What would this city be if there were no preaching, no preachers, all the churches were closed up? What if there were no influence of the gospel permeating this city? It is wicked enough as it is; but how would you like to live here, come back here in five years (all churches had been closed for five years, no preaching, no radio messages, no gospel songs), and all of this had ceased and been taken out of our city? We would not want to live here.

So the preacher is important, and he can be more important if he gives himself to the ministry and he does not have to divide himself and his time and his interest. You know one of the greatest threats to the ministry is not the time element that you may devote to other things. Say I am a preacher and have a job down the street, or I am in business and I put in eight hours a day in my business, in my job. You say that is eight hours.

That is not the big thing—the big factor in having something else is in dividing your time and your interest, having a double interest. If you can, keep free from double interests and have one single interest—and I could not emphasize this too much. It is impossible for me to emphasize the importance of keeping a single mind, a single interest, and an undivided life so that you have only one interest. I tell you, more people have been ruined because of double interests than double time. The time element would not be so bad if it were not for the interest that is involved.

There is much thought that you have to give in running a business, or doing other things if you prosper in it. If you succeed at a job, you have got to give yourself to it.

But here is a man of God, freed from all of this; he has no other interests. You will be a more satisfied servant of God if you will live like that. Do not allow yourself to get entangled with the affairs of this life! One or the other is going to win out somewhere out there in the future if you get a double interest. You say, "Well, I do not carry these double interests." One is going to win out somewhere out there in the future. You will not live with a double interest. We do not believe in polygamy in this country, but suppose we did. You could have multiple wives—men could. Do you think you could love them all the same? No. There would be one favorite. So you cannot have a double interest. You have got to settle on one.

Now the man of God ought to be free, and he should be taken care of so that he can have this single interest and not have to be bothered with other things. Let me tell you, if a church is taking care of you, it is a sin for you to be greedy and to develop a double interest. Now where a church forces it upon you, they are robbing themselves and doing you a disservice. I would not say that there are not some situations where tent-making is all right. That is the exception; that is not the rule. But nonetheless, the man of God must be taken care of. In other words, do not muzzle him.

Now what is the principle there? How much should he get? Well, do not muzzle him, whatever his need is. You know, one ox may eat more than another ox. I was preaching along this line one time in church about not muzzling the ox that treads out the grain, and a deacon came up to me afterwards, and said, "What if your ox does not tread out the grain?" I said, "Well, starve him to death. Do not feed him." But as long as he is treading out the grain, then you are to let his needs be met.

What are they? Well, that is hard to say. What are his needs? Whatever they are. And the church—the leadership of the church—should stay close enough to the pastor that they will be aware of his needs. When it comes to sending two or three children to college at the same time, the needs are going to be different than they are at other times. If he has unusual sickness, there may be a period of time when his needs are different. But all of these things should be comprehended, and the people of the church should be taught and made aware to stay up on what the needs of the servant of God are. That servant of God should be satisfied when his needs are being met. There should be a meeting of the minds. He should not be greedy.

Now I came up on the farm, and I could not describe this to you; you would not understand it because you are tractor-age people, some of you. You do not put muzzles on tractors. But we used to put muzzles on our mules and horses. Any of you remember that? You old-timers? But you see, what we did, we fed the horses in the barn. We gave them plenty, but once in a while you would have an ornery horse that could not be satisfied. He would nip every stalk of corn in the bud as he went down and plowed. You would have to put a muzzle on him. He was a greedy horse. Now when you find a greedy pastor, put a muzzle on him; but meet his needs—the principle is there. Churches ought to be aware, and be sure that the needs of the servant of God are being met. God will bless the church for it, and the work of God will prosper because of it. It is a Scriptural principle, and it is our responsibility.

272

31

May 2, 1979
Scripture: Psalm 40:1-3
Subject: "Out of a Miry Pit"

HE LIFTED ME

We will read a few verses from Psalm 40, if you want to turn there. This is a Psalm of David.

> I waited patiently for the LORD; and he inclined unto
> me, and heard my cry (verse 1).

The idea of waiting patiently suggests that the Lord did not answer as soon as David had expected or desired. There were some things that he had asked the Lord to do, and the Lord had not done them as quickly as he had hoped. Wonder if that has been true of you? Suppose it has been true with all of us?

"I waited patiently for the LORD." That means that if you do that, you believe that God knows best in the situation, and what you would like is not as important as what God knows to be right. You have faith in God to believe that God is going to do right, and that He is going to be on time—His time, not yours.

"I waited patiently for the LORD." Waiting is hard work. To be busy keeps your mind occupied, but when you have to wait— there may be seniors who are about to graduate, and you do not know just what you are going to do. A time of waiting. This will not be the only time in your life; there will be many, many periods of waiting. You do not know the answer to problems; you do not know which road to take, what choices to make. Or maybe there are no choices. Everything is just a blank; and yet, some things have got to be done. It may be that your family has got to be fed and there is nothing opening up.

There are going to be periods of waiting. I believe that the test, the greatest test that can come to a man, is the test of waiting.

Now, you may decide to go to a mission field, and it is settled. You may dread to leave home and loved ones, but still you have a fixed purpose. You have an open door. You know what you ought to do. You may not want to do it, but you know that this is something you ought to do. That is not nearly as difficult as not knowing WHAT to do, and having no open doors—just waiting. A test of your faith. Things are going in reverse for you. You have prayed, you have asked God to turn things around. He has not seen fit to do it.

You begin to wonder if it is really going to pay off to trust God. The devil will come to you with all kinds of doubts; your faith will be tested.

Does God answer? Does God hear? You read about how He answered other people's prayers in such miraculous ways. Some friend comes by and tells you that he prayed and God answered right away. And yet, you say, "I have prayed, but God has not answered yet." And after you go through that time of asking yourself, "What is wrong with me?" then you begin to ask, "What is wrong with God?" You begin to question God. You might question yourself first, but then you begin to question God. And the devil is really at work on you.

David said, "I had that experience." When you read of David's conquest, all the beautiful psalms that the sweet singer of Israel wrote, you might get the impression that everything went smoothly for David, that God was always right there. When David cried, God heard him and was right there to open the door and to give answer. But this verse suggests to me that that was not true.

"I had to wait; and I waited patiently. I learned that I could count on God, even though I had to wait."

So, if you are sick, and you can be assured that you are going to get well, you can endure suffering. But the question is, "Am I going to get well?" There is where the test comes. I am suffering, but I do not know whether I am going to get well or not. I am concerned. I cannot wait patiently because I do not have the answer. The doctor cannot assure me that I am going to get well. If I could be assured that I am going to get well, I could endure the suffering.

Well, our God can assure us that He is going to hear us, but we may have to wait patiently. There may be some trying times; a trying of your faith comes when you are having to wait. Things are not happening; things are not working out.

"I waited patiently for the LORD; and he inclined unto me, and heard my cry." Now, it is a wonderful thing when you know that God has heard, after you waited. When you know that God has heard,and God is going to take care of it, you can afford to wait. But when you have prayed and no answers come, and no assurance that God has heard, there is the test of your faith.

But David broke through, and said, "God has heard me. He has inclined His ear, and He has heard my cry, and I can wait now. God is on the way. The answer is coming. God is going to take care of me."

Now, if this should apply to some of you, maybe it will be a blessing to you. You have talked to God and the door has not opened, but you know God has heard. And you can afford to wait because God is on the way and He is going to take care of it. He will be there on time.

"I waited patiently for the LORD; and he inclined unto
me, and heard my cry."

It is a wonderful thing, when you have been through the dark valleys and the deep waters, and all is uncertainty,to come out into the sunshine knowing that God has heard and the answer has been given. By faith, you have experienced the answer, but in actuality it has not come. But the burden has been lifted, and joy has come; the assurance is there that God is at work, and you rest yourself in the Lord. Just waiting to see how God is going to do it, you know He is going to do it. You know that He is going to take care of everything, but you do not know how; you do not know when. But God has heard your cry. It is a wonderful experience.

> "He brought me up also out of an horrible pit, out of the miry clay, and set my feet upon a rock, and established my goings."

Now, I do not know what kind of pit David was in. He was down low. He was defeated. He was in a pit. I do not know whether you have ever been in one or not, spiritually speaking. I imagine you have. Circumstances had closed in on you; you tried to climb out and you could not.

I was hearing one of these men who had been traded someway from the Soviet Union—you have read about it in the paper probably—how that he was in this cell and he climbed the wall, just a straight wall. He tried it for several days and could not make it, but finally he found some way with superhuman strength to climb a bare wall. I do not know how he did it. It is unbelievable, but he climbed it and accomplished his goal. As he told the story, I said how could a man possibly climb a wall, a straight wall with no joints for fingers or toes. But you see, sometimes in God's work, you are put in a pit and there is no way to get out. Humanly speaking, you cannot climb out. The straight wall of circumstances has you completely defeated.

Well, David must have been in that situation. How did he get out? "He brought me out." See, God can climb straight walls. God can overcome circumstances that are impossible for you. David did not do it. This pit had David defeated.

"He brought me up also out of an horrible pit. . . Miry clay."

This illustration may not mean anything to you, but I will give it. Down in my part of the country, even though you would think it is all sand, down just beneath that sand is clay. Back in the days when they built log buildings, they daubed those logs that would not come together. Now they use mortar, but in those days we used clay. We would dig down beneath the sand and get to that

276

beautiful red clay, and you would dig a pit. For a big building, it took a lot of clay or mud. You would dig this deep pit, and you would have to add water and mix it, and it became miry and slippery. You could not move around in it. It was as slippery as glass. We used to get in there with our bare feet; that was a boy's delight to get in there with his bare feet and mix that miry clay with that water. It was so slippery! You tried to climb out of that pit, and you could not! No toe hold. See? No way to get out.

Well, we used to play in it as boys. But I always have this image which comes to my mind when I read this verse. Miry clay, slippery. You try to climb out of your circumstances, and you cannot climb out! You slip back into the mire.

There are circumstances, and there are going to be many of them, my young friends, in your life where you cannot climb out. It is humanly impossible. Unless we learn to trust God, believe that God will do the impossible and lift us above our circumstances and take care of us, we are going to live defeated frustrated lives.

David was in this situation. I do not know the exact situation David was describing here. It would be interesting to know. But he was describing a situation that was horrible. He described it as a pit, a "horrible pit." Out of the miry clay, God came along and brought him up. Nobody else could do it. David could not do it; his friends could not do it. There will be a lot of circumstances when your friends cannot reach you. You may pull them down with you; in their efforts to help you, they may get in the pit with you. There will be a lot of people milling around in that pit with you. But God comes along. God always comes along to lift His trusting servant out of the miry clay! Overcoming circumstances!

As long as God has a work for you to do here on this earth, God is going to see to it that you can do it. And all the slimy pits cannot defeat you. You do not have to be a victim of circumstances. If you are doing God's work, surrendered to God, He is not going to let you languish there in that pit any longer than is necessary for you to learn some lessons. You can learn some wonderful lessons in that pit. One lesson you learn is that it is wonderful when God lifts you up out of it. You have more faith in God after that experience.

I think of those disciples out in that storm that night after Jesus had put them in that boat. They were in a pit; they could not get out. Jesus came walking on the water. He took care of the situation.

So, maybe you have been in a pit. Maybe you are in one now. Maybe you are trying to get out, and the more you try to get out, the deeper you get in. You may be about to give up. You say, "If I ever get out of here, I am going to live my own life. I am not going to serve God any longer. He let me get in this mess."

Well, there are a lot of people who decide to resign; they ask God to get them out. Maybe they are sick on their bed, and they say, "Lord, if you will get me out of this pit and give me my health again, I will serve You." Then when God does this, they forget their commitment, their promise.

> "He brought me up also out of an horrible pit, out of
> the miry clay, and set my feet upon a rock, and
> established my goings."

Have you ever been mired down in your automobile in a mud hole and you spin your wheels? The more gas you gave it, the deeper you got in? You know what that is, don't you? After a while, you got on some solid ground and you began to feel that car move, and boy, how glad you were. How happy you were when you hit solid ground.

Some of you may have been spinning your wheels in the miry clay, and God has lifted you up, and you have caught solid ground. God always gives you some solid ground to get you out, when it is time to get out.

Not only that, but He put a new song in my mouth. No wonder, after being in that pit, whatever it was—discouraged. You know, this pit can be a pit of self-pity. You can get to pitying yourself down in that pit. It can be a pit of discouragement. Whatever kind of pit it is, when after a while God lifts you up, you begin to rejoice. You have never been happier in your life.

You know when you have been most grateful for good health? It is after you have been sick. A fellow who has never been sick cannot really be grateful or thankful for good health. But if you have ever been sick and thought "I might die, I do not know whether I am going to get well or not," and then one day you knew that you were going to get well. You got your appetite back, your strength back; my, you were so grateful to have good health. A new song! You praised God—oh, for a week at least, then you forgot it again. But you know, it is wonderful, that new song. When God has lifted you out of a pit, how grateful you are.

Since you have been in school, some of you have not known how you were going to pay your bill, and some unexpected money came in, and how you rejoiced. You just floated along over to the office, and you were so glad to give Miss McElhinney or whoever was there—so glad to give them that check. And you just thanked God that night. A week later you had forgotten it.

Well, that is the way we are.

But nonetheless, when God has lifted us out of a pit, that song—a new song—we know what it is. Rejoicing!

> "And he hath put a new song in my mouth, even praise
> unto our God: many shall see it, and fear, and shall
> trust in the LORD."

Reading through verse 3. May we stand, please.

PRAYER

Our Father, how precious Thy Word is. How it encourages us in our despondency. How we rejoice the many times You have lifted us out of the horrible pit. The circumstances have had us defeated. Some of us may be there now. And, Lord, if You have lifted us out before, You are going to lift us out again. Take care of us through the day, and help us not to forget that song—that new song—that You put in our mouths. Help us to keep singing as praise unto our God that many may hear, see, and come to fear the Lord. In Jesus' Name. Amen.

32

May 8, 1979
Scripture: 1 Corinthians 10:1-10
Subject: The Mixed Multitude

THE MIXED MULTITUDE

Reading from 1 Corinthians 10, the first few verses of that chapter:

Moreover, brethren, I would not that ye should be ignorant, how that all our fathers were under the cloud, and all passed through the sea;

And were all baptized unto Moses in the cloud and in the sea;

And did all eat the same spiritual meat;

And did all drink the same spiritual drink: for they drank of that spiritual Rock that followed them: and that Rock was Christ.

Before we read any more, let us just notice here that all of these people had eaten of the meat. They had drunk from the same drink; they drank of that spiritual Rock and that Rock was Christ.

In other words, if you make this spiritual, they were all Christians; they were all followers of the Lord. But notice what it says:

But with many of them God was not well pleased: for they were overthrown in the wilderness.

That suggests, of course, that there are many people who are following the Lord with whom the Lord is not well pleased. In other words, is God pleased with all followers of His? If you take this as an example, this is what it says:

> Now these things were our examples, to the intent we should not lust after evil things, as they also lusted.

We know what happened to many of the Children of Israel who started out on the journey; very few of them entered into the Promised Land. God had to let them die off. God was not well pleased with many of them.

The judgments of God upon His people, the chastening hand of God, we read about in the Book of Hebrews. Sometimes we get hung up on certain doctrines. The doctrine of grace as I preached here a few days ago, we sometimes use it as a license, saying, "Well, we are saved by grace, through faith, and we have to lose our faith before we lose our salvation. Therefore, I can just float along, drift along; I do not have to take my relationship to the Lord very seriously; just so my faith is not jeopardized. I know I still believe in the Lord. I still trust Him as my Savior, and I have some faith even though it may be vague. I have some sort of idea that I am saved (some assurance), therefore, what I do and the way I live is not too important. Just so my faith is not lost, or just so I do not make shipwreck of faith, I can come close to that as I will without losing my faith, and I will still be saved."

What an attitude! What an attitude!

Now he is giving us this example here of the Children of Israel. All of them had been delivered; all of them had gone through the experience of the Passover. That is, that night when the death angel came and the blood was applied to the door posts, they had been divinely delivered.

Then they got to the Red Sea and they had watched the waters roll back. They passed through the Red Sea with the waters on either side of them pushed back. And God delivered them out of the reach of the Pharaoh.

They had seen these miracles.

Not only that, but they had been under the cloud, and the

pillar of fire had led them. They knew what it was to have divine leadership.

Not only did God lead them safely, but they also were fed. God provided for them. They knew the miracle of the manna, and God providing for that great host of people in the wilderness. They had seen all of these miracles. Marvelous things had happened before their very eyes.

They had experienced the thrill of these miracles. I doubt that any one among them could have been there without having been thrilled. They had felt the emotional impact of all of these tremendous workings of God. They surely rejoiced as God worked these miracles. They were emotionally stirred.

You know, a lot of people feel something. They see God at work; and they experience some sort of moving within their hearts, and they may rejoice. But whatever had happened to them was not holding them steadily on course. It was not making a difference in their lives, and God was not well pleased.

The kind of religion, whatever kind of religious experience it may be, if you call it religious—that that touches the emotions without changing the heart and the life and the behavior—God is not well pleased with it. Never has been, never will be pleased. God is a holy God.

Oh, how we need today some kind of experience that will make us walk right, act right, pay our debts, not be gossipers, and just live for God like men of God ought to live. Whether you can ever preach a sermon or not, if you live right, you make an impact for God.

I do not care how good a sermon you may preach, if you do not live right, it will be of no value. In fact, you will be a detriment to the cause of Christ.

So these people had had all of these wonderful experiences. They should have been rejoicing and following the Lord with great enthusiasm, but they were not. God was not well pleased, for they were overthrown in the wilderness. God had to lay them aside.

My, how many people who started out for the Lord have had to be put on the shelf by God. God cannot use them. I would hate to be a castaway. God's judgment was upon His people who had experienced the miracle of redemption, the miracle of His guidance, and the miracle of His provisions! Still God was not pleased with them.

And notice, He gives examples:

> Now these things were our examples, to the intent we should not lust after evil things, as they also lusted.

Turn back to the Book of Numbers and you will find there a record of God's people lusting after the evil things—the things they had been delivered from!

The miracle of their redemption had physically put them out of the reach of the Pharaoh, but the redemption had not delivered them from the fondness and the love that they had for the old way of life.

The most miserable kind of religious life—if you call it that at all—is that life that has been separated by your will, or through some commitment, but you have not committed your heart to the Lord. You are still fond of the old things of the world; you think of them with a great deal of delight, and yet you are trying to force yourself to live for God. What a miserable existence!

So you read here in the Book of Numbers, chapter 11, verses 4-6:

> And the mixt multitude that was among them fell a lusting: and the children of Israel also wept again, and said, Who shall give us flesh to eat?

> We remember the fish, which we did eat in Egypt freely; the cucumbers, and the melons, and the leeks, and the onions, and the garlick:

> But now our soul is dried away: there is nothing at all, beside this manna, before our eyes.

In other words, what was the manna? The manna was God's provision. The manna was God's miracle. They had no appetite for it. Had they been left to themselves, they would have gone back immediately into Egypt to the old things they had eaten before.

God forbid that anyone should have sat here during these months with all the opportunities that have been afforded and no appetite has been developed within you for the things of God. You are just waiting until you can get free, and go back for a good mess of leeks and garlic, things that you were supposed to have been delivered from! Go back to your immodest behavior; go back where you will not have to go to church. Do as you please; skip prayer meeting. Just be completely free of all of the regulations.

Listen, a person who is going to live for God is going to have to live under discipline 365 days out of every year he lives. I could miss church three Sundays and get out of the habit of going. Anybody else could. You do not have to have many lessons before you learn it. You may say, "I go when I feel like it." No, you go when you ought to go. How you feel has nothing to do with it, unless you are sick and it is unwise for you to go. You do your duty; you do not serve God when you feel like it.

So, they wanted to go back: a mixed multitude. Is there a mixture in your heart? In one part of your heart, do you want to serve God? And in another part, do you want to live a carefree life? Are you all mixed up? What a frustration to be all mixed up. Do you have two loves? Love for the world, and some sort of love for God?

Listen, a mixed multitude! They fell a lusting, desiring the old ways of life. If you desire the old ways of life, there is something wrong with your heart. You may have never been saved, or if you have, you had better get right with God, or God will come upon you with judgment.

And I will tell you what, God does not have to put you into the pit of Hell for that judgment to be severe either. The chastening rod of God is terrible. I would tremble to think of having to live under the chastening of God because of my disobedience, my lusting after evil things, and God being displeased with me.

Here was this great host of people that had been *divinely delivered, divinely led,* and *divinely fed.* They had seen all of those miracles and experienced them as they happened. Now God was having to say, He was not pleased with them because they lusted after evil things.

Now another thing that He was not pleased with.

1 Corinthians 10:7:

Neither be ye idolaters, as were some of them; as it is written, The people sat down to eat and drink, and rose up to play.

Idolatry. Going through the motion of religion and having no meaning. I do not care whether it is in a fundamental church or wherever it is, you can be an idolator, going through the motion of worship, and that worship having no meaning, having no impact upon your life. We may be idolators more often than we think. You do not have to bow down before a graven image somewhere on a heathen mission field to be an idolator. You can be an idolator on Sunday mornings, sitting there pretending to worship when your heart is not in it! Mouthing words! But God looking at your heart and saying, "He does not even know what he is saying, and does not care; having no impact, he is not worshiping." You may just as well be somewhere in a heathen temple, going through one of their ceremonies, because it is meaningless to you, *meaningless!* A kind of religion that has no impact upon your life.

Listen, young people, that is serious business. God knows. God is looking at your heart. And God knows what is going on in your heart.

So, these people rose up to play:

And they rose up early on the morrow, and offered burnt offerings, and brought peace offerings; and the people sat down to eat and to drink, and rose up to play (Exodus 32:6).

In other words, they brought their tithes, neatly tucked in a nice little church offering envelope, and written on the outside "One-Tenth" of all they had earned that week, and when the offering plate would pass, they would drop it in. And they went through their ceremonies. They offered their peace offerings. Then as soon as it was over, they would watch their watches; and as soon as the priest let them out, what did they do?

They rose up to play.

I will tell you one thing: When you have been in the holy of holies, you do not want and you are not in the mood to play. When you have seen the Shekinah glory, and when you have seen the God of holiness, when you have been in His presence, there is a different kind of rejoicing! The levity of this frivolous sort has been replaced by a joy and a PEACE that so few seem to know about.

I get a little concerned at our National Associations. They have a big party planned. They announce and bring a preacher in and, supposedly, he has prayed and prepared and trusted that God would bless the service. He has poured out his heart, and there are hundreds of children in the balcony and in the bleachers. They have a big party planned somewhere in some hotel, to put on a big banquet of some sort, and those young people cannot wait until the preacher finishes. Everybody is on edge; Mama is on edge because she wonders, "If he does not let us out soon, my daughter or son cannot get home until one or two o'clock." I am a little concerned about that. How in the world can you have a service when everybody is waiting to go PLAY!

It is unfair competition to the preacher for a big banquet

table to be spread, waiting somewhere, and when the preacher gets finished, everybody is going to take off there. Everybody has that on his mind.

We had better reevaluate some things. I am not against the banquets, but we had better not train a generation to go and worship and as soon as the worship is over, have a game for them. I get a little concerned when I go to good churches with good pastors and in the announcements (on the Lord's Day, now), "As soon as you eat lunch, meet over at the ball park at two o'clock. We are going to practice softball." I get a little concerned. I was not raised like that. The Lord's Day has become a day of recreation; it ought to be a day of rest.

I do not know what it is going to do for our children when they see this going on as a part of the church program. We may keep it under fairly good control in this generation, but that next generation, when they come along, they are going to take it a step further. And I do not know what will be happening. WE WILL HAVE NO LORD'S DAY LEFT IN THIS COUNTRY if we keep following these trends.

Somebody needs to sit down and do a little thinking, looking into God's Word to see what God's Word expects. I wonder who is doing that. We are thinking about what "works"—so-called. We are trying to hold somebody we never have had hold of. We are trying to hold a group of people whom God has never had hold of, I am afraid.

So, they rose up to play. They had their worship, then they went into a game of some kind. And God says, "Idolatry. You just went through the motions so that you could have the games and the fun and the play."

The kind of religion that does not put a serious note in your heart is not the kind that would change your life.

Now, I am not talking about Christians going around with somber faces all the time. But I am talking about this kind of religion that makes you serious when you ought to be serious. And when you are in the holy of holies, throw your bubble-gum away. It would be all right to throw your *Juicy Fruit* away, too, even in chapel. I notice sometimes some people stay awake by the way they chew their gum. I do not know whether I had rather have you sleeping or chewing gum. I will have to decide that later. Now, it says another thing:

> "Neither let us commit fornication, as some of them committed, and fell in one day three and twenty thousand."

In other words, they had "ecumenicity." The heathen people of that day decided that they would invite God's people to a big celebration. You read about it in Numbers 25. I think I will just read that, because it is very appropriate here:

> "And Israel abode in Shittim, and the people began to commit whoredom with the daughters of Moab.

> And they called the people unto the sacrifices of their gods: and the people did eat, and bowed down to their gods" (verses 1, 2).

This was ecumenicity. The Moabites were heathen people. They worshiped heathen gods, and the Children of Israel had so backslidden until they would join the Moabites in worshiping their heathen gods. They were committing spiritual fornication.

I have seen some tremendous changes since I have been in Nashville for the last thirty-some-odd years—about forty, all told. I see some people in churches that used to not join in with the Catholics and the Jews, in their celebration. I see some of these denominational leaders in some of these denominations that used to take a stand against such things. I see them now all joined arm-in-arm, in a religious ceremony, with a people who deny that Jesus Christ ever came into the world. If there is no Christ, what are we here for?

You see these things announced in the newspaper. My, what a change. What a change! Ecumenicity. Spiritual fornication. Joining up with those who deny the Lord Jesus Christ in so-called worship, and you know they do not know the Christ that we know. They join up with the Catholics, and anybody else that happens to come along that will build their prestige, it seems. And they commit spiritual fornication.

Now, this story goes on. God's judgment had fallen, and Moses was beseeching God to know what to do.

> "And the LORD said unto Moses. Take all the heads of the people, and hang them up before the LORD against the sun, that the fierce anger of the LORD may be turned away from Israel" (verse 4).

Hang some skulls up in the sun. Listen, I would hate for my skull to be placed there because of my disobedience.

> "And Moses said unto the judges of Israel, Slay ye every one his men that were joined unto Baal-peor.
>
> And, behold, one of the children of Israel came and brought unto his bretheren a Midianitish woman in the sight of Moses, and in the sight of all the congregation of the children of Israel, who were weeping before the door of the tabernacle of the congregation" (verses 5, 6).

Here is flagrant immorality, as a part of their religious ceremony!

Let me say this to you young people. I like to see you sitting here on these benches on campus with your Bibles, praying together, reading the Bible together, but now the devil can slip in and do his damage in a situation like that if you are not careful. He can get you into such a religious mood until you will think that because you are both religious, you love the same Lord, and therefore whatever you do is all right because you are both

Christians. The devil can do his work. You be careful. Be careful.

You had better not pray over whether it is right to commit adultery or not. You do not need to pray over that. That is already settled! "Thou shalt not commit adultery!" It is not to be discussed, as an option, under any circumstances!

If you start praying about something that God has said "No" to, the devil has got you. You do not need to pray about it. Whatever God has already given a specific answer to, you do not need to pray about.

You do not need to pray about whether it is right to cheat on an examination or not. Or to steal or lie. Those are already settled.

All right. This man—thank God for him—Phinehas saw what was happening, and he took a javelin in his hand and went to the tent and slew both of them. And the wrath of God was lifted.

I will tell you whatever that sin is has got to be slain in your heart before God's judgment is lifted from you.

God was not well pleased.

> "Neither let us tempt Christ, as some of them also tempted, and were destroyed of serpents.
>
> Neither murmur ye, as some of them also murmured, and were destroyed of the destroyer" (1 Corinthians 10: 9, 10).

Nothing that God did for them pleased them. Do you know why? Their hearts were not right.

Gripers on this campus—the reason they are gripers is that their hearts are not right. Put it down. If you have got a griper on your floor in the dormitory? His heart is not right.

If nothing is right about this school—professors, etc., then that person has a heart problem, wherever you find that.

God was not well pleased with some of those who had seen all those mighty miracles.

Have you seen the miracles? Are you living so that God is pleased with you? I hope so.

May we stand.

PRAYER

Our Father, put in our hearts a spirit of love for You and also a spirit of fear, a fear of doing wrong and living out of Your will. Lord, some of our hearts no doubt need to be changed. We cannot control our hearts until they are changed. We pray that You will work such a work of grace within us that we will have a new spirit as we leave here in a few days to go to our homes to be witnesses for You. We cannot be witnesses unless You give us that spirit of love and grace that only You can give. Bless us throughout this day, in Jesus' Name. Amen.